POLITICAL PARTIES
AND REDISTRIBUTION

G000128245

This book explores the impact of political parties on income redistribution policy in liberal democracies. Rosa Mulé illustrates how public policy on inequality is influenced by strategic interactions among party leaders, rather than responses to social constituencies. Using game theory in detailed case studies of intraparty conflicts, Mulé evaluates her findings against a broad range of theories – political business cycle, median convergence, 'shrinking middle class' and demographic movements. She analyses trends in income inequality in selected OECD countries since the 1970s and provides in-depth examinations of Canada, Australia, Britain and the United States. Her methodology effectively blends sophisticated quantitative techniques with qualitative, analytic narratives. In evaluating both the impact of intraparty cohesion and ideology on redistributive policy, and trends in income inequality, this book brings a unique perspective to those interested in the study of public policy and political parties.

ROSA MULÉ is Lecturer in Comparative Politics and Research Methods at the University of Warwick.

POLITICAL PARTIES, GAMES AND REDISTRIBUTION

ROSA MULÉ

University of Warwick

CAMBRIDGE UNIVERSITY PRESS

PUBLISHED BY THE PRESS SYNDICATE OF THE UNIVERSITY OF CAMBRIDGE
The Pitt Building, Trumpington Street, Cambridge, United Kingdom

CAMBRIDGE UNIVERSITY PRESS
The Edinburgh Building, Cambridge CB2 2RU, UK   www.cup.cam.ac.uk
40 West 20th Street, New York, NY 10011–4211, USA   www.cup.org
10 Stamford Road, Oakleigh, Melbourne 3166, Australia
Ruiz de Alarcón 13, 28014 Madrid, Spain

© Rosa Mulé 2001

First published 2001

Printed in the United Kingdom at the University Press, Cambridge

Typeset in Baskerville 11/12.5 pt [VN]

A catalogue record for this book is available from the British Library

ISBN 0 521 79008 5 hardback
ISBN 0 521 79358 0 paperback

To my mother and to the memory of my father

Contents

Figures

Tables

Acknowledgments

This book has received a great deal of help. The intellectual support began with Angelo Panebianco, my mentor at Bologna University, who persuaded me to embark on this project. Anthony B. Atkinson and Frank Cowell provided the stimulus for studying income inequality and redistributive issues during my graduate years at the London School of Economics and Political Science.

I owe a special debt to Cristina Pitassi, now at UNIDO, Vienna, for helping me to come to grips with the daunting techniques of modern economics literature. Without her generous help and unflagging patience my transition from an undergraduate degree in politics and history to a postgraduate degree in economics would have most certainly failed. Athena Economides uncluttered my prose and her humour made much of the hard work fun.

There are many others who have contributed enormously. Patrick Dunleavy and Brendan O'Leary supervised an earlier draft that turned into my doctoral dissertation at the LSE. They helped me get the project off the ground and provided a unique blend of challenge, stimuli and support. Some people offered feedback for individual chapters or discussed with me the core ideas of those chapters: Jens Alber, Jim Bulpitt†, John Cairn, Dhammika Dharmapala, Roger Duclaud-Williams, Peter John, Carol Johnson, James Jupp, Paul King, Ian McAllister, Deborah Mitchell, Ines Molinaro, Michael Moran, Rodolfo Vergara and Alan Ware. I have also benefited from the comments and practical help of the participants to the Income Distribution Workshop, STICERD, between 1991 and 1994, especially Andrea Brandolini, Julie Litchfield, Magda Mercader and Stefano Toso. I thank the team of the Luxembourg Income Study for technical support.

Chapter 3 was presented at the International Political Science Association in Seoul, 1997 and at the European Forum, European University Institute, Florence, 1999; and Chapter 4 was delivered to the Departmental Research Seminar of the Political Science Program, Research School of Social Sciences, Australian National University in May 1998. I would like to thank the participants for their critical advice. I also wish to thank my colleagues at the University of Warwick for undertaking my administrative duties while I was on leave to finish this book.

Financial support from the Italian Department of Education, and the Centro Nazionale delle Ricerche is gratefully acknowledged. Extra financial resources were provided by the Research and Development Fund and the Centre for the Study of Globalisation and Regionaliz-ation, both at the University of Warwick, and the British Academy. The final version of the manuscript was written in the spring of 1998 while I was a Visiting Fellow at the Political Science Program, Research School of Social Sciences, Australian National University

John Haslam, commissioning editor at Cambridge University Press, encouraged me to rewrite the final draft. I am grateful for the construc-tive comments of the three referees of Cambridge University Press who provided their initial comments anonymously but two of them, Ian McAllister and Deborah Mitchell, later waived their anonymity and I am able to thank them personally. The title is a combination of sugges-tions from the Press Syndicate and Deborah Mitchell.

Introduction

This book began life when the political economy of income inequality in Western democracies was not a fashionable topic. Its concerns now have a perceptible timeliness. In the mid 1990s income inequality seems to be a persistent feature of many rich industrialised countries (Atkinson, Rainwater and Smeeding, 1995; Brandolini, 1998), calling for exploratory and explicative research. In view of the negative implications of inequality growth for health, crime and education (Kawachi and Kennedy, 1997; Sala-i-Martin, 1997), the search for the determinants of income inequality in liberal democracies is particularly urgent.

Perhaps the marginality of distributive concerns in scholarly work, at least until recently, rested on the relative immobility of the size distribution of income in the post-war period. This stability helped to nourish a widespread feeling that democratic countries were converging towards greater income equality. Analysts espoused the belief that universal suffrage narrowed the gap between rich and poor because 'the equality of franchise in a democratic society creates a tendency for government action to equalize incomes by redistributing them from a few wealthy persons to many less wealthy ones' (Downs, 1957: 198). A more equal distribution of power would eventually lead to the oblivion of poverty (Burkhart, 1997; Muller, 1988; Saint-Paul and Verdier; 1992).[1]

From the mid 1970s, however, prospects of declining inequality trends appeared largely misguided as innumerable findings reported that the rich were getting richer and the poor relatively poorer (Gottschalk and Smeeding, 1997; Eardley et al., 1996; Hills, 1996). The rediscovery of poverty and widening income dispersion overturned established images of stability; yet this reversal raised few doubts initially about the fundamental premises. A common first response lay on the anticyclical nature of income inequality, whereby economic downturns inevitably implied

---

[1] A more comprehensive treatment of this topic is in Mulé (1998a).

wider income differentials (Blank, 1989). The expectation was that as the economy recovered 'trickle down' effects would benefit the least well-off: in the rising tide of economic prosperity, not only the large boats of the rich but also the small boats of the poor are raised.

Hopes for benevolent tides were dashed when economic prosperity in the early 1980s failed to reverse the inequality drift in some Western countries, casting doubts on conventional wisdom. By the late 1980s there was broad agreement about the distributional changes that had taken place, but the causes of those changes were much less well understood (Richardson, 1997).

It may appear that in order to examine distributive changes research on income distribution would be intimately connected with policies to redistribute income. On the contrary, the bulk of scholarly work disregards government policies and focuses instead on international forces, especially international trade (Wes, 1996). According to this literature the rapid growth of manufactured exports from low-wage, newly industrialised countries and technological change adversely affect wages by creating a bias against unskilled workers (Freeman and Katz, 1995; Wood, 1994).

Another strand of the literature emphasises the impact for welfare provision of globalisation, the fall of socialist states and the development of the European Union (Rhodes, 1996; Esping-Andersen, 1996).[2] While I agree that international forces could be at work, such forces may sometimes be blamed too much for problems that may be domestic in origin (Fligstein, 1999; Glyn, 1998; Swank, 1998). Table 1.1 shows that in some countries the upsurge in income inequality was unprecedented, in others the movement was descending and yet in others the trend was stable.[3] The sharpest increase occurred in the United Kingdom where the Gini coefficient rose by 7.3 percentage points between 1979 and 1986. Considering the fact that income distributions change very slowly this increase must be considered substantial. However, income inequality continued to fall in Norway, Israel, Canada and France, with the percentage drop in Gini ranging from −1.3 in France to −2.5 in Norway. Table 1.1 displays a similar pattern for the Theil index, which means that results are robust to the index used.[4] The general impression

---

[2] For an excellent review see C. Pierson (1998).

[3] Income is adjusted to take into account the size and composition of households. See technical addendum for a brief discussion of the problems related to the measurement of income inequality.

[4] See technical addendum for a comprehensive treatment of these issues.

Table 1.1. *Trends in income inequality in nine Western countries*
(household post-tax–post-transfer equivalized income)

Country	Late 1970s early 1980s	Mid 1980s	Absolute change	Relative change
Gini coefficient %				
Israel	33.7	33.0	− 0.7	− 2.1
United States	33.0	35.5	+ 2.5	+ 7.0
Canada	32.4	31.1	− 1.3	− 4.0
France	30.8	30.4	− 0.4	− 1.3
Australia	30.2	30.9	+ 0.7	+ 2.3
United Kingdom	27.6	34.9	+ 7.3	+ 20.9
Norway	24.9	24.3	− 0.6	− 2.5
West Germany	23.0	26.4	+ 3.4	+ 12.8
Sweden	19.9	22.9	+ 3.0	+ 13.1
Theil index %				
Israel	20.3	18.7	− 1.6	− 7.8
Canada	17.8	16.2	− 1.6	− 8.9
United States	18.2	21.3	+ 3.1	+ 17.0
France	18.1	17.9	− 0.2	− 1.1
Australia	15.0	16.1	+ 1.1	+ 7.3
West Germany	13.9	13.5	− 0.4	− 2.8
United Kingdom	12.7	16.5	+ 3.8	+ 29.9
Norway	11.1	10.0	− 1.1	− 9.9
Sweden	6.8	10.0	+ 3.8	+ 47.0

Source: Tables and graphs are computed by the author from the Luxembourg Income Study (LIS) unless otherwise stated. Datasets for Canada 1975, 1981; Israel, 1979, 1986; United States 1979, 1986; France 1979, 1984; Australia 1981/82, 1985/86; United Kingdom 1979, 1986; Norway 1979, 1986; West Germany 1978, 1984; Sweden 1981, 1987.

gained from these findings calls into question hypotheses based on convergence in income equality.

Precisely because of the differences in inequality outcomes, neither descending nor ascending movements were the unavoidable fates. If some democracies were unable to avoid rising inequality, the reasons must lie less in international forces than in national factors, and, perhaps, in the varying policy options of their leaders. A vast array of determinants could lie behind the changing shape of the income distribution, including social services, economic climate and demographic variables. Yet distinct national experiences may also reflect national policy profiles, the impact of national institutions and the distribution of political power within a nation. Against this background, research centred on global forces suggests an absence of choice; to the extent that income inequality is declared to be driven by non-governmental forces, it has largely been *devoid of serious analyses of its political context.*

My book seeks to redress this imbalance by examining the extraordinary swings in the scope and content of redistributive policies in Canada, Britain, Australia and the USA, asking what they reveal about political games and redistribution. The study examines the ability of elected representatives to cut or expand social security benefits. Although it is not possible to read straight from changes in the distribution of a single income component to changes in the overall distribution, scholars have noted that discretionary changes in social security benefits may reinforce or mitigate income inequality movements stemming from non-governmental forces.[5] Several case studies have detected an association between cutbacks in redistributive programmes and inequality growth. For example, Gramlich, Kasten and Sammartino (1993) find that changes in government policies over the 1980s in the US pushed the Gini coefficient up by approximately 40 per cent. In a similar vein, Johnson and Webb (1992) attribute almost half the rise in inequality in the United Kingdom in the 1980s to alterations in the tax-transfer system since 1979. It is evident that in seeking to understand income inequality we need to explore the politics of income redistribution.

WELFARE STATE EXPANSION AND RETRENCHMENT

Redistributive policies are concerned primarily with the relation between family incomes and need, and this relation is defined by the design of entitlement and eligibility rules for the receipt of income transfers. In the two decades covered in this book such rules were first expanded and then contracted, albeit to a different extent depending on the political context and policy legacy of various countries. Historically, contributory social insurance was a German innovation of the 1880s when Bismarck tried to build support for his authoritarian regime among the growing industrial working-class movement. Other countries also introduced contributory systems, with the English-speaking countries and the Scandinavian peninsula marking out a somewhat different pattern, initially based on means-tested provision (Overbye, 1994). Over the 1950s and 1960s most Western countries set up new social programmes which included family allowances, the liberalisation of

---

[5] Atkinson (1996: 19–48); Gottschalk (1997: 36–59); Hills (1966: 1–18); Osberg, Erksoy and Phipps (1997: 84–107).

pension programmes, the replacement of voluntary by compulsory programmes, especially in unemployment systems, and provision for the indexation of benefits to wages and/or to price levels. In those years, most Western countries appointed commissions to develop plans and produce reports for an improved social security system after the war. By far the most influential report was the Beveridge Report which envisaged an integrated and comprehensive social security system providing a safety net from 'cradle to the grave' (Castles, 1998).

The first country to adopt a universal old-age pension after World War II was Sweden in 1946, followed by the majority of Western countries in the 1960s and 1970s. Another important trend was towards the provision of a minimum income for the elderly, although the form these provisions took differed among countries. At the same time a number of countries that had not had unemployment insurance systems before the war introduced one. Canada adopted a compulsory unemployment insurance law in 1940 which was greatly strengthened in 1971, Japan similarly in 1947 and Israel in 1970 (Gordon, 1988: 239). By the early 1950s most Western countries had a universal system of family allowances paid to families and supplementary allowances for low-income and single parents. Economic development and technological progress helped to expand the share of the pie to less-privileged groups.

One of the most significant developments over the 1960s was the heightened interest in the persistence of poverty in industrialised countries. The United States waged a war on poverty and declared efforts to create a Great Society which included new programmes for the poor along with improvements in social security benefits for pensioners. The general assumption was that the expansion of income maintenance programmes and full employment policies would eliminate poverty. Accordingly, in the major industrialised democracies cash benefits for income maintenance were vastly expanded from 6.7 to 14.3 per cent of GNP between 1950 and 1975 (Heidenheimer, Heclo and Adams, 1990: 219). These policy outputs and outcomes underpinned the general impression of convergence towards less income inequality. Western countries established social rights based on universal provisions, which contributed to the mitigation of social and gender inequalities (O'Connor, Orloff and Shaver, 1998).

Since the 1960s income transfer spending directed at those of working age rose on average about 3.5 percentage points of GDP until 1980 (OECD, 1996). Increases in the coverage and generosity of transfer programmes appear to be much more important than changes in demographic factors, such as the share of the working population, in explaining transfer spending growth. Much of the expansion is attributable to widening eligibility and/or greater take up of benefits rather than increases in rates of benefits.

The golden age of welfare state expansion began fading with the first oil crisis of 1973. Slow economic growth, persistent high unemployment rates and severe inflation placed a strain on the fiscal capacity of Western governments and created an environment which was much less favourable to welfare spending. Social security policies were forced to adjust to changing economic and social circumstances and to deflationary policies. Yet the economic recessions of the 1970s were not tackled in the same ways by all Western democracies. Austria and Sweden preferred to stimulate aggregate demand, which generated lower levels of unemployment, whereas West Germany resorted to deflationary policies (Scharpf, 1991). Several countries reacted to the economic downturn by slashing spending for antipoverty programmes and social security benefits. Politicians seemed to have accepted the conclusion that redistributive programmes caused slow growth and large deficits. 'How this proposition – the truth of which has not been proved – became conventional wisdom was left as a mystery' (Danziger and Smolensky, 1985: 262).

Conventional wisdom concealed the fact that redistributive programmes were the product of intense political choices, because it was the political community that established who was eligible for support (Castles and Mitchell, 1993). Ongoing disputes over matters that may at first seem technical and abstruse, such as the old-age pension, indexation, waiting time, are in reality conflicts for redistributive advantages among social groups (Baldwin, 1990). As Schumpeter more generally remarked, the budget is the skeleton of the state stripped of all misleading ideologies (1954: 6).

To make sense of the strategies that politicians adopt as they thread their way through a maze of political obstacles and opportunities, this book focuses on the redistributive games that elected politicians play. Of course, such an agenda is overly ambitious, and inevitably will result in over-simplification of many issues. For one thing, social security policies interact in significant ways with other public policies, such as taxation, housing, subsidies for house buyers, benefits in kind and other taxation expenditures, including relief from taxation of mortgage interest payments or pension contributions (Glennerster and Hills, 1998). Moreover, I will have to be selective and chiefly confine myself to those issues that have been unduly neglected in the literature. Most scholarly works look at the distribution of wages and salaries and disregard the contribution that government cash transfers make to inequality movements.

The importance ascribed to transfer income stems from its impact on the *personal* distribution of income, which is the take home pay that directly impinges on the living standards of many individuals. Consequently the redistributive role of government intervention cannot be overstated; its importance has far-reaching consequences for the economic well being of people in work and out of work. In the light of these considerations, it is striking that economic theories of distribution are almost wholly concerned with the *functional* distribution income, income from wages and dividends. Apart from some honorable exceptions (Brandolini, 1992), the distribution between persons seemingly raises little interest among economists. Thus the economic literature leaves unanswered the crucial question of how the income share of people out of work or unemployed, who comprise the bottom 20–30 per cent of the population, has changed. A sounder explanation includes the political sphere as a key analytical dimension in understanding variations in the personal distribution of income.

Hence, this book underwrites the idea that a comprehensive treatment of income inequality requires a multidimensional framework (Atkinson, 1997; Brandolini, 1998; Midlarsky, 1997). To this end, the study examines redistributive policies but also analyses market and demographic variables. It thus bridges the political science literature on the party policy link and the economic literature on income distribution.

The methodology applied in this book, however, significantly differs from much work on income distribution, usually based on regression analyses of interaction effects between demographic, technological and institutional factors (Blau and Khan, 1996; Freeman and Katz, 1995; Gottschalk and Smeeding, 1997). My work instead blends quantitative and qualitative techniques. The primary reason is that I am interested in the preconditions and in the mechanics of political games as well as in their redistributive effects. More specifically I seek to identify specific episodes or critical junctures when redistributive policies changed their course.[6]

My emphasis on distributive issues departs from much work in political economy. Comparative political economy has paid little

---

[6] For a strong defence of an approach to income inequality based on critical junctures see Atkinson (1997); Brandolini (1998).

Table 1.2. *Average value of income components as a percentage of average gross income in nine Western countries*

Variable	USA	Israel	Canada	Australia	Norway	West Germany	UK	France	Sweden*
Wages or salaries	75.8	66	75.5	71	69.9	63.1	72	63.2	64.5
Self-empl. income	6.7	16.8	4.5	5.6	11.1	16.7	4.5	12.1	3.7
Property income	5.8	4.4	7.2	12.5	2.7	1.1	2.7	3.6	2.7
Occup. pensions	2.6	3.4	1.8	1.1	1.2	2.3	2.5	0.0	0.0*
Market incomes	90.8	90.5	90.1	90.1	84.9	83.3	81.7	78.8	70.8
Cash benefits	8	8.5	9.1	9.3	14.1	16.5	17.2	21.2	29

Notes: Datasets as in figure 1.1. Countries are ordered according to the proportion of cash benefits in total income, starting from the lowest.
* In the data collection process occupational pensions in Sweden are treated as part of transfer payments.

attention to distributive issues and has chiefly concentrated on explaining cross-national differences in economic policies.[7] This tendency

has drawn contemporary political economists away from some of the overarching issues that absorbed many of the greatest political economists in years past. By and large, these were issues about the relationship between the state, seen as a custodian of general interest, and the market, seen as a mechanism for interchange among private interests, and the consequences of this interaction for the overall distribution of well being in society. (Hall, 1997: 195)

Perhaps 30 years of economic prosperity deflected attention from these issues, but they are hard to ignore after two decades in which income inequality has increased in most industrialised countries. By investigating redistributive games, the book contributes to the literature on political economy (Alesina and Rosenthal, 1995; Gamble, 1995b).

Governments may offset or exacerbate income inequality in many ways. They can intervene in the labour market, modify the so-called social wage, or more directly they can expand or contract cash benefits (Champernowne and Cowell, 1998). The importance of cash benefits as income source is gauged by examining the income package which separates total income into different components (Rainwater, 1993). In the mid 1980s cash benefits were the second most important income source after income from work (table 1.2). In Sweden they accounted for almost 30 per cent of gross income and about a fifth in France; in the UK cash benefits were four times the amount of self-employment income. Hence the share of cash benefits in total household gross income may be quite substantial, implying that cash income is an intermediate mechanism between market income and take-home pay. This finding adds weight to the contention that the design and selection of entitlement and eligibility rules play a vital role in inequality movements (Brandolini, 1992). Figure 1.1 shows the extent to which income inequality may change after government intervention. If we analyse inequality outcomes according to two different income concepts, post-transfer income (after government cash income) and post-transfer–post-tax income, it is evident that the major recorded redistribution in the late 1970s/early 1980s was that associated with cash income. There was a substantial redistribution in Sweden where the reduction in the Gini coefficient induced by cash transfers was over 20 per cent. Direct taxation had a low distributional impact in all the countries under

---

[7] For some notable exceptions see Birchfield and Crepaz (1998); Boix (1998).

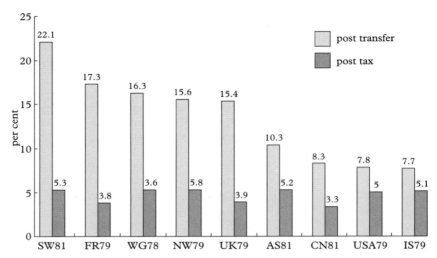

Figure 1.1. Reduction in the Gini coefficient induced by cash transfers and direct taxes in nine Western countries (adjusted household post-transfer–post-tax income)

consideration, with a more pronounced effect in Norway. In the United States, the relatively small percentage reduction in the inequality index after government intervention suggests a less-effective redistributive system.

Income transfer programmes can be characterised by the rules governing who can obtain benefits (eligibility) and the amount of benefits received (entitlements). Numerous empirical studies support the contention that cash benefits are progressive.[8] The literature confirms that, in any given year, income transfers have substantial redistributive effects, and are regarded as the main mechanism of redistribution (Harding, 1993; Ringen, 1987). By contrast, comparative research indicates that tax policy has little impact on overall income distribution, with direct taxes being moderately progressive and indirect taxes moderately regressive (Jenkins, 1995). The ambiguity of tax incidence and the possibilities of tax avoidance mean that the redistributive effects of tax policy are likely to be very small.[9] For this reason this work centres on transfer payments rather than tax policy as the main redistributive mechanism.

---

[8] On the efficacy of transfer benefits see Jantti and Danziger (1992); and Saunders (1994b).
[9] For a different approach see Johnson and Webb (1992).

THE ARGUMENT OF THIS BOOK

The aim of this book is to cast light on some of the incentives for income redistribution in a liberal democracy. Explanations of the redistributive role of elected representatives rest upon partisan theory or vote-maximising assumptions. On the one hand, the ideology of the party in power is the best predictor for the allocation of costs and benefits. On the other hand, electoral imperatives dictate variations in transfer policies which in turn affect socially undifferentiated voters.

Despite their differences, a central premise of both schools of thought is that public preferences set the agenda for redistributive policies, implying a passive response of elected representatives to their core constituencies. Politicians and policymakers give priority to the issues about which the public cares most and they try to match their proposals to public preferences. In addition, most scholars believe that redistributive policies aim at improving the relative position of one social class, itself regarded as internally fairly homogeneous. Accordingly, the population is subdivided into distinct classes, defined as lower-, middle- and upper-income groups. A further point is that both camps view political parties as unitary actors with the corollary of preference homogeneity among party leaders. No costs are attached to party competition or cooperation.

Advances in the theory of political parties, however, suggest that so simple a model may be unsuited to analysing the redistributive impact of parties in a significantly fragmented and heterogeneous society. Theoretical work on political parties has long argued that parties are not monolithic entities and are instead more fruitfully conceived of as organisations in which actors engage in coalition building, maintenance and dissolution (Belloni and Beller, 1978; Kitschelt, 1994; Laver and Shepsle, 1996; Maor, 1998; Panebianco, 1988). Within political parties actors strive for relative dominance and interact with each other in the struggle for power. In the process, governance within the party may lead to changes in decision-making rules and in the formulation of policies (Brady and Epstein 1997; Cox and McCubbins, 1993; McCubbins and Thies, 1997; McGillivray, 1997; Roemer, 1999).

This book builds on such theoretical advances and deepens them by systematically examining the making and breaking of internal coalitions, each with its own agenda, as the driving force behind the selection of redistributive policies. I argue that in devising transfer programmes party leaders may at least be concerned with gaining and retaining power in their own party as well as maximising votes or pursuing ideologies. Scholars of party politics since Ostrogorski (1902) and Michels (1959 [1915]) have repeatedly stressed the role of internal politics in the activities of political parties. Nevertheless, a common trait of current party politics literature is that the party in office, the party organisation and party in the electorate have generally been examined separately. The literature concerned with the redistributive role of parties is no exception, in that it usually examines a political party as a single variable (Castles, 1982; Rose, 1995). In contradistinction I view the political party as a multidimensional variable, particularly in terms of the structure of party competition and intraparty factors, such as party organisation, ideology and selection rules.

This multidimensional approach throws light on the fact that politicians may seek to design policies that build or recraft public opinion in order to outflank their internal rivals. In this sense, redistributive policies may be unresponsive to voters' demands, implying that vote driven policies cannot in themselves encompass the complexity of the party policy link (Mulé, 1997). Such complexity can only fully be understood in relation to those processes through which party policies emerge.

In short, the book points to the contribution that internal conflicts make to the construction of interests and the formation of coalitions. It examines the extent to which inequality outcomes may be influenced by processes of political conflicts and not generated entirely by the antecedents to that conflict, such as socio-economic cleavages.

The main problem with previous research on the redistributive impact of parties is that critically absent are the purposive actors. Political parties are typically anthropomorphised and treated as coherent actors in the political process.[10] Thus, the literature often falls prey to the functionalist argument, which postulates a purpose without a purposive actor (Elster, 1982: 454). Explorations of internal governance help to overcome this problem because they identify who are the main players; they help to understand why some redistributive proposals never reached the agenda, and perhaps why they were discarded. Inspecting the black box allows us to capture the redistributive implications of non-decisions and to examine deviations between proposed and actual changes. In this way it is possible to analyse the role of interdependent strategic action within the ruling party complementing research on electoral or ideological motives.

---

[10] This weakness is found in much scholarly work on parliaments. For a critique and an innovative study, see Huber (1996).

Views about income redistribution are especially open to this kind of refurbishing from above because inclusion or exclusion of social groups from the social safety net sets the boundaries for state-protected and risk-exposed groups (Atkinson and Hills, 1998; Barry, 1998; Goodin, 1996). Redistributive policies evoke and provoke deep tensions in political life about gender, race, religions and cultural values. Welfare states expanded in all industrial democracies partly because politicians saw social programmes as valuable resources of political legitimacy (Flora, 1986). Social security policies built direct links between ruling parties and the electorate, enabling governments to claim credit for assuring a certain degree of economic security. Entitlement and eligibility rules may thus help policymakers to manufacture social constituencies.

Another family of theories offers a different approach to policymaking, emphasising the role of policy subsystems or distinct policy communities in generating alternatives. Kingdon's (1984) theory of agenda setting provides a complex model in which separate streams of problems, policies and politics converge to produce change. Others argue that the steady diffusion of new ideas in policymaking is the real source of change (Jacobsen, 1995). From this perspective innovation in social policy stems from new information provided by intellectual and professional communities (Banting, 1979).

What is striking about conflicts over redistributive policies is how frequently they break out of these smaller communities. Over the 1970s through to the 1990s the guiding ideas of a broad range of social policies were first accepted, developed, expanded only to be repudiated, withered or contracted at a later stage. Battles over ideas were far more politicised than the routine style of policymaking that these theories describe. To make sense of social policy conflicts, then, it is necessary to examine the larger partisan struggle over ideas and assess its implications for defining social policy issues (Weir, 1998).

However, the theoretical lens employed in this book moves beyond partisan struggles. It assumes that shifting alignments within the party organisation may generate a dynamic process whereby new dominant groups attempt to translate the gains at the party level also into redistributive gains for their actual or potential supporters. Applying this mode of analysis may disclose the fact that party factions are connected to disjointed groups, rather than to social classes regarded as units. In such circumstances factions may tighten or loosen their ties with specific sections of the electorate in order to strengthen their internal position. This perspective suggests that internal processes of coalition building

impinge on the formation of privileged and less-privileged social constituencies. The main question involved in assessing redistributive policies,
therefore, is how internal conflict and cooperation affect those policies.
Focusing on internal governance exposes important dimensions concealed in previous analyses. It brings to the fore strategic and institutional factors, which may prove crucial for understanding party policies.

The argument developed throughout this book departs from the
traditional manner in which we have studied the phenomenon of the
redistributive impact of ruling parties. Conventional views centre on
interparty competition as the mechanism behind public policy formulation. I add to this tradition the notion that political competition *within*
parties is an essential element of policy change. In so doing, my interpretation places limitations upon the role of electoral and partisan politics
in the making of redistributive policies. It suggests that in their struggle
for internal power politicians spawn conflicts which may translate into
redistributive gains or losses. Since the policy impact of elite-induced
conflicts is a largely under-researched area, this book provides a step
towards filling a gap in the literature. The main contribution of this
study lies in incorporating into the analysis of transfer policies advances
in the theory of political parties, especially developments in the theory of
party goals, party competition and party organisation.

COMPARATIVE STRATEGY

Through the four cases of Canada, Britain, Australia and the United
States the book seeks to unravel the thread connecting intra-elite conflicts, transfer policies and state-protected groups. The comparative
approach is meant to show that the redistributive impact of ruling
parties is not accidental. Comparisons control whether generalisations
hold across the cases to which they are applied (Sartori, 1994). When we
try to explain a particular phenomenon by resorting to hypotheses
which are all potentially plausible, only comparisons across different
cases help in choosing the most reliable hypothesis (Keman, 1993).

The comparative method applied here is based on the most similar
system design which allows a large number of systemic variables to be
ignored, under the assumption that they are equal (Przeworski and
Teune, 1970). It offers a solution to what Lijphart felicitously defined as
the 'many variables small N' dilemma (1971: 368). This problem obtains
because comparisons of a limited number of countries prevent applications of sophisticated statistical techniques, making inferences less likely.

One alternative is to adopt the most similar systems design so as to neutralise a large number of variables.[11] In this way we employ social explanation in one of its potentially most powerful applications (Dogan and Pelassy, 1990: 132–143; Ragin, 1987: 34–52).

This study differs from recent trends in comparative politics devoted chiefly to examining the effects of policies rather than to explaining the reasons behind policy changes.[12] Explorations of the determinants of public policies were a prime concern of the old school of comparativists; instead, much contemporary comparative politics centres on policy processes or policy outcomes. A further difference from mainstream comparisons is that I explore cross-temporal variations (Bartolini, 1993). The political economy of a particular country changes over time, and circumstances in country A at time T might differ as markedly from circumstances in country B as they do from their own past in period T_{-1}. It is this emphasis on the historical origins of redistributive policies that warrants a qualitative rather than a quantitative approach. [13]

Concentrating on Canada, Britain, Australia and the United States facilitates the process of comparison because these countries share some institutional, religious, cultural and historical traditions (O'Connor, Orloff and Shaver, 1998). Such similarities minimise the danger of miscomparing because they avoid the problem of conceptual travelling, which carries the uncritical association of concepts with new cases (Sartori, 1984). Concepts suitable for analysing coalition governments may not be adequate for understanding one party governments, or vice versa. Following this line of argument, some authors contend that countries with common traits might profitably be grouped in families of nations (Castles, 1993; Collier and Mahon, 1993).

Divergences between liberal welfare states

It is by now almost academic convention to classify the welfare state regimes of Canada, Australia, Britain and the US among the so-called liberal welfare states. A liberal welfare state is a regime in which means-tested assistance, modest universal transfers or modest social insurance plans predominate (Esping-Andersen, 1990: 26). Means-

---

[11] There is a long-lasting debate over the strengths and weaknesses of the qualitative and quantitative methods, see Peters (1998).

[12] For a review of recent trends in comparative politics see Mair (1997a).

[13] Ferrera (1993) offers a useful summary of the methodologies employed in welfare state comparisons.

tested benefits are used either to decide whether a person should be exempt from or refunded a charge or allocated income maintenance benefits, such as supplementary benefits. Universal benefits are provided at the same level to all who qualify. By liberal social policy it is conventionally understood that assistance tends to be minimal, is intended to be short term and is often stigmatising in nature. Liberal regimes are centrally concerned with disincentive effects and tend to encourage private insurance.

The features of a liberal welfare state are those of an ideal type and not surprisingly the four countries differ markedly in some fundamental aspects. For one thing, public provision in the US is particularly ineffective against poverty amongst non-elderly groups and single mothers, and there is no entitlement to health coverage or housing. In the US there is a sharp conceptual and evaluative distinction between 'social security' and welfare, which confines social security to old-age insurance and to the associated programmes of survivors', disability and medical coverage for the elderly. Such programmes are seen as governmental obligations to deserving workers. By contrast, welfare is considered a set of governmental 'handouts' to barely deserving poor who may be trying to avoid honest employment (King, 1995a; Skocpol, 1995). Hence only social security has positive legitimacy as a state activity and comes close to being identified with full citizenship rights for Americans. Unlike Britain, Australia and Canada, the US has had no universal family allowances, which have been a common way for governments to support childbearing, and has a much higher proportion of the population in poverty (Rainwater, 1993). In particular, low-income children have a lower real standard of living than do their contemporaries in Western countries (Rainwater and Smeeding, 1995). High relative poverty rates and low and falling social expenditure levels express this real income deficit.

There are however many other parallels between the four countries. In the US, Canada, Australia and to a lesser extent in Britain immigration has influenced economic, social, demographic and cultural trends. The actual demographic impact of immigration has been a good deal lower in the United States over the last three decades than in Australia and Canada. By 1990 only 8.7 per cent of the US population were foreign born, compared with 16 per cent in Canada and 22 per cent in Australia (OECD, 1991). Australia has the largest immigrant population of the three 'settlement' countries and next comes Canada. Saunders (1994a) finds that in both Australia and Canada the distributional location of immigrants is largely independent of immigrant status, compared to the US. This difference has had important implications for the evolution of welfare policies. The answer to the question of 'who are the state-protected groups?' is inevitably more controversial in societies where a significant portion of the immigrant population is relatively worse off, can more easily be hired and fired and is often employed at much lower wages.[14]

Reasons for this peculiarity are essentially historical. In Australia the notion of equality has its origins in the frontier tradition, which emerged in the early years of white settlement. While this frontier spirit was also present in Canada and the US, the Australian experience fostered a degree of equality far beyond that found in the other colonies (McAllister, 1997). Several authors attribute this emphasis on equality to the successful implementation of the arbitration system, which prevented immigrants from being exploited. In Canada the general picture is similar to Australia, although immigrant families are more heavily concentrated at the bottom of the distribution than their non-immigrant counterparts. In the United States the distributional position of immigrants relative to that of non-immigrants seems worst of all. Saunders (1994a) shows that the percentage of immigrant families in the bottom 20 per cent of the distribution is almost three times that of their non-immigrant counterparts. However, there may be considerable differences in the earnings of immigrants when they are self-employed (Portes and Zhou, 1996).

Income inequality is racially based in the USA, with the historical trend showing Afro-Americans particularly disadvantaged, and more recently Hispanics as well (US Bureau of Census, 1996). Racial inequality seems to be less pronounced in Canada and Australia partly because of more selective immigration policies. The US is a much bigger society and therefore it is more likely to experience discrepancies. In Britain there is a clear-cut relationship between immigration and inequality. In this country immigrants were not selected but there was a flood of immigrants entitled to reside in the UK upon the dissolution of the British Commonwealth.

In Canada, Australia and the US their character of settlement countries has posed and continues to pose special questions of welfare or settlement policy (Castles, 1992; Jupp, 1994). For example, the politics of region and ethnic division created a different dynamics in the US and

---

[14] For a discussion on the relationship between immigration, inequality and policy alternatives, see DeFreitas (1998).

in Canada. In the US a peculiar combination of Southern agrarian interests and federal arrangements helped to maintain separate and unequal social groups; on the contrary, in Canada since the 1920s the welfare state has been the 'pot of glue' to which elites have turned to hold the country together (Myles, 1996).

Institutional similarities and differences

Apart from sociological and historical factors, the four countries share crucial institutional features. Most important of all, perhaps, is the electoral system based on the principle of 'first past the post'. Single plurality systems erect powerful barriers to entry for new parties and usually trigger bipolar competition, with either two alternating large parties or two alternating blocs. Plurality elections may also yield landslides or large defeats for an incumbent running relatively close to the opposition party.

Another institutional similarity between the US, Australia and Canada is that they are all federal systems where cental-local units are highly interdependent, and may compete with each other or cooperate to achieve social policy ends. Where policy designs and systems of decisionmaking are multitiered, institutional fragmentation may assume considerable importance in the development of social policy (Pierson, 1995). Federalism encouraged a territorial cleavage in the US over social policy between high-wage firms in the North and low-wage firms in the South (Gordon, 1994). Efforts to block social policy initiatives that would create a national labour market have been an enduring feature of the American welfare state. In Canada national social policy programmes embody the territorial cleavage and grant massive interregional transfers to the poor Maritime provinces. Explanations for this difference between Canada and the US are usually sought in the nature of the political economies of the two countries, where the sparsely populated and geographically isolated Maritimes make a low-wage social policy uncompetitive. The degree of fiscal federalism differs markedly among the three countries. A strong commitment in Australia and Canada to financial equalisation among national subunits makes for provincial experimentation with potentially redistributive policies less risky. The US has made little or no attempt to introduce any system of fiscal equalisation.

A major institutional difference between the US and the other three countries is that the latter are Westminster systems. The essence of the

Westminster model is the concentration of executive power in the hands of the incumbent party which 'wields vast amounts of power to rule' (Lijphart, 1984: 6). Westminster democracies are parliamentary systems of government in which the Cabinet is in principle dependent on the confidence of the parliament, but in reality there is fusion of power in the Cabinet. The Cabinet dominates parliament because it is composed of the leading members of the majority party in the House of Commons. Unconstrained by the need to stipulate alliances and to cooperate with coalition partners, governing parties can deploy state power for partisan advantage. They also are expected to be the most accountable (Klingemann, Hofferbert and Budge, 1994: 256).[15]

It is widely assumed that Westminster systems concentrate a disproportionate amount of power in Prime Ministers. Such concentration of power is the logic of single-party governments, because there is no independent legislative assembly and there are no coalition partners to check one another. More generally, however, in parliamentary systems Prime Ministers are the most prominent of politicians (Elgie, 1997).

Research on prime ministerial power in Westminster systems has centred on the controversy about whether monocratic control is exercised by the Prime Minister or whether more collegial decisionmaking prevails in Cabinet (Weller, 1985). Critics have noted how this polarisation of the debate artificially limits the field of study (Dunleavy and Rhodes, 1995). Prime ministerial power is exerted through control over other important levers, including a premier's ability to dominate parliament and retain the support of prominent party leaders.

A closer look at the four countries discloses many institutional differences. As Franks observes, 'there is room within the Westminster model of parliamentary government for many different configurations of power' (1989: 10). One component of this configuration is prime ministerial power. Prime Ministers vary considerably in their capacity to reshuffle or dismiss their Ministers. In Australia, for instance, it is the Labor parliamentary party that appoints Cabinet members with the Prime Minister distributing the portfolios; Prime Ministers control promotion within the ministry but not access to it. Thus Labor Prime Ministers are constrained in their capacity to remove Ministers because they do not choose them.

In Britain Cabinet Ministers are usually appointed from parliament

---

[15] This statement is more accurate for Britain than for Canada and Australia where the federal nature of the political system means that some degree of alliance building and cooperation for federal governments to get legislation through the upper house is necessary.

and the Prime Minister is solely responsible for their selection and dismissal. British premiers have extensively used their power to reshuffle and sack Cabinet Ministers. MacMillan discarded a third of his Ministers and Thatcher removed many of her staunch opponents between 1981 and 1982. The British Prime Minister, therefore, has considerable authority over most of the Cabinet.

Even more influential perhaps is the Canadian premier. Similarly to Britain, a Canadian premier can select and dismiss Ministers, although his influence is further enhanced by the pervasiveness of patronage power. Comparative research demonstrates that one important channel of patronage power is the career of members of parliament (King, 1991). The degree to which parliaments are used as a training ground for leadership affects the independence of a Prime Minister. As Weber noted, a parliament's first task is the supervision of executive leadership (1968: 1417–1420).

There is a sharp contrast between the parliamentary experiences in the three Westminster countries. In Britain and Australia Ministers are chosen from parliament and MPs have generally had a lengthy parliamentary career. Canada has marked out a different pattern. Membership of parliament is not considered necessary for those with leadership ambitions; Canadian leaders enter and exit parliament as circumstances demand (Franks, 1989). And the amateurism of Canadian MPs combines with the typical weak committee structures of Westminster systems (Malloy, 1996). Short tenure in the House of Commons primarily originates from extreme electoral volatility. Historically, Canadian political parties have proved unable to construct stable, long-lasting electoral alliances, except for the Liberal vote in Quebec (Young, 1998). Insecurity of parliamentary seats makes the prospect of a patronage appointment very appealing. Consequently patronage remains a powerful adhesive, bonding the leader and party members, affording Prime Ministers a dominant position toward parliament. By contrast, in both Britain and Australia a majority of seats is regarded as safe for one party or another. Security of tenure enhances the independence of MPs and strengthens the influence of backbench opinion. Institutional arrangements in the three Westminster countries suggest that the Canadian Prime Minister is far less constrained than the Australian or the British premier. Yet institutional arrangements only partly explain prime ministerial power. Jones asserts that the 'party is the most important factor determining whether the Prime Minister's power is enhanced or diminished' (1991: 175). Parties vary in the discretion conferred on the leader. Accordingly, by exploring the nature of intraparty government it is possible to generate predictions about the power of Prime Ministers (O'Leary, 1991: 158). The chapters devoted to Canada, Britain and Australia demonstrate that the day-to-day interaction between the party organisation and the premier critically affects prime ministerial power.

The inclusion of the United States in this book provides a counterpoint to the three Westminster countries. The former is a presidential system characterised by multiple veto points and loose political parties, the latter are parliamentary systems with the concentration of power in the executive and disciplined political parties (Lijphart, 1992). In presidential systems the separation of powers between the executive and the legislature involves greater transaction costs between the main institutional players. This cost may spiral under divided government when one party controls the White House and the other party enjoys a Congressional majority. Under divided government focused accountability is unlikely.[16]

Moreover, the US political environment is not conducive to strong European-style parties capable of controlling nominations and running political campaigns. American parties are principally electoral institutions that centre more on elections and less on initiating policy change than do most Western parties (Epstein, 1986). Members of the legislature seldom owe their election to the party and therefore numerical majorities may not translate into policy majorities; individual members are not bound either to work or to vote with their fellow party members. When party interests are in conflict with the personal interests of members of Congress there is usually a break with party policy. Unlike MPs in Canada, Britain or Australia, US legislators have substantial freedom of choice.

Scholars of American politics have engaged in a lively and controversial debate regarding the strengths and weaknesses of the US institutional players. For much of the twentieth century, Congress and political parties have been seen to be in decline relative to presidential powers (Schlesinger, 1974; Sundquist, 1981). Emancipation of presidential politics from the constraints of party organisations stemmed from the political and constitutional legacy of the New Deal when Franklin

---

[16] Mayhew (1991) argues that the ability of US policymakers to pass laws is no different under divided or unified government.

Delano Roosevelt totally dominated Washington politics (Milkis, 1993).

Coupled with the rise of strong presidential leadership was the inability of members of Congress to overcome their particularistic interests, which led them to abdicate their responsibilities in many key policy areas to the executive branch. The ascendancy of presidential power was further reinforced by the decline of American parties as central actors in the policymaking process. Political parties appeared increasingly irrelevant thanks to the diffusion of interest-group liberalism, the emergence of the candidate-centred politics, and the emphasis placed by mass media on candidates rather than parties (Krehbiel, 1996; Lowi, 1979; Wattenberg 1997).[17]

The thesis of party decline has been challenged on several grounds. Critics note that congressional reforms in the 1970s have led to statutory restrictions on the President's capacity to give direction to government in critical policy areas. They argue that the persistence of divided government makes it difficult for Presidents to garner support from congressional majorities. In addition, the relative strength of constituency interests on Congressional voting thwarts presidential attempts at controlling legislators (Hart, 1994; Jones, 1995). These findings regarding the impediments on presidential initiative and direction have added weight to Neustadt's (1990) contention that presidential power is the power to bargain successfully. The separation of powers between executive branch and legislative assemblies fosters mutual dependence between the President and the Congress, persuading them to legislate together (Peterson, 1990).

Congressional reforms in the 1970s were compounded by developments in the national party organisation, which strengthened party leadership. A major consequence is that party leadership and the standing committees now form a system of checks and balances (Cox and McCubbins, 1993; Ferejohn 1998). Party affiliation is still an important ingredient in voters' decisions and, therefore, politicians in seeking re-election also establish a partisan reputation.

The picture that emerges suggests that in the United States there is no single dominant authority. Accordingly, any assessment of policymaking in the US has to consider the effects on the system of separated powers, multiple initiative and veto points that characterise the federal government, making it an excellent case study for analysing redistributive games among interdependent actors.

---

[17] For a critique of this view see Ware (1985: 6–11).

Game theory in comparative politics

Redistributive games in the four countries are explored by using analytical tools that are of a game-theoretic nature. One reason is that a parsimonious theory/model reduces the number of key variables, thus further minimising the intractability of the 'many variables small N' dilemma (Golden, 1997; Levi, 1997). The main contribution of game theory to political science is its logical rigour which helps to highlight the problems of conflict and cooperation and to examine the strategies that change the payoffs (Schelling, 1980). As Scharpf aptly remarks

The game-theoretic conceptualization of interactions seems uniquely appropriate for modelling constellations that we typically find in empirical studies of policy processes: These usually involve a limited number of individual and corporate actors – governments, ministries, political parties, unions, industrial associations, business firms, research organizations, and so on – that are engaged in purposeful action under conditions in which the outcomes are a joint product of their separate choices. Moreover, these actors are generally aware of their interdependence; they respond to and often try to anticipate one another's moves. In other words, the game-theoretic conceptualization of strategic interaction has a very high degree of prima facie plausibility for the study of policy interactions (1997: 5).

Game theory is a variant of rational choice theory, and like all variants of this theory it assumes that individuals are instrumentally rational with consistent preferences (Elster, 1982; Hargreaves Heap and Varoufakis, 1995: 5). However, in order to profit from game theory we need not assume that actors are omniscient or have unlimited computational abilities (Rubinstein, 1998). More simply, it is sufficient that the basic notions of interdependent strategic action and of equilibrium solution be systematically introduced and that the three fundamental concepts of game theory – players, strategies and payoffs – be clearly applied. A player is either an individual or composite actor able to make purposeful choices among alternative courses of action. A strategy is a sequence of moves available to the player and his or her beliefs concerning the other player's plans. A game exists if the outcome is affected by the choices of the players involved. Payoffs are the valuation of a given set of possible outcomes by the preferences of the players. My thinking on game theory has been influenced by the following quotation from Rubinstein: 'I view game theory as an analysis of the concepts used in social reasoning when dealing with situations of conflict. This does not mean that the object of game theory is to predict behavior in the same sense as the sciences do, or indeed, that it is capable of such a function.... I fail to see any possibility of this being accomplished. Overall, game theory accomplishes only two tasks: It builds models based on intuition and uses deductive arguments based on mathematical knowledge' (1991: 909 and 923).

In this book I use a variety of models that are technically and analytically simple. These models are based on games with complete information that assume individuals know all the possible actions and how the actions combine to yield particular payoffs for each player. Games with complete information are simpler to understand and have sounder theoretical foundations than games with incomplete information (Osborne and Rubinstein, 1994).

Cross-fertilisation between game theory and comparative politics may help us to avoid one of the major 'methodological defects of rational choice theorizing that . . . generate and reinforce a debilitating syndrome in which theories are elaborated and modified in order to save their universalistic claim' (Green and Shapiro, 1994: 6). My study seeks to elude universalistic claims by endorsing an actor-centred institutionalism which is concerned with games real actors play (Scharpf, 1997). This perspective gives an active edge to choice and proceeds from the assumption that political outcomes stem from the interactions among intentional actors, but that these interactions are structured, and the outcomes shaped, by the characteristics of the institutional setting. Game theory cannot constitute a free-standing explanation because it takes strategic opportunities and rules as given (Sweet Stone, 1998; Ward, 1995); therefore it does not shed light on how bargaining costs are affected by the complexity of organisational variables (North, 1990: 27–35). Actor-centred institutionalism helps to overcome such glaring shortcomings of abstract modelling, offering a more realistic account of political games and redistribution.

THE LUXEMBOURG INCOME STUDY

A further hindrance to comparative policy analysis has been data comparability. As Heidenheimer, Heclo and Adams (1990: 10) have noted 'elementary though it seems one key problem in comparative policy studies is the difficulty of finding truly comparable measurements of the same things in different countries'. This drawback in comparative distributional analyses has been partially offset by the release of the

Luxembourg Income Study (LIS) micro-datasets. The salient feature of the LIS data is that a large number of income and demographic variables have been drawn from national, usually government sponsored, surveys and have been made comparable across the datasets.[18] More confidence can be attributed to the fact that distributional outcomes are not the result of changing concepts and definitions imposed on the data. Information is often confounded by global heterogeneity in its standard of collection. Some sources of this heterogeneity are the chosen unit of analysis, especially whether the data are based on households or individuals or whether the income figures are pre/tax or post/tax. In addition, the relative absence of data at more than one point in time gives very little leverage in addressing questions in a longitudinal framework.

We may surmount both obstacles by drawing upon the recent release of the Luxembourg Income Study micro-datasets, the only truly comparative data in the world.[19] Thus, it is now possible to compare poverty rates of subgroups of the population or inequality outcomes using internationally standardised measurements.

Another advantage is that the LIS datasets allow researchers to draw upon evidence assembled for more than one datapoint, resolving the difficulty concerning the relative lack of data at more than one point in time. It is now possible to examine trends in the pattern of income distribution over the years in various democratic countries. This book is therefore based on better and more reliable datasets than have been available in the past.

Advances in data quality coupled with progress in analytical techniques have made it easier to identify and monitor trends in income inequality. They have contributed to the development of more accurate accounts of how the structure of inequality has been changing and, most importantly, the role of different factors in the process of change. Although there are still formidable difficulties in assessing the overall effect of redistributive policies, the LIS datasets permit comparisons of the take-home pay of population subgroups, including the aged,

---

[18] It should be stressed that complete consistency cannot be assured because in each case the figures were drawn from national studies of income inequality which were not designed for the purpose of international comparison (Saunders, 1994b: 202). Comparability in the LIS datasets is achieved *ex-post*.

[19] The Luxembourg Income Study datasets have been made available since the late 1980s. They have been employed in several national and cross-national studies, see among others Atkinson, Rainwater and Smeeding (1995); Mitchell (1991).

low-income families, single parents and the unemployed. With the availability of LIS datasets I am able to explore inequality patterns at both the aggregate and at the disaggregate level, looking at poverty and inequality among and between specific state-dependent groups.

The income information in the surveys is, of course, subject to the problems of non-response and under reporting, and the reader is cautioned to bear this in mind when interpreting the results. The data are subject to a range of conceptual limitations. No information is available on net imputed rent, or capital gains, even though these are clearly important sources of income. Life-time income might have been a more appropriate indicator of economic well-being than annual income, but such an indicator is beyond the available data and the scope of this work. Finally, the LIS datasets only provided information on given points in time; a more complete picture required assembling data from official publications, including the governments' expenditure plans, reports of the Department of Social Security, Labour Statistics, OECD historical statistics and other OECD publications on employment and inequality.

At the current stage of our knowledge, moreover, policy evaluation in the field of income inequality is highly controversial. It goes without saying that innumerable intervening variables may alter the direction of redistributive policies during the stage of implementation, distorting the intentions of policymakers. Yet the statistics on poverty and inequality presented throughout this book indicate that there are distinct national experiences. It is this variety in inequality movements that warrants a detailed investigation of national factors, especially national policies. I begin by examining the political dynamics of welfare expansion in Canada (1971–1981), I then go on to explore the onset of retrenchment in Britain (1979–1991) and Australia (1983–1994) and, finally, I look at the demise of the federal social safety net in the US (1992–1996). One reason for the periodisation in Canada, Britain and Australia is the persistence of the same ruling party for a relatively long period, which presumably endowed party leaders with sufficient time to formulate and implement transfer programmes. The US chapter covers a shorter period because the Welfare Reform Act of 1996 represents a watershed in American social policy history and deserves close attention. This law abolished the federal social safety net, marking a break in the development of welfare policy since the 1930s (Lo and Schwartz, 1998; Weir, 1998). Regrettably, I had to exclude New Zealand from the study because comparable LIS datasets on income distribution are not available.

THE STRUCTURE OF THE BOOK

Chapter 1 critically evaluates different theoretical perspectives on the redistributive impact of ruling parties, based on either vote-maximising assumptions or the partisan model. It then argues that advances in the theory of political parties give refreshing insights into our understanding of redistributive policies. In particular, they bring to the fore the role of strategic games in redistributive outputs.

Chapters 2–5 offer a detailed analytic narrative of redistributive games in the four countries. [20] The relatively short time span covered in the US case study meant that long-term effects on income inequality were treated less systematically than for the other three countries. Moreover the decentralisation and fragmentation of the US institutional setting, coupled with the dramatic changes in welfare policy, required the construction of more complex redistributive games. As a result, the structure of the US chapter is totally different from the other three cases.

The first part of the chapters on Canada, Britain and Australia assesses the plausibility of some conventional views on the redistributive impact of parties. It describes variations in macroeconomic variables and transfer policies, and then argues that manipulations of entitlement and eligibility rules are not passive responses to economic cycles. Rather, ruling parties actively engage in redesigning those rules. Vote-maximising explanations are then explored, most notably the median-voter hypothesis and the political business cycle. Descriptive analysis of the distribution of disposable income appears inconsistent with the median-voter hypothesis. Similarly, the timing of modifications in transfer policies only partly matches the political business cycle. Above all, this section illustrates the limits of interpretations which suggest that policymakers give priority to the issues about which the public cares most.

The third and central part of each chapter examines transfer policies as the outcome of strategic interaction within the ruling party. Following Dowding's (1991: 53–54) suggestion, I analyse power relations between party actors by adopting a two-stage strategy. First, I trace the development of the choice situation: How did the contending factions find themselves in this condition? Were there substantial changes in the incentive structure that could have affected their bargaining position?

---

[20] For a recent emphasis on the heuristic value of analytic narratives see Bates *et al.* (1998).

The second stage centres on strategic games between factions over the content of transfer policies. More specifically, I first assess whether key structural changes have occurred. These include changes in the selection procedures for party delegates and party leaders, variations in the distribution of decisionmaking authority and institutional reforms. Historical reconstructions of the choice situation throw light on the strategic environment within which party leaders interact. I then explore the dynamics of factional strife and its impact on transfer policies.

The fourth part of these chapters undertakes a detailed analysis of inequality growth by first presenting results for three inequality indices. When dealing with summary measures it is always possible that outcomes vary between indices. As a check on this eventuality I calculate at least two and usually three inequality measures. Having established the direction of inequality movements the chapter deepens the understanding of the structure of inequality by investigating the distributional role of market and demographic variables. It would be unrealistic to neglect the role of non-governmental forces in changing patterns of income inequality. To this end, I employ sophisticated decomposition techniques based on the use of additively decomposable inequality measures, which disaggregate total inequality into various components.[21] In applying decomposition methods I follow the categorisation suggested by the Luxembourg Income Study which subdivides the total population into seven age groups (age of household head) and 20 family types, and I compare and analyse their relative weights and mean incomes. The distributional effects of within- and between-group inequality are carefully assessed in order to expose optical illusions. As Cowell put it, a drop in inequality could be an optical illusion if we have not taken into consideration demographic movements, or how income varies between and within different age groups (1995: 130). Alterations to the age structure, such as lower birth rates or the growing number of elderly, may affect the distribution of income among individuals (von Weizächer, 1995). Elderly people are over represented in lower-income groups and, therefore, the ageing of the population may widen income differentials. By the same token, rising inequality could be the outcome of changing household size and composition. In the post-war period the

---

[21] This method has a number of advantages over the approach usually adopted for this purpose, known as the 'shift–share analysis' or 'standardising' the inequality series (see Mookherjee and Shorrocks, 1982). In the shift–share method the distributional impact of demographic movements is investigated by disaggregating the distribution in year T_i and estimating what the distribution would have been like if the age structure had been the same as that observed in some other year. Shift–shares are more adequate to assess simple structural changes, but if several changes are occurring simultaneously it is difficult to identify the contribution of individual factors.

number of large families steadily declined, while the number of single households and lone parents gradually increased. Smaller households may have a negative distributional impact because they prevent income pooling.

To assess demographic effects I decompose distributional comparisons for age groups and household types into two main contributions, the 'between-group' and 'within-group' component. Disentangling the within-group and between-group inequality enables us to study more precisely the redistributive impact of governing parties: the higher the contribution of the between-group components, that is the stronger the association of the grouping factor with aggregate inequality, the more negligible the distributional role of transfer policies. Decomposition methods suggested that alterations in the size of age groups, especially the growing number of elderly, a factor which some authors find significant,[22] and the growing number of smaller household sizes had negligible distributional effects.

After scrutinising demographic movements I investigated market income. As mentioned earlier, most economists believe that the major source of inequality trends derives from wage differentials (Gardiner, 1996; Wes, 1996); therefore the final step in the examination of the structure of income inequality is to assess the role of market income (that is original, pre-transfer income). When trying to pinpoint the location of changes in a distribution, summary measures like the Gini coefficient are not adequate. For this purpose I follow Fritzell's (1993) suggestion of using a descriptive categorisation and I adopt the categories he defines.

An in-depth study of market-related differentials is of course outside the scope of this book. I simply glance over some explanations concerning the distribution of market income by focusing on families with a household head aged 20–64. The interesting aspect is whether inequality growth reflects changes in the lower or upper part of the earnings distribution (or both). The income classes are the following:

1 Market income less than 50 per cent of the median;
2 Market income equal to or greater than 50 per cent but less than 150 per cent of the median;
3 Market income equal to or greater than 150 per cent but less than 200 per cent of the median;
4 Market income equal to or greater than 200 per cent of the median.

[22] For a comprehensive review of the literature focusing on the relationship between income inequality and demographic structure see Pestieau (1989).

The cut-off values of the income classes do not give classes of equal size but one low-income category, a very broad middle category, an upper-middle- and a very high-income category. This categorisation is to provide cut-off values of unequal size, so that alterations in the share of market income at the top and at the bottom of the distribution can more easily be detected. After assessing the distributive role of market income, I then look at the distributive effects of government cash income, thus paving the way for some concluding remarks on the driving forces behind the pattern of transfer policies.

It is worth introducing a brief account of interdependent strategic action in each of the four case studies. Chapter 2 focuses on transfer policies in Canada under Trudeau between 1971 and 1981. This chapter is particularly innovative for the attention it places on opposition effects on intraparty bargaining. The emergence of the NDP as a new electoral rival turned Trudeau's internal vulnerability into a strategic advantage. Both the expansion and the contraction of social security benefits are viewed as the joint outcome of intra- and interparty competition. Under the Liberal minority government (1972–1974) expansionary programmes are interpreted as a dominant strategy in interparty competition triggered by the blackmail potential of the NDP. Internal conflicts resurfaced in the late 1970s when the u-turn from generous to stiffer cash benefits seemingly aimed at preempting the leadership threat.

In chapter 3 the redistributive game played by Conservative Party leaders in Britain is explained in terms of the shift between implicit and explicit games. The chapter focuses on the redistributive impact of sequential elections, which had been introduced by the new procedures for leadership selection and reselection. Sequential elections raised a potential threat to Margaret Thatcher during her first term, altering the direction of transfer policies advocated by the dries. This threat perception in the context of a dynamic process of bargaining accounted for the concessions of the dries, both in public expenditure growth and in the level and scope of unemployment benefits. One consequence was a curious asymmetry in the allocation of benefits, which changed the relativities between the unemployed and the elderly. Moreover, the onslaught against the culture of dependency launched during the second Thatcher term appeared as both cause and consequence of the institutional weakness of the wets and the virtual lack of interparty competition. Some organisational features of the Conservative Party, especially the cohesion and unity of the parliamentary party, accelerated the eventual demise of the wet coalition.

Chapter 4, the Australian case, advances a game-theoretic argument explaining how the emergence of a pivotal faction within the Australian Labor Party mitigated the market-oriented stance of the dominant rightwing group. A simple game-theoretic model illuminates the strategic interactions that obtain between the Centre-Left and the Right. This analysis suggested that the redistributive output was also a rational decision. The chapter develops a compelling model to account for the unions' acquiescence in the retrenchment of redistributive policies. Taking all of the above factors into account, the end product reveals an interesting phenomenon: although a right-wing faction dominated the party, its policies reflected a less radical attitude. Hence, while there was an ascendant tendency in income inequality under Labor, factional strife acted as a brake and limited its potential increase.

Chapter 5 is concerned with the Welfare Reform Act of 1996 in the United States. The central question addressed in this chapter is why and how US policymakers were able to surmount longstanding barriers against welfare reform. Applying a nested game with strategic timing sheds considerable light on this turning point in US social policy history. As mentioned above, in this chapter I concentrate on the preconditions and on the dynamics of the policy game while I do not offer a systematic analysis of market and demographic variables.

Chapter 6 reviews the material presented in an explicitly comparative perspective. It argues that demographic and market effects on income inequality can account for only a part of the overall inequality trend. Manipulations of eligibility and entitlement rules also influenced inequality growth. Differences in the policy actions and reactions of ruling parties in the four countries suggested that a plurality of incentives for income redistribution were at work, encompassing both electoral and factional politics. Their respective importance was the product of three key factors: the formation of specific linkages between party factions and social clienteles, the margin of manoeuvre that the institutional setting and the internal distribution of power bestowed on the leaders, and internal repercussions of Opposition effects. Viewing governing parties as political systems in miniature opened new avenues to analysing the political constellations that sustained and shaped the distribution of income in Canada, Britain, Australia and the US.

CHAPTER I

Political parties, games and income redistribution

> The essence of politics is redistribution, and political conflicts centre on matters of distribution.

> Karl Brunner

What are the incentives for income redistribution in democratic systems? At two opposite ends of the spectrum stand interpretations based on rational choice theory and political sociology. For the former, ruling parties redistribute income to maximise votes, for the latter, parties have contrasting distributive goals that are consistent with the interests of their core constituencies. Oriented towards the paradigm of representative democracy and pre-given electoral constituencies, the debate centres on the responsiveness of elected representatives to voters' demands. Advances in the literature on party politics, however, have exposed the limits of traditional approaches and provided a richer and more suggestive account of political games and redistribution.

The aim of this chapter is to compare, integrate and enrich traditional models with theoretical developments in the field of party politics. These developments are organised around the notion of political slack, the autonomy from voters that may give party leaders a substantial margin of freedom. Political slack signifies that information may be hidden or its disclosure postponed, rules may be changed or eluded, communication and coordination may be hindered or facilitated.[1] Above all, political slack may furnish party leaders with enough leeway to engage in redistributive games that exploit underlying dissension. In this view, redistributive policies stem from party conflicts and not from antecedents to those conflicts.

---

[1] The notion of political slack derives from the broader notion of organisational slack in the theory of the firm (Cyert and March, 1992).

TRADITIONAL REDISTRIBUTIVE GAMES: MEDIAN VOTER, POLITICAL BUSINESS CYCLE AND PARTISAN MODEL

Rational choice theorists endorsing Downsian analyses believe that voters have specific preferences on redistributive policies, and that they select parties which are closest to their position in the policy space (Denters, 1993). In plurality-rule systems, if the frequency distribution of voters is single peaked, vote-seeking parties adopt policies close to the median voter (Downs, 1957; Hinich and Munger, 1997; Shepsle and Bonchek, 1997).[2] Parties alter their position in the electoral space to capture the median voter and, therefore, one should not expect that parties alternating in power formulate distinctive redistributive policies. On the assumption that median voters and median-income groups overlap, this model posits that the middle classes benefit from redistributive efforts (Tullock, 1983: 102–106). Along these lines many scholars have conducted studies focusing on the median voter as the key to understanding the politics of income redistribution (Bishop, Formby and Smith, 1991; Colburn, 1990; Lindbeck and Weibull, 1987; Persson and Tabellini, 1994; Scully and Slottje, 1989).

For other rational choice theorists the political business cycle best explains the impact of vote-maximising parties on transfer income (Griffin and Leicht, 1986; Nordhaus, 1975). This model assumes that the 'key economic element in the electoral-economic cycle is real disposable income' (Tufte, 1978: 29). Parties manipulate instruments of budgetary policies, such as taxation and expenditure, to achieve short-term electoral benefits. Political business cycles are typically characterised by spending cuts early in the term, followed by generous benefits later in the term. The pattern is expected to recur cyclically, with parties deferring the costs of pre-election increases in the level of transfer benefits until after the election.

Vote-maximising explanations of policymaking are sometimes criticised for placing unrealistic demands on both party leaders and voters. Scarce information on what actually influences voting behaviour suggests that party leaders necessarily rely on ideological assumptions about the nature of the electorate (Budge, 1994). Incomplete information,

---

[2] Vote-maximising parties will not implement redistributive policies aimed at capturing the median voter if: (a) there are multiple issue dimensions; (b) there is a single dimension, but the frequency distribution of voters is double peaked and alienation/abstentions are significant (Lindbeck and Weibull, 1987); (c) there is a single dimension but differential alienation/abstention across two parties; (d) there are more than three parties and easy entry for new parties.

coupled with mobility between income classes that has been induced by social programmes and market forces, means that the 'median voter is never entirely certain about his future position in the income distribution' (Bishop, Formby and Smith, 1991: 53). This conclusion is also reached by Rabinowitz and MacDonald (1989), who posit that voters have diffuse preferences over certain directions, rather than an ordered set of preferences along the policy space.

What is more, conceptions of parties as vote maximising teams beg the question of what defines a given party and what determines its boundaries. They also side-step vital issues related to the birth and diffusion of parties. Vote-maximising explanations typically leave unanswered questions dealing with party identification and systematically ignore the extensive body of evidence indicating that voters identify with one party instead of another (Campbell *et al.*, 1960; Heath *et al.*, 1991). These limitations acquire added force in the light of research findings that point to the stability of voting behaviour in Western democracies (Bartolini and Mair, 1990).

The partisan model addresses some of the weaknesses of rational choice theory (Alesina, 1989). Parties are conceived as agents representing deep-rooted social cleavages in the electoral arena (class, religion, ethnicity, agrarian) (Lipset and Rokkan, 1967: 1–65). These cleavages reflect the interests of well-defined social groups and carve the electoral boundaries of political parties. In the partisan model, party strategy is directed towards garnering support within a given constituency and, through a process of integration, towards the protection of that constituency from rival parties. For political sociologists parties emerge to express and manage social cleavages through the political process. Solidarity among social groups is the seed for the growth of political parties.

Political sociologists primarily focus on socio-economic cleavages. A typical assumption is that 'parties have contrasting income distribution goals that are consistent with the locations of their core constituencies in the hierarchy of income classes' (van Arnhem and Schotsman, 1982; Boix, 1998; Brown, 1995; Hibbs and Dennis, 1988: 469). Lower-income classes, which make up the core constituency of left-wing parties, have greater exposure to rising unemployment and normally bear a disproportionate share of the social costs of economic recessions. Their relative position in the income distribution is, therefore, improved by a generous system of social security. For this reason 'vertical redistribution and the oblivion of poverty . . . are goals which one might expect would distinguish the social policy stance of parties and groups ostensibly espousing lower-class interests' (Castles and Mitchell, 1993: 116). It is important to note that redistributive struggles are considered to be inherently zero sum games, with one social class getting what the other one loses.

At first sight, the redistributive games summarised above appear incompatible. On the one hand, party leaders are portrayed as selfish and amoral vote maximisers, redistributing income in order to expand their share of votes. On the other hand, the redistributive choices of left-wing and right-wing parties are sharply differentiated, with Conservative parties exacerbating income differences and Socialist parties levelling them. These results, since they seem to be anomalies within both the rational choice and sociological perspectives, can be a starting point for reassessing the redistributive role of political parties.

ADVANCES IN THE THEORY OF PARTY POLITICS

The extant literature on the redistributive impact of parties does tackle some important questions, albeit in a framework which does not facilitate the cumulation of evidence or the systematic pursuit of theoretical models. One consequence is that some authors have questioned *tout court* the influence of parties on the redistributive process (Boyne, 1995; Cutright, 1966; Hoggart, 1987). They contend that structural imperatives, both national and international, economic and bureaucratic, limit the margin of manoeuvre of political leaders. Parties alternating in power seem to yield marginal and incremental/decremental changes in redistributive policies (Hall, 1986; Rose, 1974; 1984a).

Evidence supporting this argument can be marshalled from the experience of several liberal democracies. Contrary to expectations, the Labour governments of New Zealand and Australia have implemented substantial cuts in marginal tax rates, particularly at higher-income levels (Saunders, 1992). If party behaviour is couched in ideological terms these choices are inexplicable because regressive policies are normally associated to right-wing parties. Conversely, the Swedish Conservative government in the early 1980s adopted policies of continuity with previous Social Democratic programmes. Baldwin's (1990) important contribution on the impact of bourgeois parties in the development of welfare states adds weight to the contention that ideology is often a residual variable. The ideological divide between Left and Right over economic issues appears increasingly as an 'amorphous vessel'

whose meaning varies systematically across societies (Huber and Inglehart, 1995).

The alleged interchangeability of governing parties has stimulated a
flurry of intellectual activity around the question, 'Does Politics Matter?'
(Schmidt, 1996; Sharpe and Newton, 1984). 'Visions and realities'
(Castles and Wildenmann, 1986) of party government have even led
scholars to wonder, 'Where is the Party?' (Krehbiel, 1993). Much has
been written on the crisis and decline of parties as relevant actors in the
policymaking process (Wattenberg, 1997). Apparently brushed aside by
direct links between interests groups and public administration, ruling
parties have ostensibly failed to meet the demands of liberal democracies
(Lowi, 1979). At best, neocorporatist arrangements superseded elected
representatives by deciding on key issues which subsequently determined
most remaining areas of policymaking (Schmitter, 1974); at worst, parties
surrendered under the burden of governmental overload or resistance to
change from public bureaucracies (Peters, 1989; Rose, 1984b). Whilst the
importance of corporatism and governmental complexity cannot be
denied, such claims tend to detract from an appreciation of the influence
exerted by ruling parties in shaping redistributive policy.

Critics have noted that the emphasis on the failure and decline of
parties may largely be misconceived. They stress that parties survive and
persist through processes of adaptation and control, which stimulate
change rather than decline (Mair, 1997b). Protagonists of the decline of
parties debate seem to accept uncritically the reality of party control
over the complex web of institutions and networks surrounding the state
apparatus. Perhaps unrealistic hopes on the policymaking impact of
governing parties have sparked deep dissatisfaction among policy analysts (Patterson, 1996). If this interpretation is correct, then one should
really allude to crises of expectations rather than crises of parties. Katz
and Mair find that there is little real evidence to suggest that the age of
party has waned; 'on the contrary, their position has strengthened, not
least as a result of the increased resources that the state places at their
disposal' (1995: 25).

Discussions of party decline have prompted remarkably few re-
examinations of the nature of parties. Arguably, if research on party
government generates inconsistent results, it is less a problem of contradictory evidence and more a question of inadequate theoretical lenses
(Blondel, 1995).[3] Despite the consensus that politics matters, qualified as

---

[3] The *International Political Science Review* has recently devoted an entire issue to the theoretical lacuna
on the topic of party government (see volume 16, 1995).

it often is, Vowles and McAllister (1996: 192) note that political variables usually enter into comparative public policy research largely unexamined and frequently by the back door. Empirical research on the redistributive impact of parties seems to ignore established models of party government. For example, in Katz's well-known elaboration (1986), there are essentially three requirements of party government: 1 the most important decisions must be taken by individuals elected through party competition, or by individuals they have nominated and who are responsible to them; 2 policies must be formulated within the party in government in the case of one-party government, or after negotiations between parties in the case of coalition governments; 3 representatives nominated to the highest offices, such as Ministers or the Prime Minister, must be selected from within their party and be responsible to the electorate through their parties. In this type of government political parties control the formulation and implementation of public policies (Calise, 1989). Needless to say, this is an ideal type conception of party government, intended as a useful device for identifying empirical deviations from the model.

One aspect of this model of party government is the emphasis placed on intraparty politics. The second proposition explicitly states that 'policies must be formulated within the party in government' and the third proposition further highlights the role of intraparty politics in the selection of elected representatives. Yet with few notable exceptions (Brady and Epstein, 1997; Luebbert, 1986; McGillivray, 1997), scholars have paid little or no attention to the effects of intraparty processes on policy outputs. Before dismissing the impact of ruling parties on redistributive policies as a non-issue, an effort might be made to develop a better theoretical understanding of the ways in which competition and party politics shape these policies (Denters, 1993).

While the traditional views on the redistributive impact of parties have proceeded along the above lines, three very different approaches to the study of party politics evolved under the headings of party goals, party competition and party organisation. The argument developed throughout this book demonstrates that theoretical advances shed considerable light on redistributive games. For a start, models of party goals have moved beyond over-simplified patterns (Strøm, 1989); research on party competition has benefited from supply-side extensions to demand-side explanations (Boix, 1998; Dunleavy, 1991);[4] and theorists of party

---

[4] The term supply side is used to mean politician-driven rather than demand-driven policies.

organisation have convincingly relaxed the unitary actor assumption
(Katz and Mair, 1992; Laver and Shepsle, 1990; Maor, 1998). For the
purpose of this book, the primary contribution of these lines of inquiry is
to shed new light on redistributive games.

PARTY GOALS: TRADE-OFFS AND PRIORITIES

Party goals have figured prominently in recent research on party politics (Harmel and Janda, 1994). Few discussions of party politics manage
to get along without introducing some notion of party goals. Early
rational choice models did pay some attention to strategic goals, but
their depiction was somewhat rudimentary. Parties were portrayed as
merely vote seekers aspiring to control government (Downs, 1957).
Critics soon noted the limits of this perspective. They affirmed that
political parties sought to expand their control over political office
rather than to seek votes (Riker, 1962). The office-seeking party aimed
at enjoying patronage prerogatives and at receiving benefits from private goods beyond their electoral value. Others deplored the 'policy
blindness' of such studies because it concealed party efforts to carry out
electoral pledges; they declared that the policy-seeking party was concerned with the ideological disposition of the coalition in which it
participated (Budge and Laver, 1986; Klingemann, Hofferbert and
Budge, 1994: 27–30).

These models seem to be based on the rather questionable view that
goals are mutually exclusive; parties maximise votes, expand their
control over offices or design and administer policies. From these
standpoints a political party is dressed in a straitjacket, incapable of
bargaining or negotiating over a set of goals. Party competition reflects a
narrow, one-sided activity.

A broader definition of party behaviour sees its manifestations as
many-sided and multifarious. Vote-seeking, policy-seeking and office-
seeking evolve as special cases of competitive party behaviour under
specific institutional conditions (Strøm, 1989). Party competition is a
multiple goal undertaking, whereby leaders scrutinise a plurality of
strategic moves. Party leaders endure each of these strategic aims in
various arenas. They seek votes in the electoral arena but gain office and
implement policy in the executive–legislative arena (Narud, 1996). Such
arenas are interlinked power structures, where moves in one arena bear
consequences in another arena, nudging leaders to play nested games
(Batty and Danilovic, 1997; Tsebelis, 1990).

The perspective of party leaders as actors engaged in the pursuit of multiple goals within multiple arenas provides a refreshing improvement. Such refinement is very encouraging but it does raise important questions. If party leaders are able and willing to simultaneously pursue policy-seeking, vote-seeking and office-seeking strategies, then the question remains of how parties choose between conflicting goals. Working-class interests, for instance, cannot be fully represented when left-wing parties expand their share of votes to include middle-class votes (Przeworski and Sprague, 1986). Vote-maximising behaviour may thwart egalitarian objectives and principles. More generally, if ideologies are tied to social classes, and political parties try to appeal and attract voters from different social strata, the ideological dimension is inevitably blurred (Kirchheimer, 1966). The implication is that either reasons exist for undertaking one course of action instead of another, or alternatives must be equivalent.

A solution is to posit a 'trade-off frontier' between the achievement of one objective against another. Strøm declares that 'a theory of competitive political parties requires an understanding of the interrelations and *trade-offs* between different objectives' (1989: 570). Likewise, Budge and Laver contend that when 'we consider policy and office payoffs simultaneously, it is clear that policy concessions may be compensated by portfolios, or vice versa, in one of a number of possible ways' (1986: 498).

The idea of trade-offs between goals is compelling, but it does raise some empirical problems. For instance, although trade-offs entail no goal being subordinate to another, such 'subordination is, however, an implicit but fundamental consequence of the role that the theories typically accord to some form of "winning" criterion' (Budge and Laver, 1986: 498). A few illustrations may suffice to substantiate this claim. Perhaps the best-known example is Downs's dictum that 'parties formulate policies in order to win elections, rather than win elections in order to formulate policies' (Downs, 1957: 27–28); others find that parties are policy seekers and win elections to implement their programmes (Budge, 1994; Klingemann, Hofferbert and Budge, 1994: 27–30); yet others write that 'leaders ... want to be party leaders first, and to gain government power second' (Dunleavy and Husbands, 1985: 38–39). It is evident that party goals are generally perceived to be of unequal significance. The essence of this criticism is that party actors deliberately select their strategies with reference to a system of priorities. Thus a substantial literature challenges the view that no party goal prevails, implicit in the assumption that trade-offs are applicable to all goals.

There are at least two reasons adduced for the subordination of goals. First, it is highly plausible that party leaders have a salience ranking in their choices (Robertson, 1976). It is often unrealistic that two policy dimensions, such as taxes and expenditure, are ranked in the same order of importance. The second reason is found in decision theory and refers to the cognitive limitations of the human mind (Rubinstein, 1998; Simon, 1957: 241–260). Imperfect information and bounded rationality involve that the 'situation is searched for alternatives that are related to the main [goal] and the alternatives are evaluated in terms of it' (Lindenberg, 1988: 45). Experimental research shows that such pragmatic attitudes prevail when there is opportunity-cost time pressure (Payne, Bettman and Luce, 1996). In setting priorities to their strategic options decisionmakers resort to one primary goal.

The joint effect of cognitive limitations and salience ranking explains why some sort of hierarchy of objectives may be more commonly adopted than usually believed (Keeney and Raiffa, 1993: 41). This conclusion should not be surprising. If it were possible to simply trade-off strategic goals, it would logically follow that decisionmakers were indifferent to the achievement of one goal or the other. Consequently, party politics would be of no possible political interest because the choices made would *not* be the result of power conflicts but, indeed, a matter of indifference.

Recognising that party leaders pursue multiple goals within a system of priorities is a step towards bridging the gap between conventional models on the redistributive impact of parties. As discussed in the first section, the established debate centres on whether redistributive policies arise from vote-seeking or policy-seeking behaviour. This dichotomy seems now misleading, because both viewpoints fall prey to the objection that parties adopt a plurality of aims.

PARTY COMPETITION: ARITHMETICAL PARTICULARISM AND DIRECTOR'S LAW

The simultaneous pursuit of different goals is a key assumption of the directional model of party competition (Rabinowitz and MacDonald, 1993).[5] The model assumes that voters have a diffuse understanding of policies and argues that vote-seeking parties will offer clear policy alternatives. Convergence to the centre of the policy space may be

---

[5] See the symposium in the *Journal of Theoretical Politics* (vol. 9, 1997).

pointless if voters are attracted to candidates who are on the same side of an issue as they are. In this situation, party identification and instrumental rationality are inextricably entwined in the decisionmaking process.

Directional theory disputes the role of Euclidean distance in voting behaviour and throws light on why redistributive policies may differ when parties alternate in power. However, it endorses the assumption of exogenous preferences and hence of demand-driven strategies. Consequently, like other theories discussed so far, the directional model would be unable to answer a fundamental question: When are party leaders prepared to accept the trade-off between the government's budget constraint and social security contributions? All these theories therefore suffer from the same weakness. One reaction to this weakness is to argue that it is not really a weakness at all: income redistribution is a response to exogenous factors, such as the location of voters in the electoral space or the interests of the party's core constituency. Political parties are conceived as inputs that mechanically tie the demands of social groups to redistributive outputs.

The idea that public preferences set the public agenda has come under heavy fire for neglecting political slack, the independence of party leaders from voters (Aldrich, 1995; Dunleavy, 1991). Party leaders do not merely articulate social cleavages, but instead actively engage in defining those cleavages. Drawing upon evidence from seven European countries and 37 political parties, Iversen finds that 'the emergence of new political cleavages (conflicts over political issues) cannot be reduced to the study of the emergence of new social cleavages (divisions in people's life experiences)' (1994: 174).

Social cleavages are salient in any given society only to the extent that political parties mobilise the groups affected by those cleavages. Research findings indicate that electoral movement is positively correlated with political mobilisation, when parties mobilise voters electoral turnout is higher (Frendreis *et al.*, 1990; Patterson and Caldeira, 1988). Political parties are autonomous actors able to devise policy packages to forge new constituency identities, especially after major electoral defeats (Janda *et al.*, 1995).

This formulation may exaggerate the ease with which the electorate can be swayed by party leaders (Iversen, 1994). Stigler (1970), for instance, draws attention to Director's Law of income redistribution, which states that the middle classes have historically benefited from income redistribution, by strategically repositioning themselves in different voting coalitions. In the nineteenth century, when only excises and real property were feasible bases of taxation, the distribution of tax revenues by income class would be relatively regressive; as taxation became proportional and expenditure consisted of universal benefits, the potential rewards from redistribution rose for the lower-income classes. 'In the long run the middle classes may have been beneficiaries of this process because they were in coalition with the rich in the nineteenth century, and are entering into coalition with the poor today' (Stigler, 1970: 9). The main problem with Stigler's model is that policy change is exogenous. To make sense of Director's Law in political terms, it is sufficient to note that social groups may change their party allegiances when ruling parties actively deploy redistributive policies to manufacture electoral coalitions. Policymakers may alter the redistribution of costs and benefits to mould winning coalitions of voters.

In practice this strategy translates in adjusting social relativities and in modifying the relative position of target groups or in maintaining social relativities and in protecting the relative social and economic position of social groups (Dunleavy, 1991). Decisionmakers may enact arithmetical particularism, aimed at forging coalitions between diverse sections of the electorate.

Viewing governing parties as autonomous actors helps to clarify their role in the redistribution of income. It points to the fact that the social interests, which ruling elites caters for, are not always pre-given, but may be created and activated by party leaders. This line of reasoning shifts the debate from voter-driven to politician-driven policies, and brings to the fore issues of strategic interaction between party leaders. However, a focus on party leaders raises the question of what limits the margin of freedom of party leaders.

PARTY ORGANISATION: PIVOTAL PLAYERS, STRATEGIC DISAGREEMENT, SEQUENTIAL ELECTIONS AND CORRELATED STRATEGIES

One way to resolve the question is spelled out in the literature that views the party as an organisation. Introduced in the pioneering studies of Michels (1959 [1915]) and Ostrogorski (1902), and expanded in the early post-war works of Duverger (1959) and Neumann (1956), the conception of parties *qua* organisations has recently come back into the limelight (Katz and Mair, 1994; Maor, 1997; Panebianco, 1988).

A central tenet of these developments is that parties are miniature political systems, where the making and breaking of coalitions between contending leaders is 'the driving force of party life' (Katz and Mair, 1992: 12). It follows that there is little we can understand and discuss as long as the assumption remains that the party underworld is all alike, all made of one and the same stuff (Sartori, 1976). Yet unitary models are still the prevailing mode of analysis in most research on party behaviour (Strøm, 1998). The common justification for this approach is that simplicity is necessary in order to make the world intelligible and that the unitary actor has performed successfully in models of party competition (Laver and Schofield, 1990). But the best rejoinder to this argument is as follows. It holds if, and only if, by adding new variables the explanatory power of our results is not significantly enhanced.

Puzzles in party behaviour have prompted some analysts to re-evaluate the heuristic value of unitary models. There seems to be a growing awareness, especially among rational choice theorists accustomed to the unitary actor, that a disaggregated view of political parties may yield fruitful results. Laver and Shepsle, for instance, consider the general area of intraparty politics:

to be one of the most exciting and underdeveloped in the entire literature, since it generates the potential to provide some motivation for the actions of political parties, hitherto unrealistically seen by most theorists as anthropomorphic unitary actors. (Laver and Shepsle, 1996: 246)

To be sure, such weakness is not new to public choice analysts. Many years ago Coleman observed that leaders 'must concern themselves not only with winning an external battle, but first of all, with maintaining control of their own party as well' (1971: 35).[6] Battles for the control of the party make internal governance a key analytical dimension. Disregarding this dimension rules out fundamental questions such as, What is the range of strategies that intraparty elites can play? And, is the mobilisation of resources a response to the actual or expected bargaining position of intraparty players? In short, by assuming away any consideration of internal governance we treat as *parametric* what is instead *strategic* because we take as given interdependent strategic action within the party in power.

We are thus unable to perceive party actors as Riker's 'herestheticians', who strategically invent new policies to exploit underlying dissension, outflank contending rivals, or head off internal opposition (Nagel, 1993; Riker, 1986: 52–65); we cannot discern internal networks of coalitions that constantly exchange the resources necessary for the

---

[6] Along these lines compare Aldrich and McGinnis (1989); Aranson and Ordeshook (1972).

fulfilment of their tasks (Schwartz, 1990: 9–15); we fail to identify the different faces, or aspects, of party organisations (Mair, 1997b); and we must grudgingly endorse artificial assumptions about preference homogeneity within parties (Laver and Shepsle, 1990: 506). Available models of party competition inhibit the identification of both the range of strategic options party actors enjoy and the type of incentives they can deploy (Aldrich and McGinnis, 1989; Cox and Rosenbluth, 1996). They prevent the analysis of institutional changes within the party organisation, and the impact of these changes on strategic games. The empirical chapters in this book show that alterations in the leadership selection rules or in the electoral system for party delegates deeply affect the dynamics of political games.

Retaining control of the party should be regarded as a fourth goal party leaders strive to attain. Cox and McCubbins (1993) forcefully argue that party leaders seek party maintenance, reselection and re-election. In the light of these considerations, theorists of party organisations have pushed the argument on party goals one stage further by noting that leaders are 'motivated above all by a desire to remain party leaders' (Luebbert, 1986: 46). Innumerable examples show that battles over party platforms are often acrimonious because the outcome stands as symbolic evidence of who controls the party, rather than as a guideline for the making of public policy (Ware, 1987: 125–126). Since the outcome of party platforms reflects the equilibrium of power within the party, it follows that changes in the internal balance of power may alter party policy.

Leaving aside the debate on the definitions of power, suffice it to note that some scholars have endorsed a concept of power in the tradition of social exchange theory, where power is considered a 'relation of unequal exchange' (Maor, 1992; Panebianco, 1988: 21–25). Studying the resources of power within party organisations involves focusing upon the zones of uncertainty or unpredictable areas of organisational activity (Mair, 1994). Following this line of reasoning, party politics scholars have identified four crucial resources of power: recruitment and selection, financing, decisionmaking authority and the distribution of incentives for political participation (Panebianco, 1988: 33–36).

It is worth stressing that a conceptualisation of power only in terms of resources is insufficient (Barry 1989: 226–229). There must also be the desire to use the resources and the willingness to bear the costs of using them. Despite these limitations, I agree with the contention that 'the best starting point for the study of the relative power of groups in society is an examination of their resources, given the rules of the game they are playing' (Dowding, 1991: 77). The way power resources are controlled within the party deeply affects the margin of manoeuvrability of party leaders. Different decisionmaking regimes enhance or undercut strategic flexibility, affecting the manner in which party actors take and enforce strategic decisions. The typical distinction is between centralisation and decentralisation of power. What emerges from this discussion is that the difference in the way power is distributed within the party is a key to strategic opportunities and bargaining outcomes. Any discussion of internal governance must start with viewing party organisations as 'politically negotiated orders' (Bacharach and Lawler, 1981: 1).

Previous explorations of the party underworld have proved invaluable in detecting the party–policy link. Policy outputs may hinge on the relative strength of party factions in the legislative or executive arena (Brady and Epstein, 1997). In Ireland, for instance, Sinnott (1986) found that intraparty politics influenced key policy areas, such as capital taxation, abortion and divorce. More recently, Kitschelt notes that social democratic strategies are accounted for by intraorganisational decisionmaking (1994: 93).

Pivotal players and strategic disagreement

A complete description of the internal dynamics of parties must look at horizontal interactions among party leaders and vertical interactions between leaders and followers. Horizontal interactions between elites may be viewed as games of position, power and status (Shubik, 1984 : 655). Not surprisingly, the bulk of research concentrates on bargaining between party elites, especially between members of national legislatures (Cox and McCubbins, 1994; Weingast and Marshall, 1988).

Intraelite games are often non-cooperative because each faction is trying to maintain or expand its power to the disadvantage of other factions. Critical here is the pivotal position, which can tilt the balance in favour of one or the other faction. A pivotal player is endowed with blackmail or coalition potential deployable in bargaining games. Redistributive games can be analysed as a two-stage game, where the pivotal player enters in the second stage.[7]

One way of consolidating internal power is to establish ties with subgroups of the electorate. These ties legitimise the existence and

---

[7] A more complex game could certainly accommodate more than two stages.

power of the faction and explain why one faction may opt for maintaining social relativities, while another prefers to adjust them (Schwartz, 1994). Party leaders, for example, may appeal to different income groups by cutting taxes on one group, while offering more generous social security benefits to another group. Preference diversity implies that party leaders have more than one policy position.

Faction leaders, moreover, have to consider not only which redistributive proposal maximises electoral support, but also which proposal fosters enduring internal alliances. The 'income redistribution game which is zero-sum from the point of view of citizens need not be zero-sum from the point of view of elected representatives' (Frolich and Oppenheimer, 1984: 130). For one thing, politicians can engage in strategic disagreement which aims at avoiding reaching an agreement when compromise could alienate supporters or damage their prospects in upcoming elections (Gilmour, 1995).

Sequential elections

The discussion so far has been concerned with horizontal channels of influence. However, it may be at least equally interesting to concentrate on the process of power exchange between leaders and activists (Koelble, 1996). The vast majority of parties in liberal democracies require voluntary labour to conduct a variety of activities. Activists who join parties because they believe in a cause provide most of this work. For this reason leaders must persuade followers to cooperate by distributing ideological and solidaristic incentives (Scarrow, 1996; Ware, 1992; Whiteley, Seyd and Richardson, 1994).

Activists, moreover, may influence the selection of leaders. A telling illustration is provided by the leadership contest in the British Conservative Party in July 1995. The decision of the right-winger John Redwood to fight for the leadership raised concerns about the solidity of Major's internal support. Jeremy Hanley, then party chairman, warned Conservative MPs that Major's re-election reflected the wishes of the party constituencies. In his words, if 'MPs forget who sent them there, then they forget one of the most basic rules of politics. They were all selected by people who work very hard for the party.' As *The Guardian* editorialist continued the 'unstated warning is that any more messing around by dissidents would lead to deselection' (*The Guardian*, 5 July 1995: 3).

Research on leader–activist relations depicts leaders as vote seekers and activists as policy seekers, more committed to ideological or purposive goals (Erikson *et al.*, 1989).[8] 'The general rule is that rank-and-file, more concerned with ideology and less in line for the other spoils of office, tend to resent ... policy compromises' (Laver and Schofield, 1990: 24). We can see the potentially disruptive effect of the leader–activist divergence with a sequential elections example (Aranson and Ordeshook, 1972).

Before proceeding further, it is important to note that there are two distinct definitions of sequential elections in the literature. One refers to successive *national* elections, the other to elections of different *types* of constituencies, such as MPs, activists and voters. In this book I use the second definition. Sequential elections obtain because, in order to gain office, leaders must win more than one election, for instance intraparty elections, conventions, primaries and national elections. A typical dilemma of party leaders is to capture the median voter without alienating the median activist (Coleman, 1971; Dunleavy and Husbands, 1985). Sequential elections exemplify the quandary of party leaders when the wishes of party activists differ from those of the wider electorate.

Correlated strategies

Party leaders seek to retain control over horizontal and vertical channels of influence by simultaneously striving for power in multiple arenas and distributing incentives to members and voters. Thus, adding the organisational dimension reconciles the two antonymic images of 'party as a tool and party as a faith' deployed by rational choice analysts and political sociologists (see Pomper, 1992: 148). Like most other organisations, political parties are for the most part mixed-motive settings, where actors have tentatively consented both to cooperate and compete.

If the organisational dimension is so crucial to understanding party policies, why have we been so slow to look inside the objects of our interest? For Lawson (1990) some of the reasons are normative and methodological. Normatively, the work of officeholders is considered to be the work on which parties themselves should be judged. The most visible task of political parties is achieved by their elected representatives, often in coalition with those representing other parties. As a

---

[8] There is a lively debate in the literature on May's 'Law of Curvilinear Disparity' which asserts that activists are more radical than party elites (May, 1973). For an excellent review see Kitschelt (1989). For a recent reappraisal and empirical refutation with reference to the British case, see Norris (1995).

consequence, analysts have focused more on the relative strength of the parties in elections and less on parties as individual organisations in their own right. The second major obstacle to a closer examination of parties *qua* organisations is methodological. We have been in the habit of using readily available evidence, such as vote shares, and we have too often sought similar kinds of sources for scrutinising the internal workings of political parties.

This emphasis on the internal dimension should not obscure the fact that party organisations sometimes act as cohesive teams resembling unitary actors. The history of party politics affords ample evidence to show that certain conditions cement internal cohesion and trigger centralising pressures. It is well-documented, for example, that Bismark's anti-socialist laws helped to strengthen oligarchical control within the German Social Democratic Party (Roth, 1979). In representative democracies, moreover, it is generally believed that when electoral competition intensifies, internal wrangling wanes (Berry and Canon 1993). Unitary models have repeatedly proved their heuristic value; this book only places limitations upon them by suggesting that there are internal costs and opportunities attached to competitive behaviour.

Sudden availability of new options in the electoral arena may impinge on bargaining games within the party. Therefore threats to internal stability may stem from party competition (Mair, 1994). Correlatively, 'the *outer* moves of a party – the inter-party competition – are also a function of its *inner* moves, that is, of intra-party competition' (Sartori, 1976: 347). Party actors are constantly confronted with the need to stipulate, maintain or redefine alliances with their partners or with sections of the electorate. In a nutshell, internal and external games are interlinked.

Once we examine parties as miniature political systems, it is possible to interpret redistributive choices as the equilibrium solution of nested games played in multiple arenas with priority given to internal payoffs. This result furnishes a criterium to be used in specifying the arenas of analysis in that it indicates that the payoffs gained in different arenas are not interchangeable. Payoffs in the internal arena carry more weight because they affect the equilibrium of power between contending party leaders.[9]

---

[9] The main problem here is that payoffs in the internal arena may delicately hinge on payoffs in the external arena. An illustrative example is the resignation of the party leader following an electoral defeat. Electoral losses lend ammunition to counter-elites by exposing the weakness of the dominant coalition.

Reconstructing the history of intraelite negotiations and conflicts in the light of their redistributive impact, an area not yet adequately researched, could thus broaden the scope of debate beyond existing controversies. The time dimension is useful to shed light on correlated strategies, where the actions of player I at time T depend on the actions of player II at time T_{-1}. This approach clarifies the preconditions to redistributive choices and helps to understand policy outputs, overthrowing the paradox that, while all politics is dynamic, much political analysis is static (Box-Steffensmeir, Arnold and Zorn, 1997).

CONCLUSION: POLITICAL SLACK AND REDISTRIBUTIVE POLICIES

Scholarly work on the incentives for income redistribution in a liberal democracy has produced fundamentally different interpretations. The main theoretical division within this field is drawn between those who seek sociological explanations, on the one hand, and those who focus on instrumental rationality, on the other. Their similarities lie in the endorsement of the unitary actor model and preference-homogeneity among party leaders.

A central problem for sociological accounts remains their disregard of non-societal cleavages; their concerns contain no acknowledgement of elite-induced conflicts. This perspective reflects a general tendency in post-war political science to see the causal links between society and polity as running from the former to the latter, rather than the other way round. Established rational choice models fall prey to a similar difficulty. The autonomy of political parties in the redistributive process cannot be adequately addressed by prevailing demand-driven models, which assume that politicians are vote takers, and that their policies are dictated by exogenous variables.

Politician-driven explanations in many ways complement and integrate established models based on vote-driven accounts by suggesting that redistributive games are endogenously determined. Governing parties may try and persuade voters to sustain new redistributive programmes by engaging in arithmetical particularism or Director's Law of income redistribution (in the sense I have redefined it). Yet a central difficulty remains. Assessing whether redistributive policies are vote or politician driven fails to explain why governing parties accept trade-offs between social security benefits and budget constraints. My argument suggests that one of the routes into the problem is to look inside the party organisation and to analyse the redistributive games played by party factions. Faction leaders may develop or attenuate their ties with electoral constituencies by reallocating costs and benefits to specific social groups. This step requires moving beyond unitary models of party politics, and endorsing a conception of parties as complex organisations where bargaining is ubiquitous.

Political slack then becomes the focus of analysis. Political slack in party organisations is based on the control of at least four resources of power: selection of party delegates and leaders, funding, decisionmaking rules and distribution of incentives for participation. The individuals or factions that control these resources of power gain a strategic advantage within the party because they can deploy them in bargaining games with their rivals. The analytical gains obtained from relaxing the unitary assumption in assessing the redistributive impact of ruling parties are worth reiterating. We are able to examine how party leaders deal with internal dissent over social security policy, which is often a function of how power is distributed within the party and of the coalition or blackmail potential of contending factions. Looking inside the black box helps to understand whether party leaders attempt to design policies that build or recraft public opinion in order to outflank their internal rivals as well as to forge new electoral constituencies. Hence we are able to achieve a more integrated view regarding the party in office, the party in the organisation and the party in the electorate, thus moving beyond over-simplified accounts of party politics.

Consistent with advances in the party politics literature we can formulate several theoretically derived expectations about income redistribution. Firstly, emerging factions need supporters – party members and voters – to legitimise their struggle for internal power. Since redistributive policies define the categories in need, new redistributive programmes may forge new electoral alliances among protected or risk-exposed categories.

Second, when circumstances trigger a profound change of a party's dominant coalition, the first target of the new elite is effacing the party image connected to the dislodged leadership (Janda *et al.*, 1995). When a political party acquires a new image it testifies to the end of an era and to the success of those 'new faces' holding positions of responsibility in the internal hierarchy. The implication for income redistribution is that manipulations of entitlement and eligibility rules by the newly established leadership may aim at shedding the old party image. Refashioning the party reputation on redistributive issues might not amount to a wholesale replacement of the party's ideological tradition, but to an adjustment that blends existing policies with new purposive incentives. We should expect, therefore, that a newly established right-wing faction will push the ruling party towards less-interventionist, redistributive policies in order to estrange internal, rather than external, rivals. Correlatively, a newly established left-wing faction will attempt to expand redistributive policies and minimise the decisionmaking role of right-wing factions within the party. Thirdly, the demise of party factions brings about a radicalisation of redistributive programmes if competition is ineffective. Unconstrained by internal and external credible threats, the dominant coalition enjoys ample margins of manoeuvre to undertake radical departures from previous redistributive commitments.

The balance of power between party elites rests on the ability to control vital resources of organisational power, but this control can be affected by the options available in other arenas. New electoral rivals may weaken party factions by making inroads into their electoral constituencies, or may provide a timely challenge for the ruling party to alter its redistributive policies; weak party competition may strengthen radical groups within the party, which might otherwise be marginalised were competition effective – the British and Australian chapters offer clear examples of this. Internal realignments can also take place when generational turnovers happen at critical moments, such as during a period of prolonged opposition. The chapters on Canada, Australia and the USA illustrate the regularity of this proposition.

Of course, the interplay between internal and external circumstances is strongly influenced by the distribution of power within the political system. It matters, for instance, whether the system is presidential or parliamentary; it is important for policy outputs how easily prime ministers can dismiss cabinet members; it makes a difference to legislators' room-to-manoeuvre if their career prospects are dependent on patronage power.

In the chapters on Canada, Britain, Australia and the US we shall see how the different features of the political systems of these four countries hinder or sustain party leaders in their redistributive games. In this way, the book sheds new light on the old and important inquiry about the relationship between the role of elected representatives and redistributive policies.

CHAPTER 2

Opposition effects, blackmail and u-turns under Pierre Elliot Trudeau

POLITICAL BACKGROUND

This chapter explores the politics of income redistribution in Canada under the Liberal government of Pierre Elliot Trudeau. During his long-lasting premiership (1968–1984) Trudeau first expanded and then contracted social security benefits by redesigning entitlement and eligibility rules. This u-turn offers an excellent case study to explore how interdependent strategic action impinges on transfer programmes.

Social security provisions in North America were introduced late compared to other Western countries, and both Canada and the US are considered international laggards in welfare state expansion (Kudrle and Marmor, 1981; Myles and Pierson, 1997). However, the similarities between these two countries should not be exaggerated. For one thing, since the mid 1960s Canada has consistently offered more public support for families and caregiving than has the US (O'Connor, Orloff and Shaver, 1998; Osberg, Erksoy and Phipps, 1997). Between 1965 and 1975 new programmes were set up, the scope of existing social insurance schemes was extended, and social transfer payments were made more generous. Contributory unemployment insurance also covered the dependents of married claimants (Guest, 1997). For the unemployed without insurance coverage the government initiated the Canada Assistance Plan (CAP), which provided a guaranteed safety net for all persons in need, including Native Canadians, who earlier had been excluded from some provincial programmes.

In 1965 Pearson, then Liberal Prime Minister, had established a Special Planning Secretariat to coordinate antipoverty programmes and a federal–provincial conference to discuss the problem. Banting (1987) defines this period as the 'golden age of income security' with the implementation of various forms of social assistance and social insurance.

Concern about income security helped to usher in an earnings-related pension plan, the Canada Pension Plan, the Quebec Pension Plan and the Guaranteed Income Supplement (GIS).[1] In 1973 the government expanded Federal Family Allowances and introduced the Quebec Family Allowances.

In the early 1970s a more equitable distribution of resources was a priority among policymakers (Gillespie, 1978). Edgar Benson, then Finance Minister, had established a strong redistributive thrust to fiscal policy in his 1970 budget speech. In his words, 'steady and sustainable improvement in the standard of living of all Canadians requires ... [among other things] that we obtain a progressively more equitable distribution of the goods and services we produce' ('House of Commons Debates: 1738', 1970). Gillespie noted that the tax-reform budget of 1971 was indeed 'built upon a fair and equitable tax system' and was 'modestly redistributive' favouring policies that would improve the economic conditions of the poor relative to the highest-income families (1978: 10).

Major reforms in income security were initiated in June 1970, with the publication of the White Paper, 'Unemployment Insurance in the '70s'. The Liberal government proposed a sweeping expansion of the unemployment insurance system, transforming it into one of the most generous programmes in the world (Struthers, 1989: 237). Under the original act introduced in 1940, 58 per cent of the labour force were exempt from coverage, the most prominent among them being agricultural workers, fishermen, hospital employees, civil servants and teachers. Previous insurance schemes excluded all middle-income groups and related benefits to contributions, which meant that new entrants to the labour force and those who regularly suffered unemployment were entitled to the least benefits.

The new scheme broadened coverage to all employees, adding 1,200,000 people. Benefits were raised to two-thirds of regular earnings and their duration was not related to contributions, but to the level of unemployment. When unemployment was high and the chances of getting work low, the pay-out period was lengthened. Premiums paid by employees and employers financed the scheme when unemployment was low, but as soon as it topped 4 per cent the government began to contribute, roughly $100 million for every 1 per cent climb in unemployment. The redistributive effects of the 1971 unemployment insurance scheme showed that low-income groups received 50 per cent of all benefit paid while contributing about 14 per cent, implying a substantial

---

[1] For a comparison of the politics of pension in Canada, the US and Britain see Orloff (1993).

transfer of income to this group from the middle and upper contributors (Bailey and Naemark, 1977).

The golden age of fighting income inequality evaporated rapidly in the latter half of the 1970s. Redistributive policies were gradually scaled down, reflecting the changing budgetary intentions of the Liberal government with respect to income distribution. On 30 September 1974 Trudeau announced to the House of Commons his decision to stiffen eligibility requirements for unemployment benefits. Family allowances were first de-indexed and then curtailed in favour of an income-tested selective tax-credit programme for children. In 1978 the government reduced the level of unemployment benefits and attempts to trim pension programmes were withdrawn in response to a nationwide protest. The result was that the proportion of targeted benefits in total income security rose rapidly, climbing from 29.3 in 1975 to 37.4 per cent in 1980 (Banting, 1997).

SOCIAL CLEAVAGES AND REDISTRIBUTION

One reason why Canada was a laggard in income maintenance policies rests on the marginality of partisan polarisation along class lines (Struthers, 1989). The weakness of working-class parties and trade unions was a function of ethnic and geographical cleavages. These fault lines deflected attention and support from class issues and helped retard the elaboration of welfare programmes. In the early stages of party development the working class was difficult to mobilise because it was formed mainly by immigrants with heterogeneous backgrounds. An added difficulty was the fact that the limited federal jurisdiction granted significant regional differences in working conditions, inducing conflicts within the trade union movement (Engelmann and Schwartz, 1975: 77).

By the early 1960s, however, unionisation was well under way with about 1.4 million union members demanding political representation (Porter, 1965: 310). As a result, the New Democratic Party (NDP) was formed in 1961 from an alliance between the Cooperative Commonwealth Federation (CCF) and the Trade Union Federation. The CCF emerged in the 1930s as a Socialist movement drawing support from western farmers, the urban working class and university intellectuals (Thorburn, 1979: 6). Between 1942 and 1945 the CCF expanded almost to the level of a national party. This sudden surge of the CCF prompted the Liberal Party to begin to cultivate a left-wing image with its centrepiece based on redistributive policies (Whitaker, 1977: 156–159).

Competition from the left intensified over the years, exerting an innovative stimulus in the field of income redistribution. Change in the political atmosphere became gradually discernible. Enormous pressure from the NDP to bring down old-age poverty led to the adoption of the GIS in 1966 (Haddow, 1993). Survey findings showed that NDP supporters were more concerned with social security policies than other voters explaining why the completion of the welfare state became one of the dominant campaign themes during the 1960s (Budge, Robertson and Hearl, 1987: 78).

In those years the Liberal and the Conservative parties incessantly discussed redistributive policies such as the Guaranteed Annual Income. Leman argues that proposals for the guaranteed income were elite directed because there was little evidence of widespread public support (Leman, 1980: 58). This observation lends credence to the view that redistributive policies are not simply a response to pressures from voters; politicians may manufacture those policies to alter the incentives to vote.

Entrance of the NDP in the political arena posed an electoral threat from the left to the Liberal Party. The need to head off defections to a new party meant that in the early 1970s the Liberal Party aimed at expanding its electoral appeal to the new NDP supporters without diluting the allegiance of its core constituency. The problem was that left-wing competition brought to the fore the erosion of partisan attachments. In the mid 1960s over 30 per cent of voters were unable or unwilling to identify with a particular party, and therefore there was a sizable number of undecided voters for whom partisanship was less certain (Clarke *et al.*, 1984: 47; Jenson 1975: 549). In comparative terms Canada has a weak and unstable partisanship, which has magnified over the years (Young, 1998). Electoral volatility was further amplified in 1970 when the voting age was lowered from 21 to 18, extending the franchise to approximately one million new voters. A loose electoral basis is perhaps one reason why programmes of the governing party in Canada may be sensitive to changes in the programmes of opposition parties (Pétry, 1995). In the early 1970s a turbulent electoral arena encroached on the options available to party leaders because the nature of party competition changed from bipolar to tripolar, making redistributive games more complex.

When income inequality regained prominence in the late 1960s regional disparity was an extremely sensitive issue. As one observer noted at the time, 'the poverty of the Maritimes has occupied an

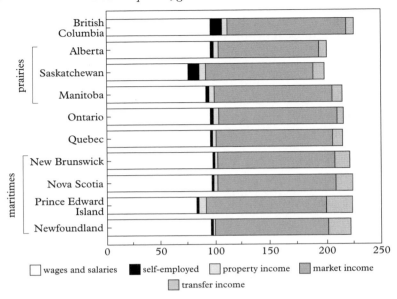

Figure 2.1. Average value of income component as a percentage of average gross
income: Canada, 1971

honourable place in the foreground of public discussion. The diffuse
poverty of the generally underprivileged has scarcely been noticed'
(Cairns, 1968: 74). Regional disparities are evident in the income package of the ten provinces (figure 2.1). In 1971 the Maritimes' mean
transfer income was much higher than the corresponding amount
accruing to the Prairies or to Ontario and Quebec. In Prince Edward
Island (P.E.I.), for instance, cash income was three times the value of
that in British Columbia, although they were probably compensating
for lower wages and salaries in P.E.I. Relying heavily on the resource-
based, seasonal economy, the Maritimes provinces utilise national unemployment benefits to maintain workers during the off season. The
geographical isolation of the Maritimes meant that very low wages were
unlikely to attract much industry to the remote region (Pierson, 1995).
Compared to the other Western provinces, Newfoundland, Nova Scotia
and New Brunswick received a larger share of transfers. To account for
regional disparities the Unemployment Insurance Act of 1978 included
the clause of 'variable entrance requirement', which entitled high unemployment regions to receive more benefits.

Geographical cleavages added a further strain to the resilience of the core–periphery cleavage. French Canadians, who inhabited the province of Quebec, had been unremittingly resistant to attempts to be incorporated into an English-speaking Canada (Noel, 1993). Although Canada had been a British colony for over a century, the Quebecois had retained their language, as well as their religion, laws, customs and education system. So the standardisation of a language, which is one of the most important steps for completing the nation-building process, has never been achieved in Canada (Kornberg and Clarke, 1992: 1–33). Observers noted that the Family Allowance Act of 1974 was a gesture to French Canadians because pronatalism has always been a powerful sentiment in French Canada (Kudrle and Marmor, 1981). The Liberal government apparently expanded family allowances to shore up its political strength in Quebec. In the light of the persistence of nation-building cleavages, social policy in Canada is not only an object of struggle and compromise among economic groups, but a critical instrument for state building (Banting, 1995).

Tensions between English- and French-speaking communities have been an elemental feature of politics in Canada for over two centuries. Not surprisingly this ethnic cleavage has deeply affected the structure and evolution of Canadian political parties (McRae, 1974: 250). Unlike political parties in Australia and Britain, and to a lesser extent in the US, which divided along class lines, party competition in Canada evolved around opposite sides of the core–periphery cleavage. The Progressive Conservative Party aggregated the interests of the English and Irish Protestants and was considered the party of government centralisation in Ottawa. The Liberal Party was associated with French-speaking Catholics and the issue of provincial autonomy. In the mid 1960s, 62 per cent of French-speaking respondents voted for the Liberals, 15 per cent voted Conservative and 11 per cent favoured the New Democratic Party (NDP). By contrast, English-speaking voters were more evenly distributed with 42 per cent voting for the Liberals and 38 per cent preferring the Conservatives (Engelmann and Schwartz, 1975: 190). Hence the Liberals had the strongest party identification because the French-speaking community was more cohesive in its vote (LeDuc, 1981).

One manifestation of provincial autonomy is that provincial organisations are the most significant unit in Canadian political parties. The Liberal Party developed as a federation of ten provincial and two territorial associations and the party headquarters – the National Liberal Federation – coordinated rather than integrated the organisational subunits. These subunits acted as independent centres of power, enhancing the potential for internal divisive forces. Provincial associations enjoyed relative financial autonomy because funds flowed independently to the federal and the provincial units (Schlesinger, 1991: 215; Smiley, 1980: 90–91).

These ancient lines of division have had greater weight than the class conflict (Engelmann and Schwartz, 1975: 75). The long-lasting salience of the core–periphery cleavage in Canadian politics represents an exception in the cleavage theory of party development, which predicts that core–periphery cleavages would give way to the class cleavage, with a trend towards similar patterns of party support across regions (Lipset and Rokkan, 1967: 15–25).

Weak party support along class lines has not only retarded welfare state development but it has also hindered the transformation of Canadian party organisations from a cadre structure into a mass organisation (Angell, 1987: 364–366). The very few studies on the historical development of the two major Canadian parties are agreed that the Liberal Party is a typical cadre party with a loose and highly centralised organisation (Azoulay, 1995; Wearing, 1981: 55). Historically, cadre parties have been extremely vulnerable to electoral competition when left-wing parties begin to mobilise the working class (Duverger, 1959; Katz and Mair, 1995). Against this background, it is not surprising that Liberal leaders considered the growing electoral strength of the NDP an alarming threat.

ELECTORAL INCENTIVES FOR REDISTRIBUTION

Electoral volatility and the growth of the NDP increased the complexity of the electoral arena. One consequence of this complexity was that four federal elections were held in 1968, 1972, 1974 and 1979 instead of two, as formally required by the five year term of the Canadian House of Commons.

In such circumstances, vote-maximising redistributive strategies were the obvious option. Gillespie (1978: 80) contends that middle-income classes gained from income redistribution because Trudeau aimed at broadening its electoral appeal. We can investigate the empirical plausibility of this contention by splitting the population into ten equal-sized groups (deciles) according to level of household income and make adjustments for family size and composition. Figure 2.2 displays the decile shares of post-tax–post-transfer income between 1971 and 1981. If

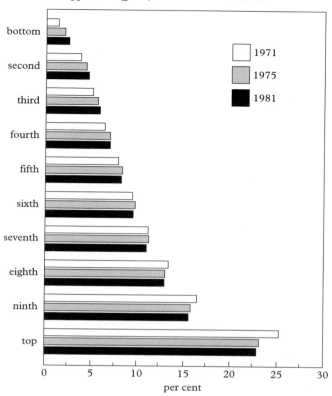

Figure 2.2. Income share of population deciles: Canada 1971–1981 (adjusted
post-tax–post-transfer income)

we consider it reasonable to position the middle-income classes between
the fourth and seventh decile, then the data show that over the 1970s the
fourth and fifth deciles were slightly better off, while the income share of
the sixth and seventh deciles declined slightly. The interesting aspect of
these figures is that the first, second and third deciles increased their
takings. More precisely, the income share of the poorest people went up
by 1.2 points between 1971 and 1981 and the income share of the second
decile rose from 3.8 to 5.7 per cent. The top tenth underwent the largest
loss with their takings dropping by 2.4 percentage points.

It is important to note that while the bottom 30 per cent of the
population was better off over the 1970s, the proportion of income
accruing to the middle deciles rose in the first half of the 1970s but
declined between 1975 and 1981. This finding suggests redistributive

effects from the richest to the poorest income strata, rather than to the median group as predicted by the median convergence hypothesis. Hence evidence from the LIS datasets only partially supports the claim that the middle-income classes gained from redistributive policies under Trudeau. The data indicate that median-voter convergence insufficiently illuminates the political forces behind income redistribution in Canada.

A different view holds that associations between voting behaviour and redistributive policies may be related to the timing of elections. Variations in social security programmes under Trudeau were sometimes compatible with the predictions of the political business cycle. Expansionary measures, including increases in the old-age pension, the guaranteed-income supplement for the elderly, veterans' pensions and the Unemployment Insurance Scheme, were introduced in the 1971 budget just one year before the federal elections of 1972. We know, however, that the model also predicts post-electoral cutbacks in transfer spending after the pre-electoral boost. Yet the Liberal government introduced a generous scheme of family allowances in 1973 one year after the election. Likewise, the PBC fails to explain why cutbacks in unemployment benefits and family allowances were suddenly activated in 1978, just one year before the 1979 general election.

All in all, the evidence assembled above provides insufficient evidence to support mainstream vote-maximising accounts of income redistribution. More generally, it seems that in Canada there is little correspondence between electoral behaviour and government economic performance because of the persistence of the linguistic cleavage reflected in the Quebequois loyalty to the Liberal Party (Guérin and Nadeau, 1998).

This is not to say that vote-maximising considerations were irrelevant for the Liberal government. On the contrary, electoral politics in Canada is seemingly of paramount importance in the formulation of public policies, but in ways that radically differ from conventional views. Thornburn, for instance, claims that in Canada reforms are first mooted by third parties and only when they appear to be appealing to the electorate are they implemented, albeit in a diluted fashion, by the governing party (1979). Such innovative thrusts of minor parties are connected to intraparty governance: when public demand for innovation is clear the risk of jeopardising the unity of the party by adopting it is minimised (Thorburn, 1979: 67). Internal considerations under the Trudeau governments appear to be at least as vital as vote-maximising concerns.

THE NEW LIBERALS AND EXPANSIONARY POLICIES

Thus, reconstructing the history of how the Liberal pro-welfare and antiwelfare coalitions evolved and consolidated may throw light on the structure of incentives that shaped the pattern of social security programmes. The preconditions for Trudeau's redistributive policies were set after the Liberal Party was dismissed from office in 1957 (Guest, 1997). The Conservative Party won a landslide victory by campaigning on a platform that included the introduction of earnings-related pensions. Such a traumatic experience as being ousted from government after over twenty years of uninterrupted tenure triggered a generational turnover in the Liberal Party, which led to internal unrest. Like in most other cadre parties, internal conflicts in the Liberal Party are not institutionalised in organised factions; rather party elites coalesce into tendencies that form and dissolve on specific issues.

In the early 1960s an old alliance among party leaders established under the leadership of St Laurent (1948–1958) was being replaced by a new generation of Liberals. These newcomers thought that indiscriminate use of patronage prerogatives and exclusive reliance on the advice and expertise of the civil service had caused the electoral defeat of 1957. They criticised the caucus for losing touch with social developments and argued that a redefinition of Liberal policies was necessary (Wearing, 1981: 47–64).

A few active left-wing reformers, such as Walter Gordon, Keith Davey, Maurice Lamontagne and Tom Kent pressed for intraparty democracy and a shift in Liberal policies towards the consolidation of the welfare state (McCall-Newman, 1982: 38–39). The old guard mainly composed of, and representing, businessmen strongly opposed social reform and believed these ideas were socialistic (Smith, 1973: 76). Internal strife between pro-welfare and antiwelfare alliances fuelled attempts at changing the internal distribution of power. Several modifications were made to enhance the authority of the national convention over the parliamentary party. In 1966 the convention was entrusted with the task of establishing 'the basic policies' of the party (Wearing 1981: 74). Previously, decisionmaking authority had always been informally given to the leader. Past Liberal leaders could formulate and enact policies with no prior consent from the extraparliamentary party.

The new Liberals wished to broaden the Liberal electoral appeal by campaigning for new social security programmes. For Smith these programmes served the twin purpose of tying party supporters with new policies and of thrusting a useful weapon into the hands of the reform wing to do battle with the conservative elements which still exercised considerable power in the caucus (1973: 216). New Liberals soon acquired responsible positions within the party. In 1961 Walter Gordon became chairman of the National Campaign committee, with direct responsibility for the recruitment of candidates and the management and financing of the party's campaign (Smith, 1973: 83). Electoral misfortunes, however, slowed down internal negotiations, delaying the formulation of redistributive policies.

The electoral results of 1963 and 1965 engendered minority governments, offering right-wingers the chance to make counterattacks to Gordon's strategies. During the Cabinet reshuffle of 1965 the internal balance of power tilted in favour of the right. A crucial step in this direction was the replacement of Gordon, as Finance Minister, by Mitchell Sharp, a representative of the financial and business community and a senior member of the antiwelfare alliance (Wearing, 1981: 68–72).

After Walter Gordon lost hold on the party in 1965 the old guard consisting of right-wingers like Mitchell Sharp, Bud Drury and Robert Winters attempted to reassert themselves (McCall-Newman, 1982: 271). Towards the end of the 1960s this group steadily enhanced its position within the party organisation, reducing the chances for welfare reform.

WHY THE GUARANTEED ANNUAL INCOME PROPOSAL FAILED

It was not until Pearson confided he was unwilling to run for election in 1968 that the question regarding the consolidation of the welfare system came back to the fore. As Trudeau put it:

I based my campaign on the central theme of the Just Society. Achieving such a society would require promoting equality of opportunity and giving the most help to those who were the most disadvantaged. Social security and equalisation payments, as well as a ministry of regional economic expansion, would give practical effect to these abstract principles. (Trudeau, 1993: 87)

New Liberals threw the weight of their support behind Trudeau, while Turner, Hellyer and Winters were backed by the antiwelfare sections of the business community (McCall-Newman, 1982: 78–97).

The depth of internal strains may easily be grasped by comparing the results of the leadership convention of 1968 with those of 1948 and 1958. Table 2.1 shows that, while in 1948 and 1958 there were three con-

Table 2.1. *Liberal conventions of 1948, 1958, 1968*

Candidates in order of rank of first ballot	First ballot	Second ballot	Third ballot	Fourth ballot
August 7, 1948				
Louis St. Laurent	61.4			
James G. Gardiner	23.4			
C. G. Power	0.4			
Total number voting	1,380			
January 16, 1958				
Lester B. Pearson	87.5			
Paul Martin	24.8			
L. Henderson	0.08			
Total number voting	1,227			
April 6, 1968				
Pierre E. Trudeau	31.8	40.8	44.6	51
Paul Hellyer	13.9	19.7	14.3	
Robert Winters	12.4	23.8	26.3	40.4
John Turner	11.7	22.6	20	11.8
Paul Martin	11.7*			
J. J. Greene	7.1	4.4	1.2**	
A. J. MacEachen	6.9	0.5**		
Eric Kierans	4.3*			
L. Henderson	0**			
Total number voting	2,366	2,364	2,357	2,352

Notes: * Withdrew as a result of this ballot.
** Eliminated as a result of this ballot.
Source: Calculated by the author from Courtney (1973: 58).

tenders for the leadership, in 1968 there were nine candidates, three times as many as in the previous contests. The figures illustrate two other aspects. First, at the previous two conventions the decision was quickly reached at the first ballot, while Trudeau won after four ballots. Second, in 1948 St Laurent gained a comfortable majority of 61.4 per cent of the total votes and in 1958 Pearson obtained an even larger majority of 87.5 per cent; by contrast, Trudeau barely attained an absolute majority of 51 per cent.

Since the total number of voting delegates was almost twice as large in 1968 than in the previous contests, this may have offered considerable potential for dissension and a higher number of contenders. A closer look at table 2.1, however, shows that internal wrangling was not merely a question of numbers: at the fourth ballot there were only three candidates left, as many as in 1948 and 1958, but the final vote was almost evenly divided between Trudeau and Winters who were, respectively, the representatives of the pro-welfare and antiwelfare coalitions.

Soon after taking office in 1968 Trudeau engaged in the strategy of conflict management that reunited the party and kept him in power for 16 years. He restaffed and reorganised the Prime Minister's Office, which Lalonde described as 'a power group supporting the Prime Minister and controlled by him' (1971: 520). Trudeau cleverly headed off internal opposition by appointing to the Cabinet members of the anti-welfare alliance, including Sharp and Drury. He then strengthened his hold on the party organisation by offering key positions in the Liberal Federation to the New Liberals, such as the new party president Richard Stanbury. Those who had taken leadership positions within the party during the Pearson period now found themselves on the sidelines. For the most part this meant people who had supported Trudeau's rivals, Turner and Hellyer, during the leadership contest (Wearing 1981: 196–197).

Efforts at concentrating power at the top were in line with the Canadian tradition of strong leadership (Franks, 1989: 23). In addition to this, however, it is typical of charismatic leaders, such as Trudeau, to resist efforts by counter-elites to strengthen the party organisation, because it would inevitably set the stage for the party's 'emancipation' from his control (Panebianco, 1988: 66–67).[2]

An illustrative example of Trudeau's success at controlling the party organisation is the failure of the guaranteed annual income to reach the Cabinet agenda. The guaranteed annual income was 'the holy grail' of antipoverty lobbies and it was approved at the 1970 policy convention with 657 votes in favour, 187 against and 117 abstentions. In principle, the deliberations of the policy conference established the basic policies of the party (Courtney, 1973: 98). Trudeau ignored altogether the deliberation of the party conference and the guaranteed annual income never reached the Cabinet agenda.[3] He justified his position

---

[2] Trudeau's behaviour is reminiscent of MacKenzie King, the Liberal leader from 1919 to 1948, who was opposed to the development of a strong party organisation. In Whitaker's vivid description: [c]onsidering the divergent crowds assembled under the umbrella of the Liberal party, [MacKenzie King] had a justifiable fear for any permanent structure which might give voice to divisive policy initiatives, not to speak of challenges to his own leadership (Whitaker, 1977: 9).

[3] For a detailed examination of the history and recent reappraisal of the Guaranteed Income see (Myles and Pierson, 1997).

some years later on the grounds that adverse economic prospects had dictated the policy decision (Axworthy and Trudeau, 1990: 39).

However compelling the economic argument might be, the very few in-depth studies of this matter conclude that the guaranteed annual income floundered for reasons related to internal governance (Wearing, 1981; Whitaker,1977). In Whitaker's view this outcome was intimately connected to the internal distribution of power:

> The Liberal party's policy process failed . . . on the issue of power. Even before the resolutions favouring a guaranteed annual income were debated and passed, the prime minister made clear in his 'accountability' session with the delegates that he was not prepared to implement such a major change in his government's approach to welfare. (Whitaker, 1977: 158)

The issue of power gained momentum after the party convention of 1970 when Allen Linden, the co-chairman of the policy committee, asked for the guaranteed annual income to be included in the party's manifesto in the next election of 1972. The Liberal caucus, however, strongly opposed this proposal. When the idea was presented to the cabinet 'Linden and Stanbury were surprised by the barrage of criticism that it encountered. The cabinet refused to have anything to do with it . . . because there *had been no parliamentarians on the policy committee, they had felt excluded from the whole process*' (Wearing, 1981: 171, emphasis added). What is more, the question of vertical lines of authority overlapped with rather delicate power considerations. As Trudeau admits in his memoirs, strategies of conflict management within the party at times yielded moderate redistributive policies:

> Throughout my first mandate, the 'leftist' reputation I had earned in Quebec during my days in opposition to the Duplessis regime imposed a certain reserve on me . . . Still somewhat shakily established at the head of the organisation, I had to be constantly aware of the possible risks involved in ranging the more traditional Liberal members against me, and of provoking a rift between the two wings . . . I had to be on my guard all the time to maintain a careful equilibrium between progressive measures and more moderate ones. (Trudeau, 1993: 165)

Trudeau was able to strike a workable relationship between the two wings of the party thanks to the wide margin of manoeuvre that the Liberal Party organisation conferred on the leader, and doubtlessly thanks to his own exceptional skills as a statesman.

THE NDP CHALLENGE AND THE 1971 UNEMPLOYMENT SCHEME

Despite prime ministerial power, internal bargaining and negotiations delayed and hampered welfare reforms. The situation changed dramatically when the electoral challenge from the NDP risked pushing the Liberals further to the right. Competition from the right of the political spectrum was nearly defunct because Conservative leaders were struggling to maintain party unity. Internal strife connected to the leadership succession exhausted their energies and attention (Penniman, 1975; Perlin, 1980).

Support for the NDP was growing in the Western provinces of Manitoba, British Columbia, Alberta and Saskatchewan where the Liberal Party was suffering from a steady erosion of its provincial electoral base. In 1971 Jim Davie, a member of the pro-welfare coalition and the programme secretary in the Liberal Prime Minister Office (PMO), succinctly remarked '[the NDP] is the danger. At the same time, a good proportion of their present support believes that there is only 50% chance that they actually vote for them on Election Day. This is our chance' (quoted in Wearing, 1981: 193). For Trudeau the main cause for defections among Liberal voters in the West was the predominance of right wingers at the provincial level:

[M]y party . . . at the provincial level, had for years tended to fall to the right. As a result, in Saskatchewan, Manitoba, and British Columbia, the Liberal Party had all but disappeared from the political stage, to be replaced by the NDP. As federal Liberals, we were worried that we might share the fate of our British counterparts, who had let themselves be pushed so far to the right by the Labour Party that there were only a handful of Liberal members left in Westminster, none of whom exerted much influence on the course of events. We were determined not to let that happen to the Liberal Party of Canada. (Trudeau, 1993: 165)

One way to fight right-wing Liberals in the provinces was to forge a shrewd offensive aimed at attracting NDP supporters. These voters tended to have lower incomes and were therefore more exposed to the risks of economic insecurity (Kornberg and Clarke, 1992: 75). Such vulnerability meant that the Liberal Party could make inroads in the NDP electorate by expanding welfare state provisions.

A significant step in this direction was to further centralise social security programmes. Federal transfers to provincially delivered services in health, education, and social assistance had formed the major part of Ottawa's expenditure growth, but in the 1970s the Liberal government increasingly used income security programmes which it alone controlled (Struthers, 1989: 237). Perhaps Trudeau's policy was tainted by an excessive universalism in a society torn by particularistic claims (Karmis, 1996), nevertheless expanding universal benefits achieved partisan social engineering by increasing the size of the state-protected population.

One instance of this strategy was the White Paper 'Unemployment Insurance in the '70s' which projected imminent labour market changes. The government argued that rapid technological changes associated with post-industrialism would threaten previously secure employment. Liberal leaders deployed this argument to overcome the resistance of those groups resenting state interference in the field of social security. Union representatives feared that state legislation would replace their protective role towards their members, undermining their representation of workers' interests. As a Liberal MP asserted:

> we have heard . . . that some of the new groups, such as the Canadian Teachers Federation did not appear to favour universality as far as their teachers were concerned . . . However, it was the committee's opinion, and my personal opinion also, that the contingency of interruption of earnings is not now restricted to certain groups in Canada, as it may have been in earlier years, and that therefore no employee should be excluded from coverage if it were possible to include him. ('House of Commons Debates', 1971: 5081)

Liberals wished to increase the size of the state-protected population by expanding coverage and by targeting specific social categories. In 1971 the unemployment scheme extended coverage to self-employed fishermen, the only category of self-employed so covered; in the fishing communities of Atlantic Canada, a region traditionally sympathetic to the Liberals, unemployment benefits constituted an important source of income.

Women were another targeted social category. It is worth noting that the NDP was the leader in putting women on the ballot and into legislatures at the provincial level (Studlar and Matland, 1996). As a response to the NDP electoral challenge, the Liberal government introduced maternity benefits, which cemented the traditional loyalty of female voters towards the Liberal Party (Kornberg and Clarke, 1992: 75). Deliberate attempts to direct the message to women were reinforced by specific pledges for female workers. In the words of David Weatherhead, than a Liberal MP:

> There are about three million working women in the labor force today and they are and have been for a long time a very vital part of our work force in Canada.

Table 2.2. *Percentages of votes and seats in Canadian federal elections,*
1968–1979

Political party	1968 votes	1968 seats	1972 votes	1972 seats	1974 votes	1974 seats	1979 votes	1979 seats
CP	31.4	27.3	35	40.5	35.4	36.6	35.9	48.2
LP	45.5	58.7	38.5	41.3	43.2	53.4	40.1	40.4
NDP	17.0	8.3	17.7	11.7	15.4	6.1	17.9	11.3
SC	0.8	0	7.6	5.7	5.1	4.2	4.6	0

Notes: CP = Conservative Party
LP = Liberal Party
NDP = New Democratic Party
SC = Social Credit

Many have worked continually for a long time, have paid into the unemployment insurance fund for a long time, and then decided to have a child.
[M]aternity leave will give the female employee significant new rights to which,
in my opinion, they are well entitled. ('House of Commons Debates', 1971: 5083)

The implementation of social security programmes favourable to
women could consolidate the allegiance of traditional voters and attract
young females who had recently entered the labour market.

Modification in the electoral and social environment changed the
options available to Liberal leaders, urging a reaction to the NDP
challenge. Competition from the Left prompted Liberal leaders to adjust
social relativities and to engage in partisan social engineering by protecting the relative social and economic position of specific social groups.

THE BLACKMAIL GAME

Expansionary social security programmes, however, failed to secure the
Liberal government with a majority in 1972. The dis-representative
effects of the single plurality electoral system meant that the Liberal Party
acquired 30 per cent fewer seats in 1972, while its proportion of votes fell
by only 15 per cent (table 2.2). On the other hand, the Conservative Party
performed much better, increasing its share of seats from 27.3 per cent to
40.5 per cent, a surge of about 48 per cent. Both the NDP and the Social
Credit gained legislative strength. The NDP obtained 3.4 per cent more
seats in 1972 and the Social Credit secured 5.7 per cent of the seats.

The new distribution of seats in the House of Commons after the general election of 1972 engendered a minority government. For one thing, the near-electoral defeat showed that expansionary social security policies were hardly the way forward, providing precious ammunition to Liberal hardliners. Leaders of the antiwelfare alliance pressed for the replacement of Benson with Turner at the Ministry of Finance. The Cabinet reshuffle signified a shift from Benson's 'modestly redistributive' budget, which had included policy instruments especially favourable towards poor families, to Turner's commitment to maintaining the status quo (Gillespie, 1978: 20–21). The new nominations sanctioned the continuing vitality of the Liberal antiwelfare grouping. Left-wing forces gaining strength in parliament, however, counterbalanced such right-wing pull.

A crucial outcome of the 1972 elections was that the Liberal minority government hinged on the external support of the NDP. This situation entrusted NDP leaders with veto power because their backing ensured the survival of the Liberal government. In Sartori's terms (1976: 122), the distribution of seats in the House of Commons endowed the NDP with blackmail potential, which it could deploy to shape policy outputs.

At this point, Trudeau cunningly turned the absence of a legislative majority into a sophisticated weapon to ease internal dissent and bolster redistributive programmes. His lucid description of the strategic game is worth quoting at length:

[B]eing a minority government allowed us to engage in a new form of politics that attracted me greatly [and] allowed me to put forward more advanced 'left wing' projects. I knew that the NDP, under David Lewis, would back me up – *in fact, the NDP supported me when some of the more conservative members of my own party did not. I was thus able to institute policies that I had been dreaming about for a long time,* and the social-democratic faction of the Opposition was forced to support them, or else deny their own social program… In this way the minority government allowed us to get social legislation through Parliament that helped less-advantaged Canadians, such as the increasing and indexing of old age pensions [and] higher unemployment insurance benefits. (Trudeau, 1993: 165/167, emphasis added)

Thus, the weakness of the government in the legislative arena became an advantage for the Liberal pro-welfare grouping, influencing the outcome of redistributive games.

The dynamics of strategic moves is illustrated in figure 2.3 which uses the graphical device elaborated by Laver and Shepsle (1990). The figure shows a policy space with two dimensions – taxes and social security

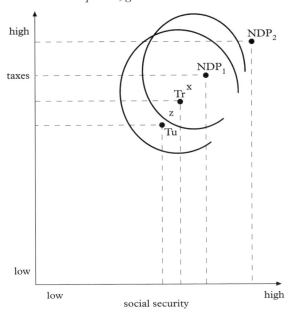

Figure 2.3. The blackmail game: Canada, 1972–1974

spending. It depicts the strategic environment between 1972 and 1974, when the formation and maintenance of the Liberal government delicately hinged on the external support of the NDP. The NDP factions are represented by the ideal points NDP_1 and NDP_2. There are at least two NDP groupings because the party was internally divided (Morton, 1986). A more radical left-wing group (NDP_2 in figure 2.3) wished to withdraw support for the Liberal minority government. Liberals were represented by the social reform faction, led by Trudeau (Tr), and the faction defending the status quo, led by Turner (Tu). The indifference curves in figure 2.3 are centred on the faction led by the party leader (NDP_1 and Tr).

Suppose NDP_1–Tr is the status quo (point x). There is one credible proposal in its win set, NDP_1–Tu (point z), but it is regarded by NDP_1 as inferior to NDP_1–Tr, so it will not receive the assent of NDP_1. This choice has consequences for the internal politics of the Liberal Party because it weakens the position of the so-called 'Turnites'. The priorities of the NDP leaders amplify Trudeau's margin of manoeuvrability, offering him more leeway in the implementation of generous redistributive policies. In such circumstances Liberal social reformers could implement redistributive policies without jeopardising the unity of the party by further alienating the business community. Redistributive policies under Trudeau in the mid 1970s can be interpreted as the outcome of a game in multiple arenas, where the payoffs in the parliamentary arena were deployed as resources in the internal arena.

This analysis demonstrates that generous cash benefits in the early 1970s were the product of strategic games both within the Liberal Party and between this party and the NDP. We have seen that these games were activated by the electoral challenge posed by the NDP and by the gradual erosion of traditional voting patterns. Tougher competition and electoral volatility elicited centrifugal drives in the party system, which pushed the Liberal government to the left. In turn, this transformation weakened internal opposition towards expansionary redistributive policies, offering Trudeau the opportunity to implement his welfare programme. In technical terms, this is a dominant strategy because irrespective of the policies devised by the NDP, the Liberals would have maximised their electoral payoffs by appealing to NDP supporters through more decisive redistributive policies. Correlatively, had redistributive policies not been implemented, it is likely that the NDP would have maximised its payoffs by withdrawing support to the Liberal minority government.

THE U-TURN

Interparty competition helped Trudeau in passing progressive social legislation but only temporarily mitigated sharp internal opposition. The main issue was that Trudeau had failed to form a majority government. Electoral losses lend ammunition to counterelites by exposing the weakness of the dominant coalition. One consequence was that expansionary transfer policies were partially offset by tax concessions to middle-upper-income families and to the business community. These concessions included the personal income tax cut, the corporate profits tax cut from 49 per cent to 40 per cent and the indexation of the personal income tax. The substantial personal income tax cut which cost the government $1,300 million in foregone revenues did not benefit the poorest families, because their income was too low for them to take advantage of either the increased personal exemptions or the minimum tax credit (Gillespie, 1978: 21). John Turner, then Finance Minister, was committed to maintaining the status quo and did not suggest redistributive policies that would improve the real economic position of the poor relative to the highest-income families.

The relationship between the so-called Trudeauites and Turnites rapidly deteriorated after the 1974 elections. Turner thought that Trudeau 'never stopped to consider [that] the economy had to be able to bear the government's social security programs' (McCall-Newman, 1982: 309). When the Liberal Prime Minister denied his support to Turner's proposals for cutting spending and implementing an incomes policy, the Finance Minister left the Cabinet and resigned on 10 September 1975 (Chrétien, 1985: 78). Turner's resignation damaged the unity of the Liberal Party because 'for years, Turner had epitomized in his person the alliance for power that had held the party together' (McCall-Newman, 1982: 241). In the winter preceding the 1979 election the Liberal adherents were asked to analyse the causes of the Liberals' difficulties; McCall-Newman reports that 'almost to a man they would begin by citing the decision in 1975 of John Turner, the former Minister of Finance, to abandon politics for the practice of corporate law' (1982: 241).

Ironically, a few months after Turner's resignation the Cabinet approved both the incomes policy and the cutbacks in spending advocated by the former Finance Minister.

> The irony was clear … Trudeau and MacDonald [the new Finance Minister] had both been more firmly anti-interventionist than the rest of the cabinet, and it had been their opposition that prevented other, more timid ministers from supporting Turner in his tough-measures stance months before. (McCall-Newman, 1982: 231)

Which factors explain this sudden and unexpected change? Trudeau gave a deterministic interpretation of these events in his memoirs. 'MacDonald came to the Cabinet and said: "There is no choice"' (Trudeau, 1993: 196). Yet this depiction leaves unanswered the question why the incomes policy was acceptable when MacDonald proposed it and considered inadequate when recommended by Turner.

One plausible answer is that the Liberal leader wished to defeat potential rivals. Turner was the only candidate to the leadership contest of 1968 to have kept a personal power base in the party and an independent public reputation (McCall-Newman, 1982: 128). All the others were either devoted to Trudeau or out of politics altogether. A further point to note is that the Liberal Party had institutionalised the core–periphery cleavage by alternating English- and French-speaking leaders, and Turner was the obvious English-speaking successor. Trudeau described those events in his memoirs as follows:

You can tell me I handled it badly ... but if [Turner's] heart wasn't in it for one reason or another, either because of his family and his economic circumstances or because I was his leader, then perhaps it was right that he leave politics. (Trudeau, 1993: 194)

In the wake of Turner's resignation from the Cabinet the antiwelfare coalition became a kind of opposition from within the party (Johnston, 1986: 35; Wearing, 1981: 236). The Liberal Party was facing its biggest crisis for more than ten years as bitter infighting threatened to fracture the internal alliance. Trudeau retreated into the Prime Minister Office (PMO) and came to regard his staff there as the only group whose loyalty was unquestioned (Wearing, 1981: 236). Cabinet members were taken by surprise when Trudeau and his closest advisers unexpectedly announced cutbacks in both family allowances and unemployment benefits. In a vivid recollection of those events, Jean Chrétien, then newly appointed Minister of Finance recounts that

Since Trudeau's announcement came as a surprise to me, the press jumped on the idea that the Prime Minister had pulled the rug out from under his Minister of Finance. The people who had criticized Trudeau for not being concerned with the economy now abused him from interfering with Chrétien's territory, and I was made to look like a fool. I've never quite decided whether it was a breakdown in communications or a power play by the PMO. (Chrétien, 1985: 177)

Chrétien suspected that the scaling down of welfare spending might have been the outcome of a power game, lending support to the view that power games between party leaders affect redistributive policies. Cutbacks in transfer payments showed that internal rivals had no alternative policy to offer. Hence the u-turn from an expansionary design in the early 1970s to a restrictive stance in the late 1970s, can be interpreted as an optimal strategy in the intraparty arena. It can be viewed as an instance of correlated strategies, in which the actions of player I at time T depend on the actions of player II at time T-1.

Trudeau was playing a game in multiple arenas consisting of two distinct strategies, one pursued in the electoral arena and the other in the internal arena. In the early 1970s redistributive policies were activated and social cleavages gained new political expression partly because they furnished a weapon to the reform group. By skilfully

Table 2.3. *Trends in income inequality: Canada, 1971–1987*
(adjusted household post-tax–post-transfer income)

Year	CV	Gini	Theil
1971	72.5	39.1	26.1
1975	63.7	36.0	21.8
1981	62.5	34.3	19.5
1987	59.7	30.6	15.8
Percentage change			
1971/1975	− 12	− 8	− 16
1975/1981	− 1	− 5	− 10
1981/1987	− 4.4	− 10.7	− 18.9
1971/1987	− 17.6	− 21.7	− 39.4

balancing internal and external pressures Trudeau was able to both maximise votes and defend his leadership position. Expansionary redistributive policies in the early and mid 1970s were a function of sophisticated power plays in the executive and legislative arenas. In the latter half of the 1970s, by contrast, the leadership threat convinced the Liberal leader to espouse restrictive redistributive policies.

INCOME INEQUALITY: DEMOGRAPHY, MARKETS AND INCOME TRANSFERS

Redistributive games under Trudeau evolved while the gap between rich and poor was progressively narrowing, with the sharpest decline occurring at the beginning of the decade (see table 2.3). Taking into account that income distributions change slowly, the reduction in inequality between 1971 and 1975 is remarkable, suggesting that redistributive policies had profound effects. Another point to note is that the Theil index, which is a bottom sensitive index, dropped in this period by 16 per cent, indicating that lower-income groups were better off. The overwhelming impression gained from table 2.3 is that of a general decline in inequality growth over the 1970s, which continued into the 1980s.

Unfortunately income distribution in Canada has been under-researched and the few ventures in the field report contradictory results. Dodge (1975) found less inequality in the early 1970s, corroborating my results, but Gillespie (1978: 24–25) claimed that no

Table 2.4. *Population decile share of post-tax–post-transfer income and adjusted post-tax–post-transfer income: Canada, 1971–1981*

Decile	Post-tax–post-transfer income			Adjusted Post-tax–post-transfer income		
	1971	1975	1981	1971	1975	1981
bottom	0.8	1.3	1.8	1.3	2.0	2.5
second	2.6	3.2	3.6	3.8	4.4	4.7
third	4.3	5.0	5.2	5.1	5.7	5.9
fourth	6.2	6.6	6.8	6.4	7.0	7.0
fifth	8.1	8.3	8.3	7.9	8.3	8.2
sixth	10.0	10.0	9.9	9.4	9.7	9.5
seventh	11.9	11.7	11.6	11.1	11.2	11.0
eighth	14.0	13.6	13.4	13.3	13.0	12.9
nine	16.9	16.3	16.2	16.4	15.7	15.5
top	25.1	24.0	23.3	25.2	23.1	22.8

redistribution took place during that period. The explanation for my different results is straightforward: Gillespie's income definition does not make any adjustment in household composition using equivalence scales. However, if there is significant heterogeneity of household types, then my approach is more appropriate. The reason is that it makes an appropriate adjustment to the weighting of households' representation in the distribution of income as the demographic structure of the population changes.[4] To evaluate the discrepancy in the results produced by the two methods I have calculated the decile shares for both unadjusted and adjusted (equivalent) disposable income in Canada between 1971 and 1981 (table 2.4). When measured by unadjusted income the bottom decile gained only 0.5 per cent between 1971 and 1975, while when employing adjusted income their share rose by 0.7 per cent. Since the total income share for the bottom decile is approximately 1 or 2 per cent, a difference of 0.2 per cent may be significant. Table 2.4 also shows that adjusting income for family size and composition may substantially reduce the measured income accruing to the top decile. From 1971 to 1975 the rich people lost 2.1 per cent of their adjusted income share, while they lost only 0.9 of their unadjusted income. The data cited above demonstrate that applying different income concepts produces different results.

[4] For a discussion of the implications of different equivalent scales see Coulter, Cowell and Jenkins (1992) and technical addendum.

Table 2.5. *The contribution of changes in within- and between-age-group
components to the trend in total inequality: Canada, 1971–1987
(adjusted post-tax–post-transfer income. Theil index)*

Year	Total inequality	Within-age-group inequality	Age effect (between-group inequality)
1971	26.1	23.1	3.0
1975	21.8	19.6	2.2
1981	19.5	17.0	2.5
1987	15.8	15.2	0.6

A further difference between Gillespie's work and mine is that his
estimates are calculated from the 1969 Consumer Finance Survey. My
results draw from the Consumer Finance Survey of 1971, 1975 and 1981
available through LIS and provide more updated information on the
distribution of post-tax–post-transfer income. My estimates should be
more reliable because they are derived from up-to-date samples and are
calculated using more sophisticated methods.

Demographic effects

During the 1970s demographic expansions characterised most Western
countries, including Canada, and the baby boom of the 1960s continued
into the following decade. It makes sense, therefore, to assess the
distributional effects of the age structure. I evaluate age effects by
looking at inequality trends within and between age groups. In the
computations I use the Theil index because it is amenable to decomposition into different components, while other indices, such as the Gini
coefficient, cannot be disaggregated so easily (see Cowell, 1995). From
table 2.5 we can see that the within-group component had a stronger
impact on the decline in aggregate inequality than the grouping factor,
implying a relatively marginal distributional role of the 'baby boom' of
the 1960s. It should be pointed out, however, that the rate of change was
faster for the age effect.

A second demographic variable worth examining is the family structure. Over the 1970s household size and composition in Canada underwent major changes. The processes which brought about the decline of
the traditional family composed of a couple with children were similar
to those in other industrialised countries. Greater mobility and higher
rates of marital breakdown led to large increases in the number of

Table 2.6. *The contribution of changes in within- and between-household types to the trend in total inequality: Canada, 1971–1987 (adjusted post-tax–post-transfer income. Theil index)*

Year	Total inequality	Within-household inequality	Between-household inequality
1971	26.1	23.0	3.1
1975	21.8	18.5	3.3
1981	19.5	17.4	2.1
1987	15.8	14.1	1.7

one-parent families and to the declining proportion of couples with children. Usually the distributional impact of smaller households is negative, because it prevents income pooling. We should therefore expect a stronger effect of between-household inequality on total income inequality. Decomposition results by family size reported in table 2.6, however, do not substantiate this hypothesis. Over the 1970s between-household inequality declined only marginally, while the sharpest drop occurred in the within-group component from 23.0 per cent in 1971 to 17.4 per cent in 1981. Even accounting for the greater rate of change in between-household inequality, developments in family structure had a fairly low distributional impact in Canada during the 1970s. The income decomposition analysis reveals that what dominated were the contributions from changes within-age and within-household type subgroups. Thus, demographic effects played a negligible role in the downward inequality movement.

Market effects

A more thorough analysis of demographic changes would require a detailed investigation of immigration movements in that they may exert a major economic impact by either increasing or decreasing the supply of labour, and by affecting the size and location of the labour force. However, this investigation lies beyond the scope of this work. In addition, in the cases of Canada and Australia we have seen that immigrant status is not correlated with the distributional location of immigrants. We can therefore explore market effects in a general way. Figure 2.4 shows that the proportion of workers in the middle-market income class rose while the proportion in the upper and lower tails of the distribution declined. More precisely, the number of people with market

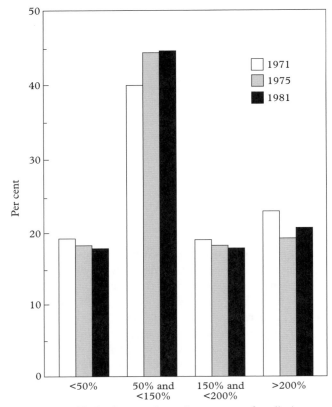

Figure 2.4. Proportion of the population in different market income classes: Canada, 1971–1981 (head of household aged 20–64)

income below 50 per cent of the median declined by 1.4 percentage points between 1971 and 1981, while the proportion in the top income class dropped by 2.2 points. A salient feature of figure 2.4 is that the distribution of market income is more concentrated towards the middle. In Canada there was a tendency towards depolarisation in the 1970s, with a falling percentage of workers with low and high incomes associated with growth in the middle of the distribution. Inequality fell in the period under consideration partly because market differentials were less scattered.[5]

[5] Wolfson (1993) has pointed out that income polarisation and income inequality are two different concepts. The population included in analyses of income polarisation is not representative of the

Table 2.7. *Gini coefficient (per cent) for selected income definitions: Canada,*
1971–1987

Year	Market income (1)	Post-transfer income (2)	Reduction from transfers (1)–(2)
1971	47.0	39.9	7.1
1975	43.6	35.4	8.2
1981	42.6	34.4	8.2
1987	44.2	34.5	9.7
Percentage change			
1971–1975	− 7.2	− 11.2	−
1975–1981	− 2.1	− 2.8	−
1981–1987	+ 3.7	+ 2.9	−
1971–1987	− 5.9	− 13.5	

The distributional impact of government transfers

Having established that market effects had a strong distributional impact, the last step is to examine the contribution of government cash
benefits. Table 2.7 sets out the inequality index before and after government intervention. It shows that the drop in the Gini coefficient induced
by cash transfers in 1981 was 8.2 per cent; this was the same as in 1975
but higher than in 1971, when it was 7.1 per cent. Government cash
transfers continued to mitigate income inequality in the mid 1980s. The
data unambiguously indicate that market income inequality grew
between 1981 and 1987 from 42.6 to 44.2 per cent but post-transfer
inequality remained virtually even. It is evident from table 2.7 that the
impact of transfer payments on income inequality was fairly stable over
the 1970s, and modestly rose by 1.5 per cent in the 1980s despite the
Liberal government curtailing unemployment benefits. However,
the most significant result is that government direct intervention on
income inequality mitigated considerably the effects of growing market
differentials. The rate of change of post-transfer income inequality
between 1971 and 1987 was − 13.5, much faster than the change in
market income inequality of − 5.9. This difference shows that transfer
payments offset the movements in market income.

whole population because it comprises of only the labour force, and in most studies only the male
labour force. It also goes without saying that the share of the population with middle-level
incomes going up or down partly depends on how 'middle' is defined.

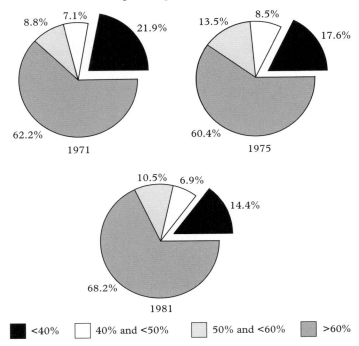

Figure 2.5. Percent of female household heads below or above different poverty lines:
Canada 1971–1981 (adjusted post-tax–post-transfer income)
Note: Legend refers to income as a percentage of median income

Some subgroups of the population increased their economic welfare.
Figure 2.5 illustrates that over the 1970s the proportion of female
household heads below the three poverty lines declined significantly.[6]
More precisely, the proportion of poor women dropped from 21.9 per
cent in 1971 to 14.4 per cent in 1981. Female poverty rates fell under all
three cut-off points. By 1981 there were 6 per cent more women
enjoying a relative non-poor standard of living, probably as a joint result
of government intervention and increasing labour market participation.
These figures justify the use of different cut-off points in that they show
how estimates are sensitive to the exact placement of the poverty line.

---

[6] One way of defining relative poverty is in terms of 'economic distance' from a specified average
standard. The most widely used economic distance measure is one half of median income, which
has the advantage of taking directly into account changes in society through changes in median
income. See the technical addendum.

CONCLUSIONS

Social security programmes in Canada over the 1970s have usually been conceived of as vote-maximising devices. Explanations based on vote-driven models of transfer policies offered important insights on the driving forces behind redistributive policies, but left unaddressed too many anomalies.

This chapter attempts to puzzle out the reasons behind those deviations. Under the Liberal minority government of 1972–1974 expansionary programmes are interpreted as a dominant strategy in interparty competition. Entrance of the NDP in the electoral arena provided incentives for Liberal leaders to mobilise voters. Competition from the left of the political spectrum threatened to capture actual and potential Liberal voters. By contrast, competition from the right was nearly defunct because Conservative leaders were struggling to maintain party unity. Internal strife connected to the leadership succession exhausted their energies and attention. This chapter shows that Liberal leaders played redistributive games by availing themselves of the opportunities offered first by the NDP electoral challenge and then by its blackmail potential. Opposition effects are notoriously strong in Canada because of weak and unstable partisan allegiances.

Most importantly, the NDP challenge impinged on the outcome of bargaining games between the Liberal pro-welfare and anti-welfare coalitions. We saw that by deftly exploiting the NDP's blackmail potential, Trudeau was able to overcome opposition within his own party against generous social security programmes. Internal conflicts resurfaced in the late 1970s with the u-turn from generous to stiffer cash benefits, seemingly aimed at pre-empting the leadership threat. Income redistribution after 1975 could partly be understood as Trudeau's reaction to his fear of being outmanoeuvred by the Turnites.

While looking inside the party organisation sheds considerable light on distributional outputs, results from the LIS datasets indicate that neither the age structure of the population nor shrinking household size had significant distributional effects. Market differentials seemed more relevant, suggesting that the distribution of market income had equalising effects. Further decomposition of aggregate inequality, however, pointed to the key redistributive role performed by social security policies.

CHAPTER 3

The arithmetics of politics under Margaret Thatcher

POLITICAL BACKGROUND

The aim of this chapter is to analyse the politics of income redistribution in Britain under the Conservative governments of Margaret Thatcher. Most political commentators have concentrated on the economic advances of the Thatcher era, rising prosperity, the spread of home ownership, the drastic drop in inflation, and the reduction of the budget deficit. It is now clear, however, that the economic benefits have not been equally spread, with the rich becoming richer and the poor relatively poorer (Atkinson, 1995b; Goodman, Johnson and Webb, 1997). In February 1998, the latest evidence of the 'Rowntree Inquiry into Income and Wealth Distribution in the UK' provided a devastating account of the process, showing that income inequality in the mid 1990s reached a higher level than recorded since the war (Hills, 1998b).

This amplification of income inequality surely stemmed from a plurality of causes. When the Conservative Party returned to power in 1979 with the biggest turnover of seats since 1945, the economy was in the throes of the most severe recession since the 1930s, with double digit inflation and soaring unemployment. As a trading nation Britain had been vulnerable to world-market trends, but the economic crisis of the late 1970s had been exacerbated by Britain's demise as a great power (Gamble, 1995a: 33).

Many supporters of the Conservative government viewed the welfare state as a main cause of the sluggish economy. Conservative intellectuals believed that 'egalitarianism [had] accompanied Britain's economic decline' (Joseph and Sumption, 1979: 12). The welfare state allegedly imposed a burden on the taxpayer, stifled incentives to work and to save, and undermined individual self-reliance. Transfer payments were deemed the principal reason of expenditure growth and budget deficits.

The government's decided attack on the culture of dependency in general, and unemployed people in particular, derived from its conviction that transfer benefits generated disincentives to work. Nigel Lawson, the then Chancellor of the Exchequer, claimed that the social security system encouraged 'idleness and irresponsibility' (quoted in Gilmour, 1992: 125) and thwarted virtues of hard work and drift. Thatcher reinforced this opinion in her memoirs:

Both for public spending reasons and in order to deal with the 'Why Work?' problem (namely, the disincentive to work created by the small disparity between in-work and out-of-work incomes), we had already agreed to tax short-term social benefits as soon as possible. In the interim we decided to reduce these benefits – unemployment, sickness, injury, maternity and invalidity benefits – by 5 per cent. (Thatcher, 1993: 55)

Thatcher's comments conceal the fact that there was scant empirical evidence to sustain the belief that transfer benefits generated disincentives to work. In 1977 only 50 per cent of those eligible were claiming Family Income Supplement (FIS) while 24 per cent of supplementary benefits remained unclaimed; in 1979 only 60 per cent of those eligible were claiming the one-parent benefit ('Social Security Statistics, Great Britain', 1981: 253).

The take-up rate was therefore well below 100 per cent, casting doubts on claims of fraud and abuse by benefits' recipients and on the alleged disincentive effects of transfer benefits. Yet fraud and abuse continued to be the spectre used to justify draconian cuts in spending (Lister, 1991: 94). Paradoxically, these remarks were uttered while official estimates reported that the supplementary benefit unclaimed was running at 25 per cent, which meant that 410 million pounds a year went unclaimed (*The Guardian*, 5 November 1986). The Conservative manifesto of 1979 was nevertheless committed to cutting public expenditure and to 'rolling back the state'. These pledges were to have serious repercussions for social security spending, which in 1978/1979 represented nearly half of public expenditure on the welfare state. Part of the problem was that the system was supporting three times the number of people who had depended on it in the mid 1940s, when the National Assistance Board was set up (Donnison, 1982: 11). Claimants of supplementary benefits had risen from one million to almost five million reflecting major demographic movements. The number of elderly, single parents and students entitled to benefits rose faster than the rest of the population. Despite these changes no thorough overhaul of social assistance policies had taken place (Dilnot, Kay and Morris, 1984: 23–26).

Structural issues were not the chief concern of the Conservative government. Instead its assault on the welfare state grew out of the philosophical underpinning of the New Right (King, 1987). Although the New Right is a label attached to a diverse ideological and political movement, its adherents are united by a rejection of the assumptions of the policy regimes underlying social democracy. Gamble argued that 'poverty, unemployment and disadvantage [were] no longer conditions demanding remedy through government programmes' (1989: 11). As Thatcher put it, the underlying strategy was to 'let our children grow tall and some grow taller than others if they have it in them' (Quoted in *The Independent*, 10 February 1995). Clearly there was little or no place for redistribution in this ideological framework.

In some respects New Right ideas were not new. Welfare spending had been curtailed under the Labour government in 1976–1979 after the International Monetary Fund made new loans conditional on the reduction of government outlays (Hills, 1998b). Though it is widely thought that the Thatcher governments represented a distinct break with welfare state policy, their radical nature should not be exaggerated. Over the 1980s, professional and managerial classes tempered the Conservative governments' attacks on the welfare state by protecting universal social services, such as the National Health Service (Klein, 1995; Le Grand and Winter, 1987).

Instead the real break with the past came about in social security policies (Atkinson, Hills and Le Grand, 1986; Hill, 1990; Lister, 1991). Thatcher was distinctive because 'none of its predecessors had dared to cut social security spending' (*The Economist*, 22 December 1979: 13). Under the Social Security Acts of 1980, 1982, 1986, 1988 the Conservative governments established new rules which made take-up benefit more limited and difficult (King, 1995a: 168–173). During the period 1979–1988, 38 changes in the rules governing unemployment benefits were made, which significantly reduced their scope and coverage (Atkinson and Micklewright, 1989). As one analyst observed '[t]he practice of *laissez faire* has not permeated social security. Since 1979 there have been almost annual Acts concerned with social security policy as well as countless changes in regulation and policy' (Bradshaw, 1992: 86). Furthermore, while the generosity of welfare provision was cut back, the number of beneficiaries increased substantially. Table 3.1 shows that between 1980/1981 and 1981/1982 the number of unemployment benefit recipients grew by 25 per cent, yet the government had reduced both the coverage and the level of unemployment benefits. The fall in

Table 3.1. *Estimated numbers receiving social security benefits: United Kingdom, 1977/78–1985/86 (thousands)*

Year	Retirement pension	ub*	Sickness benefit	Invalidity benefit	Child benefit	One parent benefit	FIS
1977/78	8,430	620	540	550	13,680	210	85
1978/79	8,530	570	560	600	13,480	290	85
1979/80	8,680	550	490	620	13,330	370	80
1980/81	8,880	960	435	620	13,160	430	95
1981/82	9,015	1,220	445	660	13,145	470	125
1982/83	9,075	1,200	450	700	12,935	505	160
1983/84	9,095	1,260	175	730	12,720	540	175
1984/85	9,145	1,180	170	740	12,510	570	170
1985/86	9,260	1,170	170	740	12,330	600	170

Note: *ub = unemployment benefit.
Source: 'The Government's Expenditure Plans', 1983/4 to 1985/6 (Cmnd 8789).

numbers receiving sickness benefits was the result of the transfer to employers of responsibility for payment during the first eight weeks of sickness in a tax year. Recipients of child benefit also dropped substantially, probably as a consequence of tighter eligibility criteria (Hills, 1987: 92).

Policies towards low-income groups

These developments were in stark contrast with the post-war consensus on the desirability of maintaining and expanding a comprehensive system of social insurance. The notion of consensus is a difficult one, in that there was never complete bipartisan agreement between members of the main political parties, or within the parties themselves, and differences of substance have pervaded all policy areas. In the field of social security, strands within the Conservative Party were critical of the whole trend to welfare statism, and a major area of disagreement between the two main parties was on social security (Glennerster, 1998).

The depth of such controversy, however, should not be overstated. David Donnison, then Chairman of the Supplementary Benefits Commission, thought that every government since World War II, no matter which party was in power, had claimed that they wanted to support the family, to maintain – or return to – full employment, and to get people off means tests (1982: 207). Thus, consensus had a broad denotation, it meant 'accommodation between different interests and values, which set a framework and priorities for post-war policy to which all parties in practice adhered' (Gamble, 1989: 3). The origins of consensus on the basic principles of the social security system must be sought in the Beveridge Report published in 1942 which proposed a shift away from the traditional means-tested benefits towards a more universalist system (Dilnot, Kay and Morris, 1984: 9–12). Universal benefits meant that social security was to be provided at the same level to all who qualified; by contrast, means-tested benefits were paid only to those in need.

Political leaders made considerable efforts to defend the innovative spirit of the Beveridge plan. Although the return of the Conservative government in 1951 marked a retreat from the universalistic model of social policy, the commitment to full employment was strong (Glennerster, 1995: 70–94). In the mid 1960s the Labour government expanded the social security system by incorporating an earnings-related tier into the structure of unemployment benefits (ERS) and by establishing the Supplementary Benefits Commission to report on the conditions of poverty. In June 1970 the elections returned a Conservative government committed 'to develop and improve Britain's social services to the full' ('Conservative Manifesto', 1970: 3). Prime Minister Heath initiated some new universal benefits, notably the constant attendance allowance for the disabled and the new pension for those over 80 who could not previously qualify.

The Labour government of 1974–1979 made further progress in social security policy by introducing non-contributory invalidity benefits, and the first benefit intended for the one-parent family. Compared to Canada, the USA and Australia, support to reproduction in Britain was less fraught with the politics of internal racial and ethnic divisions (O'Connor, Orloff and Shaver, 1998). Prime Minister Wilson undertook the most important explicit reform of the Beveridge plan in the field of pensions. In 1975 the government brought in the state earnings-related scheme (SERPS), which gave retirement pensioners an earnings-related pension in addition to state pensions. The scheme introduced a 'ratchet' according to which pensions were indexed to prices and earnings, whichever rose faster.

By 1979 a system of annual review of benefits had been established which resulted in uprating national insurance benefits in line with wages and prices, whichever grew faster. For the entire post-war period British party leaders agreed on the definition of poverty (Banting, 1979: 74).

Economic hardship was caused by a variety of factors, including personal misfortune, low wages, large families, disability, sickness, etc., and the solution proposed was setting a national minimum standard of living. Convergence on redistributive policies over the 1950s and 1960s allegedly showed that party politics and electoral considerations had little influence on the final decisions (Rose, 1984a). Social policy was either the product of incremental/decremental decisionmaking or the result of pressure group activity.

The Thatcher experience, however, presents a radically different picture. According to a book-length study of Social Security Bills in Britain, Thatcher's premiership marked out a different pattern:

> The primary role of bureaucrats in formulating [social security] policy options has been maintained but the emphasis has changed: the parameters within which reform is perceived as possible have been determined by politicians rather than administrators. (Ogus, Barendt and Buck, 1988: 11)

Such observations validate the view that in the 1980s the core executive control over the state apparatus was much stronger (Richardson, 1994). With the advent of a Conservative government in 1979 a new, more active and impositional style of government was attempted. Thatcher made skilful use of advisers to extend her influence in the government and in her party, by establishing links with right-wing think-tanks and intellectuals. Through this network of advisers Thatcher launched an offensive against the social security system. She wanted to reverse the trend in social security policies by reducing the role of universal benefits and increasing that of means-tested benefits. This controversy between selective and universal benefits was not new in British politics and within the Conservative Party (Glennerster, 1998; Weale, 1990); but Thatcher was the first party leader to elevate it to a primary policy objective.

Most importantly, in the early 1980s, the link between the value of social security benefits and earnings was broken. Instead of cash benefits rising with national prosperity at times of wage increases, they increased only in line with price inflation. This meant that their value would fall in relation to the income of those in work.

The Conservative government did not merely introduce new policies to affect transfer benefits. There were also areas where the method of calculation of the benefits was changed. In 1986, for example, the government succeeded in substantially reducing the value of pensions just by modifying the formula for deriving them. As set out in section 6 of the Pensions Act, the formula changed from 25 per cent of the best 20 years of earnings to 20 per cent of the lifetime average, and the pension inherited by the spouse was halved (Ogus, Barendt and Buck, 1988: 207). The halving of inheritance rights on a partner's pension will presumably have the greatest impact on lower-income families.

In other areas, the *lack* of change was just as important. Despite the sharp rise in unemployment in the early 1980s, no variations were made on the level and duration of unemployment benefits. The cumulative effect of these measures was that between 1978–1979 and 1983–1984 the number of social security claimants increased by 138.4 per cent but spending on income-related benefits rose by only 110.6 per cent in real terms (Atkinson, Hills and Le Grand, 1986: 30). This indicated a real decline in the benefit per claimant, created by the abolition of the earnings-related supplement and the taxation of benefits.

Stringent entitlement rights reduced the number of people with National Insurance benefits by 10 per cent, and so a much larger proportion of the unemployed were dependent on supplementary benefit. In addition, the data collected on state transfers in Britain show that between 1975 and 1985 average take-home pay rose by 2 per cent, whereas the real value of social benefits for a single unemployed person rose less than 1 per cent per annum on average (Atkinson, Hills and Le Grand, 1986).

Lastly, the tax system was made more regressive than ever. There was a shift away from direct to indirect taxation by replacing the previous split rates of Value Added Tax (VAT), 8 and 12.5 per cent, with a single rate of 15 per cent. Later this figure rose again to 17.5 per cent. Indirect taxation is a regressive tax in that it has little relation to a taxpayer's ability to pay. Redistributive taxation is almost always direct taxation, because the more you earn the more you pay. Yet the Conservative government initially cut the top marginal tax rate on earned income from 83 to 60 per cent, and later reduced it to 40 per cent. It also gradually lowered the basic rate of income tax from 33 to 25 per cent. Raising the Value Added Tax to 15 per cent added about 4 per cent to the Retail Price Index, at a time when inflation was resurgent and the oil price soaring. Higher indirect taxation was needed partly to finance reductions in income tax at both the top marginal tax rate and the basic rate. Most strikingly, Hills (1987) reports that the cuts in direct taxes had been entirely paid for by cuts in the generosity of benefits relative to national income.

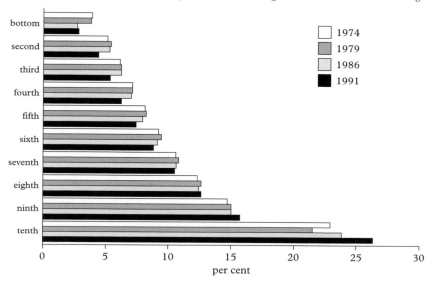

Figure 3.1. Income share of population deciles: United Kingdom, 1974–1991
(adjusted post-tax–post-transfer income)

ELECTORAL INCENTIVES FOR REDISTRIBUTION

One reason why the Conservative government redesigned entitlement rules may be sought in vote-maximising strategies. It is widely believed that during the post-war period British party leaders agreed that convergence towards 'the middle ground' ensured electoral success (Kavanagh and Morris, 1994). Available data suggest that middle-income groups were net gainers from redistribution (figure 3.1). Between 1974 and 1979 the income share of the fourth decile was stable, but the fifth, sixth and seventh decile increased their takings, corroborating the median-voter hypothesis. The second and third deciles also were better off, but the share of the bottom tenth slightly declined. Hence, before the advent of the Conservative government, the distribution of disposable income reflected the predictions of the Downsian model. From 1979 to 1991, however, the figure delineates a consistent decline in the income share of the middle-income groups, refuting median-convergence hypotheses. Rather than concentration towards the median of the distribution, the LIS data reveal sharp widening gaps between rich and poor.

It is reasonable to believe that middle-income classes benefited from taxation policy, especially from the shift to indirect taxation, and from access to universal social services. Probing the validity of these claims, however, lies beyond the scope of this work. As far as measured income is concerned the available data presented in this chapter testify that under Conservative rule middle-income classes were worse off.

While the results are incongruent with median-voter assumptions, evidence for the political business cycle in the United Kingdom between 1979 and 1991 is ambiguous. In 1979 the Conservatives pledged to curb government outlays, but between 1979 and 1981 spending increased by 2 per cent, partly as the effect of soaring unemployment. Further deviation from the model was the government's reduction of the scope and level of benefits after 1981, regardless of the timing of elections. Highly controversial policies were enacted in 1982 just one year *before* the general election of 1983. From June 1982 the earnings-related supplement for unemployment and sickness benefit was abolished; a few weeks later unemployment benefit and supplementary benefit paid to unemployed people (with the exceptions of additions for children) became taxable.

The impact of these changes was immediate. Official estimates reported that the combined effect of taxation and the 5 per cent cut in unemployment benefit of 1980 meant losses ranging from £140 in 1982–1983 for a single person to £481.80 for a married couple; unemployed people with very low incomes lost £1.75 a week in real terms for a couple and £1.10 for a single person (*The Times*, 9 July 1982: 2).

Under the Social Security Act of 1986 there was a radical shift in the centre of gravity to means-tested benefits, with benefit levels reduced and entitlement rights stiffened one year *before* the general election of 1987. This Bill abolished lower-rate benefits which enabled those individuals not meeting the full contribution conditions to receive a half and a quarter rates of national insurance. As a result many people failed to qualify for national insurance benefit on account of insufficient contributions. In May 1986, over 800,000 of the 3 million people unemployed had insufficient contributions to receive any unemployment benefit (Atkinson and Micklewright, 1989).

More consistently with the PBC, the Social Security Act of 1980 cut the real value of child benefit by 9 per cent, despite pre-electoral promises to increase it (Lister, 1991). It also severed the link between wage movements and benefits discussed above. Other instances corroborating the predictions of the PBC were the abolition of the child dependency addition to unemployment benefit in 1984, one year after the 1983 elections, and the social security cuts introduced by the passage of the Social Security Acts of 1988 and 1989, following the successful election of 1987. Hence in a few cases manipulations of transfer policies do appear compatible with the PBC; however, the timing of several other benefits changes does not substantiate the model. In the following sections I propose an explanation rooted in three factors: the geographical distribution of poverty; the shift from implicit to explicit games; the introduction of sequential elections.

Electoral geography and Director's Law

The inadequacy of conventional vote-maximising models to explain the link between electoral competition and income redistribution might rest on the peculiarity of the British electoral geography.[1] The majority of Conservative voters live in the South, whereas Labour supporters are chiefly concentrated in the North. Over the 1980s the geographical distribution of votes coincided with differences in the principal bases of poverty. In the South the elderly were the most likely to be poor; poverty in the North was more likely to be associated to redundancy and joblessness (Green, 1996).

Research centred on the geographical location of poverty in Britain is still in its infancy, and therefore the connection between the principal bases of poverty and electoral geography has been under-researched. It may well be that redistributive costs and benefits have been apportioned between risk categories in order to mould electoral coalitions in specific areas of the country. Borrowing from Krieger (1986: 86) we can describe this strategy as arithmetical particularism which relied on making sectional appeals, either to different social groups or to different geographical areas. Arithmetical particularism enabled Conservative leaders to adjust social relativities by changing the economic position of target groups. In this light, social security policies altered economic relativities between benefit recipients by penalising the unemployed while being more protective towards pensioners. The high priority given to the elderly, relative to other claimants, is reflected in the consistently declining proportion of pensioners requiring means-tested help for their living costs, which fell by 2.8 percentage points between 1979 and 1990 (Evans, 1998: 275). This drop was partly the consequence of increasing receipt of private and occupational pensions paid in addition to state pension. By contrast in the same period the percentage of unemployed with no unemployment benefit rose by 21.6 points (Evans, 1998: 278).

A good example of the asymmetric distribution of benefits is that in

---

[1] Unfortunately the LIS datasets do not include the geographical variable for Britain, so I draw on published information on the geographical distribution of poverty and inequality in Britain.

1981 the government increased pensions in line with inflation plus an additional 2 per cent for the amount by which the inflation of 1981 was underestimated, whereas unemployment benefits were indexed without getting the extra 2 per cent. Electoral strategies meant that middle-class social benefits, such as health and pensions, were carefully protected (Boix, 1998: 201). But this observation fails to acknowledge that pensions were curtailed in the medium–long term through de-indexation, which meant the relative position of pensioners to the working population worsened. Nigel Lawson, then Chancellor of the Exchequer, lucidly describes pension policy in his memoirs:

> The most controversial decision announced in the 1979 Budget was the repeal of the Labour Government's legislatively enshrined formula for uprating pensions in line with prices or earnings, whichever rose faster... As earnings normally rise faster than prices, Labour's commitment was an expensive one ... We decided to switch to straightforward indexation in line with prices. On the other hand the 1979 Budget increased pensions by 19 1/2 per cent. This increase was designed to compensate and to soften the blow of the change in the form of indexation. (Lawson, 1992: 36–37)

The real value of pensions, at least, did not decline (Hills, 1998b). Other state-dependent groups were less lucky. As noted earlier, one of the first casualties of the Thatcher government was the abolition of the earnings-related supplement (ERS) for the unemployed, sick and widows introduced by the Labour government in 1966. In addition to this under the terms of the Social Security Act of 1980, 4 per cent was cut from short-term contributory national insurance benefits, including injury, unemployment, sickness and invalidity benefits. This reduction in the level of unemployment benefits suggests that a much larger proportion of unemployed people were poor and therefore dependent on supplementary benefit.

Income polarisation between North and South was reflected in different patterns of dependence on supplementary benefits. In the North the number of beneficiaries grew from 15.7 per cent in 1979/1980 to 20 per cent in 1983/1984, an increase of 4.3 percentage points, while in the south-east it increased from 9.4 per cent to 9.7 per cent, a rise of 0.3 points (Walker and Walker, 1987: 47–48). Hence higher unemployment, low-paid jobs and poverty were of different magnitude and significance in the two regions (Green, 1996; Johnston and Pattie, 1989).[2] Arithmeti-

---

[2] The spatial distribution of poverty, is of course, more nuanced than the account offered in this chapter. There are urban–rural differences, as well as differences between large metropolitan centres (see Green, 1996; Noble and Smith, 1996).

cal particularism helped Thatcher to capitalise on the geographical distribution of poverty.

The North had a higher proportion of individuals living in poor households (Borooah *et al.*, 1991: 98). The economically fortunate were instead living in the south and formed a sizeable proportion of what Galbraith dubbed the 'contented electorate' (Galbraith, 1993: 15). Although the north–south divide pre-dates the 1980s (Fiedhouse, 1995), Walker claims that the Conservative government 'has helped to widen and deepen these divisions, sometimes to a catastrophic extent' (1987: 13). Other redistributive measures limited the availability of benefits to women in general, and married females participating in the labour market in particular (Hill, 1990: 5). Specific changes that increased women's dependence and the extent of gender inequality included variations to pensions and maternity benefits and to women's eligibility to unemployment benefits. Alterations to the States Earnings Related Pension Scheme diminished its value for elderly women and the universal maternity grant was replaced in 1987 by a means-tested benefit. At the same time statutory maternity pay was introduced to be administered by employers with a new qualification test, which excluded large numbers of pregnant women (McDowell, 1989). Tougher conditions to establish a claimant's availability to work afflicted women with pre-school children who had to demonstrate that they had already made arrangements for child care before being entitled to benefits (Jones and Millar, 1996). These measures worsened the financial hardship of women because unemployment is not equally distributed among groups in society, and women are a particularly vulnerable group that experience high poverty rates (Harkness, Machin and Waldfogel, 1996). Cutbacks in the real level of child benefit affected the standard of living of lone mothers.

These facts suggest that the Conservative governments carved the boundaries between categories of people in need and deliberately chose to implement harsh measures against subgroups of the state-dependent population. Arithmetical particularism coupled with the adjustment of social relativities helped the Conservatives to promote alliances between sections of the middle class and beneficiaries. Much has been written about how the middle classes were wooed through housing policy and tax policy (Dunleavy and Husbands, 1985; Jowell *et al.*, 1997). The government encouraged council tenants to buy their homes by offering favourable terms, which presided over one of the biggest booms in the housing market ever experienced. Social engineering was further promoted by selling off council houses so as to produce a major growth in Conservative voting among manual worker households. This chapter adds to those scholarly works the finding that transfer policies under Thatcher were also politician driven.

New electoral coalitions were forged by policy manipulations, which explicitly denied benefits to specific groups while granting them to other less stigmatised groups. Analysts have observed that by stigmatising benefit claimants the Tories 'have tried in a muted ... way to extract political advantage from a widespread populist suspicion of the state dependent population' (Dunleavy and Husbands, 1985: 24). Conservatives engaged in vote mobilisation to build the electoral coalition that kept them in power (Boix, 1998).

This process of coalition building among sections of the electorate was facilitated by weak interparty competition. Divisions within the Labour Party over proposals of internal constitutional change absorbed the energies of the Labourites. In the late 1970s and early 1980s Labour's strategy shifted further to the left (Whiteley, 1983: 2–6). Such policy radicalisation opened a political vacuum in the centre of the ideological space, soon filled by the formation of the Social Democratic Party (SDP). Throughout 1981 and 1982 the SDP in alliance with the Liberal Party produced sweeping by-election successes, and was an apparently dominant force in shaping public opinion (Budge *et al.*, 1988; Dunleavy and Husband, 1985: 67).

Entrance into the electoral arena of a new political rival tempered internal opposition against the anti-egalitarian stance of the 'dries' because several Tory moderates were acutely vulnerable to the Alliance's advance in their constituencies. 'By 1981 an election was within sight, and the rise of the SDP/Liberal Alliance was worrying the "wets", especially as many of them were, by chance, most exposed to the Alliance's advance in their constituencies' (Riddell, 1983: 46–47). In November 1981 the by-election in the Conservative stronghold of Crosby on the Lancashire Coast produced a swing of 25 per cent and returned to parliament Shirley Williams, a prominent leader of the SDP. In March 1982, another SDP leader, Roy Jenkins, took the Tory seat at Hillhead, Glasgow. The Alliance's success seemed to be related to its moderate image (Rasmussen, 1983). Although the establishment of the SDP inflicted heavy damage on the Labour Party, 14 per cent of Alliance voters identified with the Conservative Party, and a much higher proportion would probably have voted straight Conservative had there been no SDP alternative (Crewe and King, 1998: 290).

Modifications in the electoral arena affected the internal dynamics of the Conservative Party by changing the options available to Conservative groupings, enhancing the internal position of right-wingers. Furthermore, the Falklands war boosted Conservative support, contributing to the landslide victory in 1983. The electoral results established Thatcher in her political leadership and showed that opposition parties were not a serious electoral alternative.

This situation had far-reaching consequences for social security policies. Lack of credible electoral rivals meant that the government had only been prepared to make compromises in policies when pressure was exerted from within its own supporters (Ogus, Barendt and Buck, 1988: 11). A telling example was that in 1986, Norman Fowler, then Secretary of State, was forced to reverse his intention to pay the new family credit to husbands rather than wives, because it 'upset the formidable Tory women. When they have allies like that, the poor hardly need the poverty lobby' (*The Economist*, 28 June 1986). Intraparty politics clearly influenced the way redistributive policies were selected.

EXPLICIT GAMES AND THE ANTIEGALITARIAN CRUSADE

One reason why the political dynamics of social security policies under Thatcher has been under-researched might be the Conservative government's recurrent emphasis on macroeconomic policies. Thatcher confirms in her memoirs that the hardest battles were fought on the grounds of economic policy (1993: 27). Monetarism was a dominant media theme which observers quite understandably were curious to investigate. By contrast, the shift to a residual social security system went largely unnoticed. As analysts noted at the time, little by little the social security system had undergone major changes of principle without any widespread public recognition (Atkinson and Micklewright, 1989). However, the growing awareness that economic benefits have not been equally spread, with the poor getting poorer and the rich richer, justifies the attempt to reconsider the internal dilemmas of the Conservative Party in those years in the light of their redistributive implications.

A preliminary step in this direction involves tracing the evolution and consolidation of strategic games between Tory leaders. To this end, it is useful to borrow Schelling's distinction between tacit and explicit games (1980: 21). Tacit games are those where players watch and interpret each other's behaviour; partners cannot or will not negotiate explicitly; by contrast, in explicit games the conflict of interest is publicised and overt.

Tacit and explicit games are not thoroughly distinct definitions, and combinations of the two games may exist.

Scholarly work has long recognised the pervasiveness of tacit games within the Conservative Party. As one observer noted 'Conservatives . . . engage in ideological conflicts using sophisticated codewords and themes which resonate with the cognoscenti but cannot easily be picked up by outsiders' (Dunleavy, 1993: 124–125). Tacit games enhance loyalty and unity because they promote close cooperation and coordination (Schelling, 1980: 54–67). The Conservative Party has long been re-garded as highly cohesive with few rigid factions and widespread con-sensus about long-held beliefs (Aughey and Norton, 1981: 51; Rose, 1964; Webb, 1994: 110).

This pattern of internal coalitions changed in the 1970s, with a substantial number of Conservative MPs disagreeing on the same issues (Norton, 1978: 244). There had been more dissenting MP votes under Edward Heath from 1970 to 1974 than in the previous 25 years, between 1945 and 1970. One reason was the increasing professionalisation of parliamentary roles which strengthened backbench influence (Searing, 1994)

Among the Conservative ranks the difference with pre-1970s dissent was not just a matter of quantity, but also of quality. Internal unrest was reflected in a shift from tacit to explicit games, which fostered the formation of more stable alignments. The intensity of internal rifts has stimulated several attempts at classifying ideological groups in the Con-servative Party (Aughey and Norton, 1981; Baker, Gamble and Ludlam, 1994; Crewe and Searing, 1988; Dunleavy, 1993; Garry, 1994).

Difficulties in classifying Conservative groupings and charting an ideological map might be resolved by bringing into sharper focus the key internal disputes on the eve of Thatcherism, in the early 1970s. Crewe and Searing (1988) find that the Conservative Party consisted of a variety of subgroups but that political thinking in some subsections could be quite highly crystallised. Their results showed considerable distance on the political values of two ideologically opposed groups, namely the Monday Club on the Right and Pressure for Economic and Social Toryism on the Left. Between these sharply defined ideological communities, a few more flexible groupings filled the terrain, providing a general structure of Conservative ideology based on four pillars; progressive and traditional Tories on the one hand, and liberal and corporate Whigs on the other. Progressive Toryism had paternalistic roots. It repudiated laissez-faire, favoured programmes for reducing the extremes of poverty and wealth and espoused a vision of the state as trustee for the community. Its support for the welfare state was closely connected to its conception of community. Traditional Tories were cynical about social planning and skeptical about the virtues of social progress. Their primary concern was strong government and leadership.

Liberal and corporate Whigs sought to preserve private property as the most effective means to achieve their aims. Liberal Whigs believed that government intervention distorted the marketplace and undermined economic growth, while corporate Whigs believed in the economic advantage derived from a close partnership among government, trade unions and business. From the early 1950s to 1974 the dominant coalition within the Conservative Party melded elements of corporate Whiggery with progressive Toryism. Thatcher ascendency to power hinged on an alternative alliance, which connected liberal, free enterprise Whiggery with traditional, authoritarian Toryism (Crewe and Searing, 1988).

Various hypotheses have been advanced to explain the quantitative and qualitative twist in internal revolt. Some authors claim that the party was facing a generational shift and young Conservative MPs had a less deferential attitude towards party policy (Budge *et al.*, 1988: 60). Generational turnovers, however, are usually deemed insufficient conditions for tilting the internal balance of power because they do not always trigger variations in bargaining strength between party elites (Panebianco, 1988: 33–45). Others maintain that internal bickering was fuelled by the authoritarian and confrontational personalities of Heath and Thatcher (Norton, 1978: 217–255). Explanations in terms of personalities are limited because they sidestep the crucial question regarding the dynamics of power within the party organisation.

SEQUENTIAL ELECTIONS

A more convincing view holds that the new pattern of internal strife was the outcome of leadership selection rules introduced in 1965, with the main innovation being MPs' participation in electing the party leader (Shepherd, 1991: 103). Prior to 1965 the Conservative leader was not chosen by election but 'emerged' out of informal discussions from the party ruling caucus. It is widely believed that enormous powers were concentrated in the hands of the leader, who could enjoy security of tenure, the right to appoint the heads of the professional party organisation and the control of policymaking. All authority and policy emanated from the leader. This procedure portrayed a public image of internal cohesion and accommodation. In 1965 the procedure for selecting the leader was changed with the requirement that the leader obtained an overall majority plus 15 per cent of the votes cast. Once elected there was no provision for the formal removal of the party leader and consequently the leadership selection rules of 1965 did not alter significantly the relationship between the leader and the party.

This relationship was profoundly modified after the two resounding electoral defeats of February and October 1974. Widespread recrimination against concentration of power in the hands of the then leader, Edward Heath, led to the introduction of new selection rules (Behrens, 1980: 32; Punnett, 1993: 262). First, the 15 per cent of votes requirement on the first ballot was replaced by a requirement of 15 per cent of all eligible voters, in addition to an absolute majority. Second, provision was made for regular election at the beginning of each new parliament and in each subsequent session. From 1975 the Conservative leader had first to ensure re-election as leader and therefore satisfy the wishes of the faithful MPs.

One consequence was that the formal security of tenure of the party leader was brought to an end, which signified an increased dependence of the leader on the support of MPs. It may be argued that Conservative leaders never enjoyed security of tenure, and that the new rules merely formalised the realities of existing relationships. Several Conservative leaders had been informally ousted by the members of parliament. Alec Douglas-Home, Harold MacMillan, Anthony Eden, Winston Churchill and Neville Chamberlain all resigned as a consequence of loss of confidence among their close allies (Bogdanor, 1994: 86–96).

Nevertheless, detailed descriptions of the leadership selection suggest that the new rules marked a departure from previous experience. Bogdanor, for instance, concedes that 'neither Mrs Thatcher, nor perhaps John Major, would have been selected under the old methods' (1994: 96). There is scholarly consensus on the fact that Thatcher was elected not because there was an extensive commitment to her views but rather because she was the only serious candidate willing to challenge Heath (King, 1985: 97; Riddell, 1983: 21; Shepherd, 1991: 176–177). Estimates of the proportion of Thatcherites on the eve of Thatcher's election based on responses on three values, strong government, free enterprise and discipline, indicate that her supporters ranged between 10 and 25 per cent (Crewe and Searing, 1988: 371).

The new procedures impinged on the high degree of cohesion which had historically characterised Tory leadership. Jim Prior, a leading Conservative figure, described the situation frankly:

the traditional ways in which the old 'inner circle' used to organize the Party informally and discreetly, born of the values of duty and loyalty – could no longer work. Whenever Willie Whitelaw and Francis Pym used to get together, they still seemed to think that the party could be run as they had run it ten or fifteen years earlier. Although they undoubtedly could wield some power and used all their skill to keep Margaret's Shadow Cabinet reasonably cohesive, it could never be the same again. (Prior, 1986: 103)

Apart from loosening internal cohesion, the selection rules increased the dependence of the Conservative leader on the party (Norton, 1978: 24). The fact that the leader was now directly dependent on the favours of the Conservative MPs heightened her sensitivity to the views of back-benchers, 'the probability of removal may be low; but the risks to the individual [leader] are high' (King, 1991: 29). Conservative leaders were now compelled to face the problem of sequential elections. Sequential elections create a dilemma for party leaders because in order to gain or retain office, leaders must win the favours of different types of constituencies, including MPs, party activists and voters. Potential threats of candidates standing against the incumbent could prove damaging for the party's image giving some leverage to dissidents within the parliamentary party (Norton, 1978: 25). This claim was substantiated by the Conservative leadership contest held in July 1995, when the visibility of the leadership battle tarnished Major's victory because '218 votes meant that 109 Tory MPs did not cast their votes for Major' (*The Economist*, 8 July 1995).

Comparative research on the leadership selection found that the 'process of selection may constrain the style and behaviour of those selected, either because of the resources required, or because of the need to ensure reselection where that is necessary' (Marsh, 1993: 229). Thus sequential elections may have encroached on Thatcher's policymaking authority and perhaps affected her influence on redistributive outputs.

Sequential elections and redistributive policies

The ideological chasm within the Conservative Party was often depicted as a battle between 'wets' and 'dries'. Thatcher, for example, describes in her memoirs 'the passionate and obstinate resistance mounted by the "wets" to the fiscal, economic and trade union reforms of the early 1980s' (1993: 105). The press reported how 'Mrs. Thatcher was particularly infuriated at having to make 'wet' decisions at the last minute to pull the government back from what seemed a certain short-term disaster', such as countermanding a partial deindexation of pensions (*The Economist*, October 1981). Clearly the distinction between 'wets' and 'dries' is an overly simplified account of the variety of Conservative thinking which was much more nuanced (Douglas, 1989). Tory rebels were by no means a homogeneous group but it is plausible to assume that the public was influenced by press reports or public speeches and perceived internal strife in bipolar terms. For this reason and for analytical convenience my analysis focuses on the redistributive effects of strategic interaction between these two rival groups. Some members of the 'dry' coalition were overtly inegalitarian and believed that wide differences in income were both natural and desirable. In the words of Joseph and Sumption, the cornerstone of the new strategy was 'to challenge one of the central prejudices of modern British politics, the belief that it is a proper function of the State to influence the distribution of wealth for its own sake' (1979: 1). The novelty and radicalism of Thatcherites was the rejection of the social democratic message, which suggested that the state was seeking to reduce inequalities. With the advent of Thatcherism inequality was 'welcomed and praised, and promoted through fiscal policy' (Gamble, 1989: 14).

The 'wets' were less sympathetic to such views. They claimed that the Tory tradition, going back to Disraeli, stressed the primacy of community over individuality (Gilmour, 1992: 142–177). Concern for the poor was of long standing within the party with roots going back to the Tory democracy of the nineteenth century (Banting, 1979: 74–75). They also believed that some degree of state intervention for the relief of poverty was necessary, and that less-privileged groups should be protected.

The leadership selection procedures had transformed the 'dries' into a dominant minority, but still a minority, within the party and thus contributed to the factional quarrels in the 1980s (Budge *et al.*, 1988: 69). Arguably, this minority status enhanced their ideological spurt, so unusual among Conservative leaders. Radical policies go deeply against the grain of Conservative thinking, which was traditionally tinged with moderate tones. 'Margaret Thatcher was a Conservative rarity in her readiness to identify Conservatism in unambiguous ideological terms' (Whiteley, Seyd and Richardson, 1994: 127). Minority groupings are sometimes more radical than majority ones because purposive incentives develop to compensate for other incentives controlled by the larger group (Panebianco, 1988: 3–15).

The crusading spirit of the 'dries' helped cement their internal divisions. A large number of Conservative figures, such as Rhodes Boyson, Lord Beloff, Paul Johnson, Alfred Sherman and Alan Walters, had changed their political allegiances at least once before, and thus might be expected to do so again (Denham and Garnett, 1994: 270–271). These people had been recruited from varying sources, some had been Liberals, others Labour supporters. 'Since their beliefs were shaped more by their antipathies than by a common positive vision, the need for a constant unifying enemy was particularly urgent for them' (Denham and Garnett, 1994: 271). Internal rivals were instrumental to the viability of the 'dry' coalition.

Thatcher's account of her conflicts with Jim Prior, Minister of Employment and leading 'wet', clearly illustrates the instrumental role of the ideological drive:

> For all his virtues, Jim Prior was an example of a political type that had dominated and, in my view, damaged the post-war Tory Party. I call such figures 'the false squire'. ... In order to justify the series of defeats that his philosophy entails, the false squire has to persuade rank-and-file Conservatives and indeed himself that advance is impossible. His whole political life would, after all, be a gigantic mistake if a policy of positive Tory reform turned out to be both practical and popular. Hence the passionate and obstinate resistance mounted by the 'wets' to the fiscal, economic and trade union reforms of the early 1980s. (Thatcher, 1993: 104–105)

The 'wets'' reaction was epitomised in Prior's belief that the 'dries'' inegalitarian stance was 'a very simplistic approach... In a world increasingly interdependent and with a people used to a welfare state, it looked an unpromising scenario' (Prior, 1986: 119).

Although the bitter battle over redistributive policies was cast in economic terms, several observers have noted that the main goal of the Thatcherites was to reshape the party image and re-educate the nation. For Deakin 'ultimately the economic arguments were means to a still more ambitious end – Keith Joseph's insistence that the party must move away once and for all from its previous position' (1987: 86). Gamble aptly affirmed that the 'appeal to monetarism was much more than a set of techniques for controlling the money supply' (1995a: 100). Bulpitt argued that the 'dictates of party management, political argument, electoral success, and above all, the necessity to find a future governing competence, ensured that a link would be made with the statecraft of monetarism' (1986: 33). These authors agree that the Conservative appeal to monetarism was not entirely guided by economic reasons.

Evidence substantiating these claims is provided by Thatcher's belief that a staunch defence of monetarism was a pre-condition to shaping the attitudes of the electorate:

I was utterly convinced of one thing: there was no chance of achieving that *fundamental change of attitudes* which was required to wrench Britain out of decline if people believed that we were prepared to alter course under pressure. (Thatcher, 1993: 122, emphasis added)

Against this background it is not surprising that 'Thatcherism', whatever its meaning, became part and parcel of the Conservative identity (Jessop *et al.*, 1988: 6). Fashioning both the party image and voters' attitudes corresponded to the same strategic line.

A further consequence of the minority status of Thatcherites was that on coming to office the Prime Minister had little choice but to appoint as Cabinet ministers Heath's most able and effective supporters, including William Whitelaw, Jim Prior, Ian Gilmour, Peter Carrington and Quintin Hogg. Thatcher also brought in people like Peter Walker, the symbol of Heathite interventionism, and Christopher Soames, a typical traditional Tory. As *The Economist* commented in the wake of the Cabinet formation 'the significant thing is not that there is a strong moderate faction in Cabinet, but that, with only a handful of exceptions, the Cabinet is itself a moderate faction' (22 September 1979: 15). The Prime Minister ensured that four key posts were given to her closest supporters. Geoffrey Howe was appointed Chancellor of the Exchequer, John Biffen, Chief Secretary of the Treasury, Keith Joseph, Secretary of State for Industry and John Nott Secretary of State for Trade.

Divisions inside the Cabinet grew steadily worse and much of the debate centred around public expenditure (Behrens, 1980: 70). Prior's reaction to the 1979 Budget eloquently expressed this dissension: 'It was really an enormous shock to me that the budget which Geoffrey [Howe] produced the month after the election of 1979 was so extreme' (Prior, 1986: 119). The general emphasis on aggregate public expenditure may be misleading if it assumes that all spending counts equally (Esping-Andersen, 1990). Budget cuts during the first Thatcher term were not equally distributed. Soon after the Conservatives took office, the Treasury pressed for cuts in welfare outlays proposing the reduction of the annual uprating of benefits in order to save £600 million; but the proposal was abandoned in the face of strong opposition from the Social Service Secretary, Patrick Jenkin (Young, 1991: 212).

As the economy slumped and unemployment soared the government's stubborn concern with inflation and the minimalist state provoked an outright revolt within both the Cabinet and backbenchers. In 1981 the unemployment rate stood at 13 per cent and most Cabinet members were expecting less-stringent monetary rules. Concerns were raised about the redistributive effects of the government's macro-economic policies. 'The biggest revolt is over Sir Geoffrey's decision to index unemployment benefit next year 2 per cent below the inflation rate' (*The Economist*, October 1981). Francis Pym, a leading Tory 'wet', claimed that for the most part internal disputes gravitated on the interaction effects between economic and social policy:

[t]o insist that unemployment is an urgent social problem in need of immediate and imaginative attention may or may not require a new economic policy, but it undoubtedly requires a sympathetic social policy ... it is undesirable for any Government to make a hard and fast choice, or to appear to do so, between economic and social policy. (Pym, 1984: 111/112)

Thatcher's reply to mounting opposition from her Cabinet was epitomised in her famous dictum 'I have only one thing to say. You turn if you want to. The lady's not for turning' (Thatcher, 1993: 122). The Budget provoked open dissent and criticism among many Tory leaders. Even Thorneycroft, Thatcher's own choice as party chairman, sided with the dissidents and was removed before the Annual Conference held in Blackpool in 1981.

The Blackpool Conference displayed the two faces of a divided cabinet. Michael Heseltine, Secretary of State for the Environment, criticised the right-wing emphasis on independence and self help because 'self help [had] a limited meaning in an inner city community where 40 per cent of the young kids may be without work' (*The Times*, 16 October 1981: 2). Controversy over the relationship between the Conservative Party and sections of the British population was sparked by different opinions regarding the party image. Hardliners wished to mould it as the party of free-market principles, initiative and duty; while the 'wets' believed that the government should not relinquish its responsibility for acting as a brake on income inequality.

Arguably, however, the most significant aspect of the Blackpool Conference was the surfacing of the dilemma of sequential elections:

The unease of Tory members of parliament [contrasted] strongly with the loyalty and enthusiasm of constituency delegates for Mrs. Thatcher, and more particularly for Thatcherism. The . . . more applause she won at Blackpool the less appeal she had to the broader electorate watching television. (*The Economist*, 17 October 1981: 29)

Had the Conservative leader satisfied the wishes of moderate Cabinet ministers and those of the wider electorate, she would have annoyed the party's rank and file. Thatcher skilfully deployed different sources of power to quell the revolt within the party. First, she immediately appealed to party activists in order to mobilise their support. In her words:

The dissenters in the cabinet had been stunned by the 1981 budget proposals. It was clear that the Party in the country must be mobilized in support of what we were doing. The forthcoming Central Council of the Conservative Party provided an opportunity for me to do this . . . I got a good reception. For the moment at least, the Party faithful were prepared to take the heat and back the government. (Thatcher, 1993: 138–139)

Thatcher's demagogic appeal to activists helped to boost party membership, after years of relentless decline. Her close attention to the rank and file raised activists' perception of their importance for the party organisation. Survey findings suggest that since the early 1980s Conservative members have been feeling more influential in the decisionmaking process of the party organisation (Whiteley, Seyd and Richardson, 1994).[3]

Thatcher gauged the mood of many Conservative activists correctly. 'Above all', wrote *The Times*, 'Mrs.Thatcher has given voice to many grassroots Tory views about unions, law and order, scroungers and capital punishment' (11 March 1986: 3). In their survey of attitudes among Conservative and Labour members, Whiteley, Seyd and Parry (1996) find that the Tory leader was especially popular among young Conservative members who were more committed to political principles. Their results show that young Conservative activists were less favourable to the redistribution of income and wealth and less supportive of government expenditure to relieve poverty. Therefore Thatcher was able to promote and reinvigorate the loyalty of party members through attacks on scroungers and on the welfare state.

---

[3] These results seem to reject McKenzie's (1963) claim that Conservative activists are not relevant actors in the decisionmaking process. Yet, they also qualify Kelly's (1989) contention that activists significantly influence policymaking. Activists do play a role, but not a very significant one.

The second strategy Thatcher deployed to ease the strains between 'wets' and 'dries' was to relax public expenditure. Growth in government outlays in the early 1980s was doubtlessly the effect of automatic stabilisers, but it was also the outcome of internal opposition: 'The relenting on cuts took some of the edge off the cabinet anger... It is regarded as signalling the start of the "wet appeasement"' (*The Economist*, 24 October 1981: 29). For Shepherd, Thatcher always tempered her radicalism with an overriding desire that the Conservatives should hold office with her as their leader (1991: 178). Faced with the pragmatics of power, the Conservative leader restrained her policy ambitions. Hence by appealing to the party faithful and by pacifying the 'wets', Thatcher was able to forge an internal alliance and to retain the leadership despite the fact that she had joined a minority coalition.

The equilibrium within the Conservative ranks, however, became gradually more precarious. Profound divisions over macroeconomic policies were heightened by noticeable differences in social policy. Peter Bottomley, then Conservative MP for Woolwich West, complained that unemployment benefits were 'now worth less than at any time in the past decade. The last thing we can afford is to be accused of dishonesty' (*The Times*, February 1982). In such conditions, it is not surprising that 'the Government suffered one of its biggest backlash revolts of the present parliament... when 13 Conservative MPs voted to restore the 5 per cent that was cut from unemployment benefits in 1980' (*The Times*, 18 March 1982: 1). The press reported that the revolt was 'the most determined piece of internal dissent Mrs Thatcher [had] suffered' (*Financial Times*, 14 July 1982). When 18 Conservative MPs voted against the refusal to restore benefits cuts, the government's majority fell to eight. Rebels included Dennis Waltern, Cyril Nebyon and Julian Critchley, five others abstained. It was clear that any further pressure would risk splitting the party asunder.

BREAKING THE INTERNAL ALLIANCE ON SOCIAL SECURITY POLICIES

Tensions reached a climax in the summer of 1981 during the discussions preparing the budget. The Treasury requested spending cuts for 1982–1983, below the totals derived from the March White Paper. Thatcher recounts in her memoirs how this proposal sparked 'one of the bitterest arguments on the economy, or any subject, that I can ever recall taking place at Cabinet during my premiership' (Thatcher,

1993: 148). The renewed outbreak damaged the party image to the point that:

decisions came to be seen as victories by one side or the other . . . and it was quite impossible to convey a sense of unity and purpose in this climate . . . Some ministers were trying to discredit [the government's] strategy itself. (Thatcher, 1993: 130)

Fierce reactions to the 1981 Budget acted as a springboard for a Cabinet reshuffle. According to Francis Pym, 'Margaret Thatcher saw this crisis as a personal challenge to her resolve and became doubly determined not to give an inch on the economic strategy' (Pym, 1984: 8). In September 1981 the Prime Minister dropped three well-known 'wets', Ian Gilmour, Lord Privy Seal, Christopher Soames, Leader of the Lords and Mark Carlisle at Education, and brought in three men on whom she could rely, Norman Tebbit, who was appointed Minister of Employment, Nigel Lawson, Minister of Energy and Norman Fowler, who became Minister of Health and Social Security.

In 1982 the Conservative government asked the Central Policy Review Staff to report on measures apt to resolve the problem of ever-increasing public expenditure. When the Policy Review proposed to dismantle the welfare state they found a determined rejection from Cabinet members. The prime minister's press office issued a denial that Mrs Thatcher had anything to do with the plan.

As the recession wore on, internal turmoil exploded and the Cabinet's cohesion began to break down. At this critical point two institutional features insulated Margaret Thatcher from losing control of policymaking. The constitutional role of Prime Ministers in appointing and reshuffling their Cabinets was 'undoubtedly one of the most important ways in which a prime minister [could] exercise power over the whole conduct of government' (Thatcher, 1993: 25). Another salient aspect was the strong institutionalisation of the Conservative Party, which concentrated power in the hands of the dominant coalition and hindered the formation of stable organised factions (Panebianco, 1988: 130–141). The joint effect of prime ministerial prerogatives and strong institutionalisation mollified the 'wets' resistance to Thatcher's policymaking authority.

The Cabinet reshuffle and the electoral landslide of 1983 crushed the 'wets' as a coherent force within the party. Thatcherite ideas became so dominant that social policy ceased to be a divisive issue among MPs during the second Conservative term (Garry, 1994). To put into effect

Thatcher's low spending and antiprogressive policies, a prerequisite was defeat of moderate 'wets'. In this new scenario, the Fowler Report of 1986[4] could easily mark a retreat from any serious commitment of insuring individuals against risk (Lister, 1991). The Fowler Report was described at the time as the most radical since Beveridge. The *Financial Times* hailed the Fowler Report as the cure for clamping down on the 'Costa del Dole' (21 August 1985: 3). Its major proposals were cuts in child benefit and the phasing out of SERPS which meant a far less secure and independent old age. This report was brought into full implementation in 1988 and marked an important turning point in the history of the British social security system (Hill, 1990: 56). Evans (1998) finds that after the introduction of the Fowler recommendations, between 1987 and 1991, means-tested benefits fell by about 10 per cent against a general increase in incomes of 5 per cent for all. The third Thatcher term was dominated by the aggressive policy of John Moore pressing for further cuts.

INCOME INEQUALITY: DEMOGRAPHY, MARKETS AND INCOME TRANSFERS

It is important to investigate how measured income inequality fared while the Conservative governments were scaling down redistributive policies. The United Kingdom is one of the few LIS countries with datasets going back to the mid 1970s and this information provides a unique opportunity to trace inequality trends over a long period of time. From table 3.2. we see that the pattern of inequality growth in Britain is divided into two periods, 1974–1979 and 1979–1991. In the first period between 1974 and 1979 inequality indices clearly drop. The striking feature of table 3.2 is that under the Conservative government there was a clear reversal of the trend. Between 1979 and 1991 all indices rose, with the growth ranging from 10 per cent to 30 per cent.

This unanimity of the three indices is important because it reduces the possibility that results are dependent on the particular index used. As we have noticed in the previous chapter it is useful to look at a different way of examining the evidence. Table 3.3 presents inequality growth in terms of income shares by quintile group. Between 1974 and 1979 the bottom 20 per cent slightly increased its income share from 8.9 per cent to 9.2 per cent. However, this rise was less than half the increase

---

[4] For a thorough examination of the Fowler Report and its effects on social security claimants, see Evans (1996).

Table 3.2. *Trends in income inequality in the
United Kingdom, 1974–1991
(adjusted household post-tax–post-transfer income)*

Year	CV	Gini	Theil
1974	67.3	28.7	14.8
1979	53.8	27.6	12.7
1986	64.7	30.3	16.5
1991	93.9	34.8	22.9
Percentage change			
1974–79	− 20	− 4	− 14
1979–86	+ 20	+ 10	+ 30
1986–91	+ 45	+ 15	+ 39

Note: * Percentage changes are rounded.

Table 3.3. *Quintile income share: United Kingdom, 1974–1991
(adjusted household post-tax–post-transfer income)*

Population quintile	1974	1979	1986	1991
bottom	9.0	9.2	8.0	7.2
second	13.2	13.3	13.2	11.5
third	17.3	17.6	17.0	16.3
fourth	22.9	23.4	23.0	23.1
top	37.6	36.5	38.8	42.0

enjoyed by the other three quintiles. The income accruing to the second and third quintile rose respectively by 0.7 per cent and 0.8 per cent, while the fourth quintile expanded its share by 0.5 per cent. Hence the poor gained less from the redistributive process than the middle-income groups. It is also evident that before the advent of the Conservative government income differentials were less marked, with the top quintile losing a fraction of its takings. Under Thatcher the picture was almost symmetrical. In the 1980s the income share of the bottom quintile shrank by 2 per cent, the top quintile gained 3.5 per cent and the middle groups were slightly worse off.

Snapshots of a few years, however, hamper the identification of the turning point in the trend. Several authors have suggested that the period between 1977 and 1980 marks the start of a sustained and substantial increase in the dispersion of incomes (Hills, 1996; Jenkins, 1991).

Table 3.4. *Contribution of changes in within- and between-age-groups to the trend in total inequality: United Kingdom 1974–1991 (adjusted household post-tax–post-transfer income. Theil inequality index)*

Year	Total inequality	Within-age-group inequality	Age effect (between-group inequality)
1974	14.9	13.4	1.5
1979	12.8	11.4	1.4
1986	16.5	15.9	0.6
1991	22.9	21.6	1.3

Demographic effects

The age profile of the British population has been regarded as an important determinant of income inequality in the years between 1965 and 1980. Mookherjee and Shorrocks (1982) report that the growing number of elderly contributed to rising inequality to the point where subtracting the age effect from aggregate inequality meant a reversal of the trend. Recent findings, however, suggest that the age effect is much less significant in the 1980s (Jenkins, 1995; Stark, 1989: 181–182). Table 3.4 sets out the results of the age decomposition between 1974 and 1991. Again, the pattern highlights a sharp contrast between the 1970s and the 1980s. Clearly the age effect was roughly stable during the 1970s, while there was a downward trend from 1979 to 1986 and an upward drift between 1986 and 1991. Since aggregate inequality in the same period grew to 16.5 per cent, the age factor seems negligible. Inspection of table 3.4 reveals that what dominated was the contribution from changes in inequality within age groups. This analysis shows that the age profile of the population had a low distributional impact. It thus corroborates research showing that demographic changes have contributed relatively little to the changing shape of income distribution in Britain. These conclusions, however, should be qualified because the rate of change in within-group inequality between 1986 and 1991 is greater than for between-group inequality.

The second demographic variable we analyse is the household size and composition. We have seen that different household types may affect the distribution of income when their concentration varies. In Britain, as in many other industrialised countries, there has been a secular decline in average household size. Reasons for the decline in average household size include greater mobility, a trend towards

Table 3.5. *Contribution of changes in within- and between-household types to the trend in total inequality: United Kingdom, 1974–1991 (adjusted household post-tax–post-transfer income. Theil inequality index)*

Year	Total inequality	Within-household inequality	Between-household inequality
1974	14.9	11.5	3.4
1979	12.8	9.9	2.9
1986	16.5	14.2	2.3
1991	22.9	19.8	3.1

younger people living independently from their parents and higher divorce rates (Kiernan, 1995). The impact of these changes is likely to reduce equality all the more because they prevent income-pooling and increase the number of low-income single-adult households, especially those of single parents. Table 3.5 shows that between 1974 and 1991 there was an upsurge in within-household inequality that rose from 11.5 to 19.8 per cent. The level of inequality between household types was rather stable, implying that the growing proportion of smaller households had fairly marginal effects on total inequality. These results indicate that demographic movements in Britain over a period of about fifteen years had low distributional consequences.

Market effects

The marginality of demographic variables in changing patterns of income inequality strongly suggests that other forces were at work. Wage differentials, for instance, have received great attention from analysts of the distribution of income in Britain (Jenkins, 1995). Several studies have detected a clear link between the propagation of income inequality and wage dispersion (Gardiner, 1996; Gosling, Machin and Waldfogel, 1996). Consequently, they concentrate specifically on the spread of wage differentials during the last 20 years. Figure 3.2 represents the proportion of the population in four income classes for the period 1974–1991. The picture that emerges is unambiguous. Between 1974 and 1991 the proportion of the population with less than 50 per cent of median income almost doubled. Furthermore, while the proportion of poor workers grew by 4.3 percentage points between 1974 and

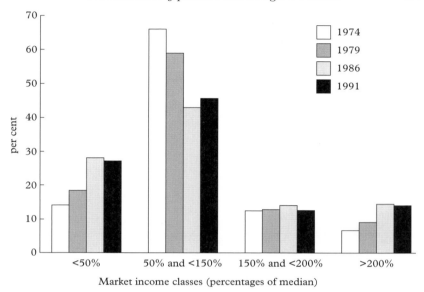

Figure 3.2. Proportion of the population in different market income classes: United Kingdom, 1974– 1991 (head of household aged 20–64)

1979, its growth accelerated under the Thatcher government, climbing by 8.7 points between 1979 and 1991. At the same time, the proportion of the richest income category with more than twice median income more than doubled, again with the highest increase of 5.4 percentage points between 1979 and 1986. On the other hand, upper-middle-income earners were much less affected, since their number rose slightly from 13.1 per cent to 14.1 per cent and then declined to 12.9 per cent in 1991.

A noteworthy feature of figure 3.2 is that over the 1980s the distribution of market income was more spread away from the middle: the falling percentage of workers with middle-range earnings was associated with growth in the lower and upper tails of the distribution, corroborating the hypothesis on the shrinking middle class (Cowell, Jenkins and Litchfield, 1996; OECD, *Employment Outlook*, 1993). Income polarisation mainly reflected structural and technological changes and there was an expansion of the secondary labour market, with an increase in temporary and part-time workers employed in low-skilled jobs.

Table 3.6. *Gini coefficient (per cent) for selected income definitions: United Kingdom, 1974–1991 (adjusted household income)*

Year	Pre-transfer income (1)	Post-transfer income (2)	Reduction from transfers (1)–(2)
1974	43.3	31.9	11.4
1979	46.9	31.5	15.4
1986	53.6	34.9	18.7
1991	53.2	38.3	14.9
Percentage change			
1974–1979	+8	−1	–
1979–1986	+14	+11	–
1986–1991	−1	+10	
1974–1991	+23	+20	

Table 3.7. *Cumulative percentage of the unemployed and total population below three different poverty lines: United Kingdom 1974–1986 (adjusted household post-tax–post-transfer income)*

Percent of median income	Unemployed population			Total population		
	1974	1979	1986	1974	1979	1986
Less than 40 per cent	20.5	13.2	14.4	1.8	2.7	4.2
Less than 50 per cent	30.7	21.6	23.0	6.9	5.7	7.1
Less than 60 per cent	38.5	30.0	36.0	15.5	13.8	13.0

Income transfers

The distributional role of market forces can better be understood by looking at variations in the Gini coefficient induced by government intervention. Table 3.6 displays the results of the Gini coefficient for selected income definitions. It shows that market income inequality rose almost consistently throughout the period and declined slightly between 1986 and 1991. At the same time, inequality in post-transfer income dropped modestly between 1974 and 1979 and rose thereafter with a surge between 1986 and 1991. The fact that post-transfer income inequality increased while market income inequality decreased is an indication of the importance of transfer payments. This difference suggests a less-effective role played by cash transfers in reducing income differentials.

Detailed analyses of the composition of the poorest income group indicate a declining proportion of poor elderly over the 1980s but a higher proportion of poor lone parents and unemployed (Goodman, Johnson and Webb, 1997: 98–110; Land and Lewis, 1997). Hence the elderly have experienced lower risks of slipping into poverty whereas being unemployed or a lone parent has carried a higher risk of being relatively poor.

CONCLUSIONS

Over the 1980s income inequality in Britain grew faster than in many other countries, suggesting that national factors played a crucial role. By decomposing the structure of inequality it was possible to highlight the low distributional impact of demographic variables, such as the growing number of elderly and the smaller size of households. On the other hand, income polarisation in the market sphere increased income inequality. Widening market differentials, however, were not offset by government intervention. During adverse economic conditions social security acts as a brake, but in Britain its influence in reducing inequality has been increasingly limited over time (Evans, 1998).

The Conservatives sustained pre-transfer income inequality with a raging attack on the 'culture of dependency'. It is worth stressing that the relative position of benefit recipients, with respect to the working population, declined considerably. Because average income increased, the relative value of the basic pension fell from 47 per cent of average income in 1983 to 37 per cent in 1990, and the number of poor pensioners below half the average income increased substantially after the mid 1980s. The decline in the relative value of unemployment benefit over the period since 1983 has been from 36 to 28 per cent of average income. More generally, Hills found that over the whole period from 1979 to 1995 the incomes of the poorest 10–20 per cent were little or no higher in real terms, despite overall income growth of 40 per cent (1998b).

However, Conservative policies concealed an asymmetry in the distribution of costs and benefits among high-priority and low-priority beneficiaries. More favourable attitudes towards pension benefits protected the elderly relative to other claimants, while cutbacks in the level and scope of unemployment benefits exposed the unemployed to the risk of poverty. The latest evidence assembled by the *Rowntree Inquiry into Income and Wealth Distribution* shows that the real value of the basic pension over the 1980s stayed much the same (Hills, 1998b). In contrast, the real value of unemployment benefits dropped.

In trying to understand changes in redistributive policy we looked at a variety of interpretations. Much of the evidence cited seemed incongruent with conventional vote-driven views of income redistribution. Neither the median convergence hypothesis nor the PBC sufficiently illuminated the reasons behind Thatcher's redistributive policies. Politician-driven explanations, instead, were much more powerful. They pointed out that Thatcher capitalised on the geographical distribution of poverty and was able to forge new coalitions of voters between people in work and the deserving poor, such as pensioners. Conservative leaders engaged in sophisticated applications of arithmetical particularism, whereby specific state-dependent groups, including women, lone parents and the unemployed, were penalised while others were protected. As predicted by Director's Law of income redistribution, social groups enter or exit electoral coalitions if redistributive policies alter their incentives to vote. The Conservative governments manipulated redistributive policies to mobilise sections of the electorate into a winning coalition of voters.

Explanations of Thatcher's redistributive policies, however, have focused too exclusively on electoral considerations. The bulk of research on the Conservative Party has paid little or no attention to the redistributive impact of strategic games between contending party leaders. My account suggests that alterations of transfer policies over the 1980s reflected strategic repositioning between 'wets' and 'dries'. The main factors behind this shift were the introduction of the leadership selection rules, the evolution of explicit games and the weakness of electoral rivals. In addition, the dilemma of sequential elections impinged on the options available to the feuding partners. By raising Thatcher's threat perception, sequential elections facilitated the internal compromise on social security benefits between 1979 and 1981.

If we divide the Thatcher era in its three terms it is easy to see that the radicalisation of social policy followed shifts in internal realignments. Two Social Security Acts passed in 1980 introduced the first cuts, most significantly by severing the links between wage movements and benefits. At this stage internal opposition was buoyant and Thatcher was still in quest of legitimacy, so the 'dries' whittled down several proposed cuts. The chapter concentrates on the first term because this period represented a critical juncture during which internal opposition was virtually eliminated.

The landslide victory of 1983 and the demise of the 'wets' as internal opponents meant that 'the politics of interest, of faction, of groupings and collaborations within the party, which a leader might ignore at her peril, had entirely vanished' (Young, 1991: 332). It was not until the 'wets' abandoned the internal battle that the Conservative government undertook the most radical departure from post-war social security policies with the ratification of the Fowler Report. This policy radicalisation was encouraged by the weakness of interparty competition and the lack of a credible alternative to Conservative rule. To evaluate the significance of the 'wets'' demise for income redistribution, suffice it to note that the rate of change of income inequality was much faster between 1986 and 1991 (table 3.2.).

Ample freedom of manoeuvre meant that Thatcher's second term could be dominated by the Fowler Report which was tempered only by the opposition of the Conservative Women's National Committee. During the third term, internal dissidents were either ousted or marginalised, and the government could thus press for further social security cuts. My account of the trajectory of social security policies under Thatcher complements other sociological explanations which have stressed the fact that the government wanted to scale down expectations of what the state could and should provide (Hill, 1990).

This chapter indicates that the growing gap between rich and poor in Britain is neither accidental nor a mere product of 'natural' differences. Market forces, weak electoral competition and internal repositioning contributed to the accelerating pace of income inequality. Variations in redistributive policies were partly initiated by alterations in elite-voter alignments, which were in turn triggered by the formation and demise of intraparty coalitions.

There are several interesting differences between the British and the Canadian case. Backbench influence was stronger in Britain because MPs are not subject to patronage power to the same extent as they are in Canada. Moreover, the dilemma of sequential elections mitigated Thatcher's radical stance in the first term. A further difference is that the politics of welfare expansion differs radically from the politics of retrenchment because the latter activates vested interests in established redistributive policies (Pierson, 1994). Finally, party competition in Britain was much weaker than in Canada, where the NDP offered external support to the Liberal minority government.

CHAPTER 4

Right-wing ascendency, pivotal players and asymmetric power under Bob Hawke

POLITICAL BACKGROUND

In 1983 the Australian Labor Party (ALP) returned to office after a lengthy period in opposition. Under the leadership of Bob Hawke the party succeeded in winning four consecutive elections, breaking the historical pattern of short-term Labor governments followed by long-term Liberal–National Party coalition governments. During this period Labor set out to defy the stance which had been adopted under previous Labor governments by engaging in deregulation and in scaling down social security benefits. Similar pressures towards rolling back the state were encountered in other OECD countries, but enthusiasm for economic rationalism[1] mostly came from the political right, from Reagan in the USA, Thatcher in Britain and Mulroney in Canada. What is surprising is that in Australia the manager of retrenchment was a Labor government.

When Labor took office in 1983 the economy had been struck by the most severe recession since the 1930s; inflationary pressures were mounting and unemployment was soaring. Adverse terms of trade meant that the budget deficit in 1983 reached almost AU$4.5 billion compared with an estimate of less than AU$1.7 billion.[2]

A salient feature of Australia's vulnerability was the structure of her trade: a small economy dependent on a narrow range of exports (Easton and Gerristen, 1996). As the price of raw materials plummeted in the late 1970s, Australia registered large monthly current account deficits which precipitated the AU$ depreciation in February/March 1985. The

---

[1] The term economic rationalism has never been clearly defined although it is widely used in the Australian academic literature to indicate a minimum role for government and a maximum role for the market.

[2] The outgoing Fraser Government had suppressed the true estimate of the deficit. This was an important element in subsequent elections, since the ALP were able to recast themselves as the party of fiscal responsibility.

perceived economic imperatives were to improve international competitiveness, reduce protective tariffs, restructure Australian industry,
and deregulate the financial market. For Bob Hawke 'restructuring the
economy – creating a more competitive, diversified, productive and
export-oriented Australian economy – is the only sure way towards
lower unemployment and higher living standards' (*Labor Times*, 1983: 2).

The general thrust of these developments was to reduce the size and
scope of government intervention. A radical swing to economic ration-
alist policies within the federal bureaucracy placed particular emphasis
on smaller government, lower taxes and a more targeted system of
government cash benefits. Treasury officials became deeply convinced
about the merits of economic rationalism, deregulation of the labour
market and in particular of less state involvement (Pusey, 1991). In the
words of Paul Keating, then Federal Treasurer:

the logic of our economic policies leads to an expectation of smaller government as a proportion of the economy over future years ... Australia's need for
budgetary restraint in the years ahead occurs precisely because the private
sector is expected to expand solidly. Public stimulus in this context is not only
unnecessary; it would be positively harmful to the prospect of sustained growth.
(Keating, 1985: 20)

Sound economic management apparently required cutbacks in welfare
spending. Over the 1980s government outlays fell by about 4 per cent of
GDP and social security spending declined. This slowdown was partly a
consequence of economic developments, most significantly a growth in
employment that was impressive by international standards. The trend
was reinforced, however, by redistributive policies directed specifically
at curbing expenditure by improving the targeting of transfer payments.

Policies towards low-income families under Hawke show some clear
patterns. A move to retrenchment followed by less-restrictive policies
and a failed attempt to shift the burden from direct taxation to indirect
taxation. To explain these developments I first look at the redistributive
games typical of unitary models of party competition and then I explore
the role of strategic interdependence within the party in power. Some of
the findings are consistent with results in the British chapter, especially
the limited role of electoral competition in the dynamics of income
redistribution under Hawke. Labor sometimes wooed voters with expansionary social policy but sometimes it did not. A more comprehensive explanation examines the replacement of the dominant coalition
within the ALP, underscores the role of a new pivotal player able to

moderate Labor's shift to the right, and evaluates the development of asymmetric power between the ALP and the trade unions.

Policies towards low-income groups

The processes generating and redistributing income in Australia have several unique features as compared with those of other OECD countries (Jackson and Bozic, 1997). The most relevant factors are a social security system financed from general revenue and paying flat-rate means-tested benefits, and a tax system that relies heavily on personal income taxation but raises total revenue in relation to GDP which is low by international standards. Entitlement for social security benefits in Australia has been conditioned by the private means of those eligible. Comparative research on the welfare state indicates that the Australian social security system is one of the most selective in Western countries (Mitchell *et al.*, 1994; Saunders, 1994b: 21–33).

This selectivity was one component of the strategy of 'domestic defence', which distinguished Australia from other capitalist states from as early as the beginning of this century (Castles, 1988: 91–108). Domestic defence involved strong regulative intervention to protect labour, such as a full-employment policy, restrictive immigration, industrial protection and an arbitration system. Early mobilisation of the working class led to compulsory conciliation and arbitration of industrial disputes, which aimed at defending living standards by achieving a minimum wage. One consequence was that unemployment benefits have been funded from general revenue and have not been related to the claimants' previous earnings.

A significant implication of the strategy of domestic defence is that cash transfers have been of secondary or residual importance in securing social policy objectives, in sharp contrast to the social democratic concern for universal welfare (Beilharz, 1994). In the main, Australia has been characterised as a laggard in the expansion of the welfare state because it has one of the lowest expenditures in transfer benefits amongst OECD countries. Trends in government outlays, however, may conceal that Australia enjoyed high levels of employment and a young demographic profile. These factors contributed to the development of a wealthy and relatively egalitarian society.

It was not until the 1970s that Australia underwent deep socioeconomic changes. As in most Western countries, the decline of the traditional family of wage-earning father, non-earning mother and dependent children affected the distribution of income. Higher rates of marital breakdown increased the number of one-parent families (Gibson, 1990: 180). As a result the coverage of social security programmes was steadily improved.

Expansionary social security outlays were also a reaction to change in the rate, duration as well as distribution of unemployment. In 1975 only 19 per cent of unemployment beneficiaries received benefit for more than six months, by 1985 this proportion had increased to 53 per cent and 35 per cent of beneficiaries had been in benefit for over one year (Cass, 1986: 5). In 1975 there were 161,000 people in receipt of unemployment benefit, comprising 2.6 per cent of the labour force. By 1985 the number of beneficiaries was 561,000 comprising 7.8 per cent of the labour force.

This sharp increase in welfare dependency and poverty was an apparently major concern among Labor leaders. Bob Hawke proclaimed in the electoral campaign of 1983 that 'Half of the three million Australians who depend on government welfare assistance – our aged, our disabled, our invalids, widows and single parents – are on payments below the poverty line. No Labor government can tolerate this situation' (*Australian Financial Review*, 17 March 1983). Yet one of the salient features of the Labor government's approach to social security policy was greater targeting of those most in need. Table 4.1 shows that the number of social security beneficiaries grew until the early 1980s, but the advent of Labor to power coincided with a reversal of the trend. Under Hawke the recipients of the old-age pension declined by 1 per cent and family allowance beneficiaries dropped by 11 per cent.

Cutbacks in government outlays were justified on the grounds that resources had to be diverted to 'productive' rather than 'unproductive' sectors. The new creed of the Hawke–Keating alliance was that socially protective activities hindered wealth production. As Hawke wrote in his memoirs, the then Federal Treasurer, Paul Keating, 'shared my desire for a modern, relevant party committed to economic growth rather than merely more equitable shares of a diminished cake' (1994: 235). A crucial step in this direction was to forge an industrial relations system more flexible to the demands of international markets. Consistent with this perspective the government implemented policies which primarily benefited those involved in relations of production.

In 1983 the two principal instruments of the Hawke–Keating economic strategy were initiated, the Accord and deregulation of the financial system. Financial deregulation, the float of the exchange rate

Table 4.1. *Trends in the number of social security beneficiaries: Australia, 1980–1996 (thousands)*

Year ended 30 June	Old-age pension	Disability support pension	Sole parents benefits*	UB**	Special benefit	Sickness benefit	Family allowance
1980	1,321	229	161	309	21	40	2,073
1981	1,347	221	194	313	19	48	2,092
1982	1,367	216	208	374	16	50	2,120
1983	1,390	220	224	633	20	62	2,155
1984	1,358	240	234	588	18	62	2,179
1985	1,331	259	246	562	18	62	2,191
1986	1,324	273	250	568	18	64	2,153
1987	1,322	289	248	553	19	70	2,136
1988	1,328	296	238	478	22	75	1,948
1989	1,334	307	239	389	25	79	1,927
1990	1,340	306	248	419	27	79	1,890
1991	1,375	334	265	676[a]	29	71	1,911
1992	1,446	378	287	852	34	44	1,929
1993	1,515	406	298	914	28	46	1,933
1994	1,581	436	313	878	25	47	1,827
1995	1,578	464	324	801	20	47	1,804
1996	1,602	499	342	812	18	33	1,812

Notes: * In November 1980 the six month waiting period for Supporting Parent's Benefit was abolished resulting in a substantial increase in number. Sole Parent's Pension replaced the Supporting Parent's Benefit in March 1989. Figures do not include benefits from March to June 1989.

** UB = unemployment benefit.

[a] Unemployment benefit was replaced by Job Search Allowance and Newstart Allowance in July 1991.

Source: Australian Department of Social Security, DSS Customers, 1997, various tables.

and the entry of foreign banks to challenge Australia's financial institutions were declarations of Labor's belief in the irresistibility of market forces. But the Labor government did not leave market forces to set wages. The hallmark of its economic strategy was an incomes policy, the so-called Accord, which provided widespread consensus among business pressure groups and trade unions (Singleton, 1990: 121–154). Strictly speaking the Accord was not a neocorporatist arrangement in that formal bilateral agreements took place only between trade unions and the Labor governments while business groups were informally consulted (Castles, Gerristen and Vowles, 1996).

Cooperation between the unions and the government seemingly showed that Labor's redistributive strategy was congruent with its tradition (Mishra, 1990: 79–92; Travers and Richardson, 1993). However, it should be noted that previous Labor governments introduced social security policies that were an advance on those of their conservative predecessors and devoted an increased proportion of government expenditure to them (Johnson, 1989: 101). Under Curtin and Chifley several important measures were introduced, including child endowment in 1941 and the widows' pension in 1942. When Labor returned to power in 1972, the Whitlam government expanded income support for the poor and progressively abolished the means test for persons over 70 years old.

These developments buttress the contention that Labor traditionally aimed for more social and economic equality and favoured a method of more effective social control over the dynamics of the economy to achieve these aims (Maddox, 1989: 161–179). Consequently the emphasis on targeting and selectivity appeared a retreat from social equity and social reform (Gibson, 1990: 180–203). By the late 1980s virtually all income support payments in Australia were subject to means tests, with the main exception being the invalidity pension to blind individuals. Hence the overall direction of Labor social security policies in the 1980s challenged the philosophical underpinning of the ALP platform and principles (Beilharz, 1994; O'Leary and Sharp, 1991). Several explanations have been advanced to shed light on Labor's redistributive policies. A widespread view holds that reductions in government outlays were triggered by economic imperatives, which led Hawke to place redistribution of wealth second to wealth production (Duncan, 1989: 20). The dramatic drop in real GDP growth in the early 1980s was associated with sharp rises in unemployment and inflation rates compelling Labor leaders to resort to deflationary policies.

One problem with interpretations based on macroeconomic variables is that policy actions did not always follow the economic cycle. When the economy recovered it brought about an impressive surge in real GDP, rising employment rates and a relative slowdown in inflation, but Labor's redistributive stance remained largely unaffected. Draconian spending cuts combined with economic recovery meant that government expenditure was heading back towards the level that had prevailed in the early 1970s, before Whitlam's expansionary policies. Partly because of a severe current account crisis, the 'Hawke government... became one of the most fiscally conservative governments that Australia has had' (Parkin and Bade, 1990: 637).

Tight fiscal policy was unrelated to Labor's flirtation with monetarism because the Reserve Bank had abandoned monetary targeting in the mid 1980s. In the wake of deregulation and financial innovations, monetary aggregates became unreliable indicators of the money supply and made interpreting the growth rate of monetary aggregates too difficult. In such circumstances the abandonment of monetary targeting was a conscious decision not to use the money supply as an instrument to curb inflation (Argy, 1992: 202). The upshot of this discussion is that there is little evidence to support the contention that economic imperatives dictated variations in social policies. Labor governments devised containment strategies independently of macroeconomic cycles or Reserve Bank objectives, leaving open the question of what accounts for the pattern of redistributive policies.

ELECTORAL INCENTIVES FOR REDISTRIBUTION

In turning our attention to the political dimension we should note that party competition in Australia is essentially bipolar. The Australian political system is perhaps the best example of non-plurality majoritarian systems (Lijphart, 1994: 143). These systems are quite similar to plurality systems except that they tend to create two blocs of parties instead of a two-party system, and parliamentary majorities for one of the blocs rather than for one party. In Australia there are officially three government parties, comprising the right of centre Liberals, the primarily agrarian National Party and the left of centre Labor Party. Competition is bipolar because the National Party has competed against Labor in virtually permanent alliance with the Liberals. The National Party is a small organisation with its main base in Queensland and the rural parts of Victoria and South Australia. Its programmes have a narrow set of concerns and thus the National Party can hardly be regarded as a serious contender for power without the Liberals.

During the 1980s these two blocs contested four general elections and Labor won all of them. On 5 March 1983 the ALP returned to power with a majority of 75 to 50; in the second electoral victory on 1 December 1984, the Hawke government secured a reduced majority of 82 to 66 seats; the electoral contest on 11 July 1987 returned a third Labor term with a slightly larger majority of 86 to 62 seats and in 1991, the last election under Hawke's premiership, the ALP gained 78 seats while the Coalition secured 69 seats, a much closer result than the previous three.

A similarity with the British case is that electoral success was facilitated by the weakness of party competition. Tensions between the Liberal Party and National Party, stemming from the desire of the National Party to go its own way, prevented the Coalition partners from forging a credible alliance against Labor. Hawke's unpopular redistributive policies carried low risks in the mid 1980s because the Opposition was in a shambles (Kelly, 1992, part 3).

The national Liberal Party came increasingly under attack from several state branches. John Bjelke-Petersen, the belligerent premier of Queensland and staunch supporter of single-rate taxation, launched a fierce campaign against prominent Liberals, such as Senator Peter Baume, Ian Macphee and Max Burr. Disputes about the leadership succession racked the Liberals from 1983 onwards. Andrew Peacock, the Liberal leader who replaced Fraser in 1983, had to hand on the leadership to John Howard in 1985, but returned to his position in 1989 after Howard was ousted.

Internal wrangling fuelled disunity and eventually induced Liberal leaders to embrace radical free-market ideas. Leading Liberal figures, such as Peacock, Howard, Macphee and Chaney argued that the core of Australia's economic problem was the system of arbitration, regulation and protection that had characterised the Australian settlement. For the first time in its history the Liberal Party was abandoning its guise as pragmatic reformer of the free enterprise system. The Liberals' pledge to dismantle the old edifice and to attack vested interests was reflected in their wish to establish a comprehensive legal alternative to the Conciliation and Arbitration Commission. Their greatest single challenge to the status quo was to replace the centralised industrial relations model with a decentralised system where market forces would set wage rates (Kelly, 1992). Liberals promised to break down the conciliation and arbitration framework created in 1904 which has nourished the culture of employer–union dialogue ever since.

The Liberal shift to the right had two major consequences. It doomed its immediate electoral prospects and provided Labor with margins of discretion previously unknown. Defining discretion as the range of potential policies that can be selected, the Liberal radicalisation expanded Labor's issue space. By moving far to the right the Liberal Party opened a vacuum in the right-of-centre policy space which endowed ALP leaders with greater strategic flexibility.

Summing up, the Hawke governments operated within a political and economic context characterised by a severe current account deficit, a social security system based on targeting and selectivity, and weak electoral rivals. The ALP secured a comfortable majority in 1983, a reduced majority in 1984 and tighter majorities in 1987 and 1990. All these elements contributed to furnishing the setting within which redistributive policies evolved over the 1980s.

Convergence towards the centre of the electoral space has been a long-standing interpretation of Labor policies in the post-war period. The ALP made inroads into the Australian middle class since the late 1960s, not only to win more votes but also to redress the bias associated with malapportionment (Hughes, 1994). Labor's electoral drawbacks lay in the over-representation of rural districts combined with the vote–seat distortion resulting from the geographical concentration of its constituency. However, explanations of Labor policies which rest on electoral geography are less poignant in the light of five successful elections (Charnock, 1994).

Psephologists observe that Australian parties converge to the centre because they feel confident about the votes of their core constituency. A well-known feature of Australian politics is that a majority of seats are regarded as safe for one party or another. In the 1980s a seat was 'safe' if a swing of over 10 per cent was needed to lose it; it was 'fairly safe' if the swing was between 6 to 10 per cent, and 'marginal' if it was less than 6 per cent (Wright, 1986: 130). The relative stability of the electoral arena combined with compulsory voting means that 'parties seek support among the "swinging" voters, and this has added to the impetus of both Labor and non-Labor to spread to the "centre" of politics in Australia' (Bean and Butler, 1991: 98). However, other observers note that the votes gained in the 1980s were at considerable cost to the level of support in older Labor electorates (McIntyre, 1991).

Hypotheses based on centripetal competition would lend credence

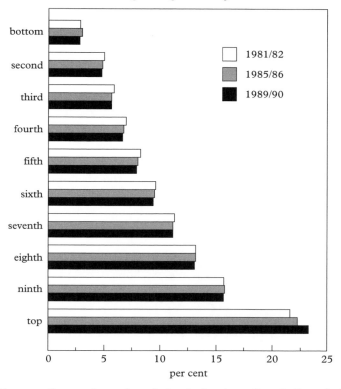

Figure 4.1. Income share of population deciles: Australia 1981/82–1989/90

to the view that redistributive policies mainly benefited middle-income classes. On the usual assumption that median-income groups and middle-class voters overlap, we would expect that median-income deciles increased their takings. Close inspection of the data does not corroborate the median-voter hypothesis because the middle deciles lost approximately 0.3 per cent of their takings (figure 4.1). Although the decline is slight, it does run contrary to expectations, casting doubts on the hypothesis of the 'middle-classing' of Australian society. This contention is reinforced by the fact that the richest tenth increased their share by 1.7 per cent. A different view holds that associations between voting behaviour and redistributive policies may be related to the timing of elections. In Australia there is a three-year electoral cycle and this should be taken into account when interpreting the evidence. A detailed examination of social security policies suggests that some changes were compatible with the predictions of the political business cycle. In the 1984 Budget, for instance, the Labor government accepted the unions' proposal of a tax cut of AU$7.60 a week for incomes between AU$12,000 and AU$25,081, which presumably favoured union members. For Carew 'the tax cuts were blatantly tailored to favour the ACTU's constituency' (Carew, 1992: 83; see also Kelly, 1992: 143–145). Labor leaders were probably responding to ACTU's (Australian Council of Trade Unions) concern regarding membership decline by protecting unionised members.

In line with the predictions of the PBC, the Labor government promised to eradicate child poverty during the electoral campaign of 1987 to shore up its traditional working-class support (Warhurst, 1988). Since the public perceived the decline in living standards to be connected to spending cuts, Brian Howe, the Minister of Social Security, announced a family package aimed at protecting the needy. For Hawke the new family package ensured that by '1990, no Australian child will be living in poverty' (Hawke, 1994: 403). The package was to cost $405 million in a full year. Of this $234 million was to be spent on a family allowance supplement of $22 per week, to be paid to mothers from 1 November 1987. An additional teenage (13–15 years) supplement of $6 per week was to be paid from 24 December ($69 million). The Family Plan was well received both by welfare lobbies and Labor voters at large. Before the general election of 1984, indexation was restored for the single adult rate.

Apart from generous benefits being introduced before elections, other restrictions were enacted after elections as predicted by the PBC. One year after the 1983 election, unemployment benefits for those aged 18–20 were excluded from full indexation and an asset test for those aged 25 and over was introduced which operated alongside the normal income test. The Women's Electoral Lobby noted a range of measures which discriminated against women, such as stiffer eligibility rules to enable the parent to qualify for allowances (Simms, 1988).

In past elections women had been more likely to support non-Labor parties, so during the electoral campaign of 1983 Labor strategists stressed women's issues and were rewarded with electoral gains for the Labor Party (Curtin and Sawer, 1996). A section on women was inserted in the party platform for the first time in 1982, reinforcing a wide-ranging women's policy, including detailed legislative and machinery-of-government proposals. The ALP consulted women's organisations before the launch of the official policy document.[3] Yet the emphasis on gender issues had practically disappeared after the next election in 1984 (Simms, 1993: 30).

These facts corroborate the predictions of the PBC but other modifications were in stark contrast to the model. Most striking was Hawke's announcement of the assets test for pensioners during the 1984 election campaign speech. The Australian McNair Anderson exit poll reported that pensioners concerned with the assets test contributed to the swing against the government of 1.4 per cent (Galligan, 1985b: 177). One year before the election of 1987 the government announced what the press defined as the 'harshest budget for decades' (*The Guardian*, 20 August 1986). A few months before the election of 1987, the government introduced work tests which narrowed provisions by increasing review and surveillance of both eligibility and entitlement rules. It is reasonable to assume that changing bureaucratic procedures may 'be a more politically acceptable way of restricting scope than direct (and transparent) legislative changes to eligibility criteria' (Saunders, 1991: 113). What is important here, however, is not so much the form of the changes, but rather their timing. Introducing these modifications before the election of 1987 is incongruent with PBC explanations of income redistribution.

Furthermore, in the run-up to that election, the Federal Treasurer, Paul Keating announced the so-called 'mini-budget' which estimated that $400 million was taken off social welfare spending. The measures included tighter eligibility criteria for pensions, the abolition of unemployment benefits for 16 and 17 year olds, and means testing family allowances. A salient point is that welfare benefits are usually targeted at the poor groups whereas taxation policy is often targeted at the rich. Although this book is not centrally concerned with taxation policy, it should be noted that between 1975 and 1982 wages and salaries increased by 98.8 per cent and the tax paid on these income sources increased by 148.1 per cent. By contrast, income from rent, dividends and unincorporated enterprises rose more quickly, by 125.4 per cent, but the tax paid on it rose only by 73.6 per cent (Bryson, 1988: 496). The imbalance between income sources was mostly because the wealthier sections of the population were favoured with a network of tax exemptions. It is remarkable that Labor did not substantially alter this balance during the 1980s.

All in all, the development of social security policies under Hawke

---

[3] For a reassessment of ALP's attitude towards gender issues see Sawer (1998).

provides inconsistent evidence supporting the PBC. This conclusion is reinforced by time series analyses of Australian fiscal policy which show that associations between elections and transfer policies often yield unexpected signs (Swank, 1992). As we found in the Canadian and the British chapters, investigations of the median-voter hypothesis and PBC have shed light on some policy changes but have left unanswered questions regarding why Labor manipulated redistributive policies in ways that are incompatible with these models. The Labor governments seemingly devised policies that demand-driven interpretations cannot adequately explain. In the following sections I argue that there were essentially three main determinants of redistributive policies under Hawke which were: the ascendancy of the right-wing faction within the ALP in the early 1980s, which refashioned the party image; the emergence of the centre-left faction as a pivotal player; and the lopsided relationship between the ALP and the unions.

POLITICAL RENEWAL SHAPES SOCIAL POLICIES

Redistributive policies under Hawke reflected a fundamental process of internal realignment unparalleled in Labor history, which saw the once dominant left-wing group displaced by the right-wing group. By the early 1980s right-wingers had dislodged left-wingers in most of the party's policy committees (Wheelwright, 1983: 47–40). Internal realignments had momentous consequences for Labor's redistributive policies because the differences in the social policy aims of the left and the right were fairly sharp. The similarity with the British Conservative Party is striking. ALP right-wingers endorsed free market principles, neoclassical economics and the minimalist state. Hawke, for instance, believed that the left was 'simply out of touch with the realities of the nation and of the world in which we lived' (1994: 102). Keating's biographer, Edna Carew, recounts that the Federal Treasurer was concerned 'with "making the pie bigger" not squabbling about who was getting what size slice' (1992: 58).

Left-wing Laborites valued the socially protective activities of the government and believed in social reform and income redistribution. Left-wingers had sustained Whitlam's redistributive policies and were delivered a hammer blow by the scale of Labor's defeat in 1975 (McAllister, 1992: 124). The debate that opened up within the ALP after the ensuing electoral débâcles of 1977 and 1980 moved away from recrimination to consider whether the centralising 'big government' approach of Curtin, Chifley and Whitlam was appropriate. By 1980 'the party leader could even declare in the heat of an election that Labor was the party of low taxation' (Jupp, 1982: 127). Internal backlash against the left culminated in the right-wing push to secure the leadership of the Labor Party by replacing Bill Hayden, who was supported by the left, with Bob Hawke in 1983. The defeat of Hayden sanctioned the last severing of ties with Whitlam's government and with its redistributive policies (Jaensch, 1989: 82). Right-wingers wished to reshape the party image to attract either previously unsympathetic or indifferent voters. In such conditions, it is reasonable to suggest that they designed redistributive policies to adjust social relativities by altering the economic position of targeted groups (Johnson, 1996). Hawke and Keating embarked on a new programme of radical social policy change and sought to use that change as an instrument of political renewal (Castles, Gerriston and Vowles, 1996). As Hawke pointed out 'ahead of us lay the polemical exercise of persuading the Labor Party to abandon the tired certitude of an earlier age and to prepare for the future' (Hawke (1994: 252). Against this background Labor espousal of free market principles was less dictated by Treasury officials and more by strategies of internal realignment.

There was, however, a high degree of convergence in outlook, philosophies and cultural style between the Labor government and senior civil servants; but this intersection of approaches is a long way from demonstrating the compliance of elected representatives to senior public servants or to the economic policy elite as some scholars maintain (Quiggin, 1998: 81). On the contrary, the resignation of the Treasury chief, John Stone, in 1984 after Hawke and Keating dismissed his tighter budget proposals shows that public officials were far from captivating Labor leaders.

My account indicates that espousing a distinct redistributive strategy was instrumental to reshaping New Labor as the party of wealth production led by the right-wingers. Intraparty warfare propelled the redefinition of social policies because right-wingers were consolidating their internal position by devising redistributive policies in stark contrast to those endorsed by left-wingers. Reformulation of social policy signalled that Labor was embarking on a new course aimed at brushing away the legacy of the previous Whitlam government. Hawke confirms this point in his memoirs:

Labor's years of ambitious bidding for government from the Opposition benches followed by the profligacy of the Whitlam years had given it a reputation for financial recklessness. From the beginning we were determined to eradicate this perception. This meant that many of our moves would be unpopular. (Hawke, 1994: 293)

Unpopular moves included cutbacks in welfare spending to reconstruct Labor's reputation against the ramshackle image of the 1970s. Stiffer eligibility rules were an integral part of this strategy despite its electoral price:

> In 1984 our resolution to clamp down on middle-class welfare caused a furore; this centred on our decision to apply an assets test to pensions and to impose an income test on pensioners over seventy years of age. *We pressed on with this reform despite electoral misgivings in our own ranks.* Some colleagues wanted to abandon the move when the heat was turned up. I refused to budge because it was intrinsically correct. (Hawke 1994: 293, my emphasis)

This quotation offers compelling evidence that party leaders sometimes pursue policies inconsistent with vote-seeking behaviour and more in line with policy-seeking strategies. The move to reimpose an incomes test on pensioners aged 70 and above had been strongly opposed by the then Minister of Social Security, Senator Don Grimes, who argued that it would be immensely unpopular (*National Times*, 13 May, 1983). But in Hawke's view, policy seeking involved shedding the old ideological baggage and distributing new symbolic incentives by curbing social security benefits.

Party officials openly acknowledged symbolic manipulations. In the words of Bob Hogg, then National Secretary, 'there has been a number of ... symbols that have been removed or changed' (1991: 54). Traditional ideological wording relating to income distribution and redistribution, such as 'the democratic socialisation of industry', were replaced with appreciations of the private sector. 'The market mechanism', Keating wrote, 'is a powerful engine of economic growth ...competition can facilitate the transformation to a structure that encourages growth. The benefits of the market economy are therefore widely appreciated by this government' (1985: 20). In addressing the issue of international competitiveness, economic management and free market principles the Hawke–Keating alliance was destroying the institutional pillars on which Labor's support had always been based (Kelly, 1992: 15). Labor's new course helped to mitigate the age-old hostility of the Confederation of Australian Industry (CAI) for left-wing governments, marking a further break with the past.

At the same time as right-wingers were consolidating their own power at the top of the ALP, factional politics within the party became institutionalised and centralised. One major difference between the ALP and the British Labour Party is the fact that factional politics in the ALP had historically been based on state branches. These branches controlled two vital resources, the flow of funds and preselection procedures. From the late 1960s, however, the ALP has steadily become a party where power is concentrated within the federal parliamentary organisation and the National Executive, at the expense of state branches. 'The general scenario is one of a Party historically rooted in its State Branches becoming a national party' (Manning, 1995: 11).

Centralising forces culminated in the early 1980s in a crucial institutional change. The Melbourne Conference in 1981 abolished the equal representation of state branches at the federal level and introduced proportional representation (O'Connell, 1991: 150). Proportional representation for the election of state delegates to national decision-making bodies enhanced the power of the national organisation with respect to state organisations (Lloyd and Swan, 1987; Stokes and Cox, 1981). The impact on the ALP was dramatic.

Cross-state alliances quickly developed and a national system of factions emerged. Power shifted significantly 'from the so-called "machine" itself largely controlled by unions, to a "system" of factions' (Manning, 1995: 12).[4] Explanations for the rise of national factions rest on their ability to absorb potentially destabilising internal conflicts after a period of dramatic social and economic change (McAllister, 1991: 218). Others view their emergence as a manifestation of the rapid decline in the blue-collar workers and the continuing increase in white-collar employment (Burchell and Race, 1991: 11).

Formal factions were established at the same time as pressures were mounting for modifications of the 'Objective' – the statement of Labor's policy aims first drafted in 1890. At the Melbourne Annual Conference in 1981 the debate centred on whether the ALP should be committed to extensive nationalisation and collective ownership if elected to power, or whether 'democratic socialisation of industry, distribution, production and exchange' should be undertaken to the '*extent necessary* to eliminate exploitation' (Lloyd, 1983: 244). Eventually the Conference agreed to the socialisation of the means of production only 'if necessary', with 28 votes in favour and 22 against.

This resolution was a milestone in the evolution of New Labor and its redistributive commitments because the Objective was a symbol of what the ALP stood for, both for Laborites of many generations and for their political rivals. 'The Objective was essentially an intra-party statement, the product of discussion and compromises within the party, important

---

[4] Formalised factions came to prominence in the states of Victoria and New South Wales in the 1950s and 1960s (Wheelwright, 1983). However, organised national factions only emerged after Labor took office in 1983 (Bean and McAllister, 1989).

as an expression of the party to the party' (Jaensch, 1989: 87). Redesigning the Objective was tantamount to legitimising the new balance of
power because right-wingers effectively controlled most ALP policy
committees.

THE CENTRE-LEFT AS PIVOTAL PLAYER IN REDISTRIBUTIVE GAMES

The intended social policy changes spurred the formation of a new
faction, the Centre-Left, chiefly supported by individual members
rather than unions (Maddox, 1989: 9–20). For John Cairn, then Premier
of Victoria, the Centre-Left represented an anxiety about the extremism
of the other two dominant groups (1995: 82). Ideologically, the new
faction positioned itself between the Left and the Right. As stated in its
manifesto:

> The Centre Left is committed to democratic socialist principles. As such, its
> distinguishing characteristics are the pre-eminence it gives to social, economic
> and political equality, *the emphasis on achieving this through redistributional programs.*
> (*Position Statement*, 1984, my emphasis)

The Centre-Left soon became a coherent and influential grouping that
controlled a quarter of the parliamentary party and a third of the
Cabinet. Among its prominent members were Cabinet Ministers Hayden, Young and Walsh, Health Minister Blewett, Senator Cook and
Button and Dawkins.

One salient feature of factional development was that real power in
the ALP now lay in Faction Caucuses where faction delegates took key
decisions on how they voted and what they did within the formal organs
of the ALP – Parliament, Conference, Executive, Pre-Selection machinery (Lloyd and Swan, 1987: 103). National factions were parties in
miniature with a fee-paying membership, regular conferences and elected party officials. Party and political offices were apportioned to particular factions in accordance with their strength (Bean and McAllister,
1989: 80). All factions to some extent represented a particular ideological position within the party, 'but this was corrupted enormously by the
exigencies of power politics, patronage and feudal empire-building'
(Burchell and Race, 1991: 15). Hawke recalls in his memoirs how
important it was to appoint to positions of responsibility prominent
factional leaders, such as:

Peter Barron who was an important link with the Right, the dominant faction within the Labor Party – and in particular with the New South Wales branch. Robert Hogg, from the Victorian Left of the party, also joined my staff in those early days and was an effective factional counterpoint to Peter. (1994: 164)

The distribution of power between the three factions was institutionalised in a 'hierarchy of states within a state' which mirrored the place of the respective factions in the second Hawke government (Pusey, 1991: 106). Labor leaders subjected the civil service to strong political control. Most of the political consultants appointed in the first year had worked for ministers rather than in the department. They were for the most part more senior than individuals appointed to ministerial staffs and were drawn from academia and a number of professions (Wilenski, 1986: 194–195).

Cabinet ministers of the Right faction controlled the central agencies, the Department of the Prime Minister and Cabinet Finance and the Treasury. At the other end of the spectrum, the ministers of the Left held the less-strong programme and service departments. Ministers of the Centre-Left faction controlled the 'market' departments, the Department of Finance and the four departments of Trade, Resources and Energy, Primary Industry and Industry, Technology and Commerce.

While the partition of ministerial posts reflected factional power at the top, state branches influenced the functioning of the party by providing funding and voluntary work for the factions.[5] The Right had been represented in New South Wales, the largest state in the federation, and had been strongly backed by the Australian Workers' Union (AWU) (Hagan and Turner, 1991). Support for the Left had mainly developed in Victoria, where Bob Hawke pursued his political career. Predominance of the Right and the Left in New South Wales (NSW) and Victoria meant that the Centre-Left could only penetrate smaller states such as Queensland, South Australia, Tasmania and Western Australia.

Right-wingers steadily improved their strategic position in the key national organs of Parliamentary Caucus, Conference and Executive (McAllister, 1991). By the mid-1980s the Right became the most numerous group with 40 per cent of parliamentary members against the Left's 35 per cent. In the 1987 federal election 25 per cent more right-wing candidates were electorally successful than the candidates of the Left (Bean and McAllister, 1989: 89).

The consolidation of right-wingers reflected the growing strength of the NSW state-branch. Between 1984 and 1986 membership increased

---

[5] For the importance of funding arrangements in the formation and consolidation of party structures see Mulé (1998b).

Table 4.2. *ALP state-branch membership, 1978–1986 (percentages)*

State	1978	1980	1984	1986	Absolute change 1984–1986
NSW	34.0	38.5	33.2	39.0	+ 5.8
Victoria	24.6	25.0	24.7	21.0	− 3.7
Qld	13.0	10.5	13.0	14.0	+ 1.0
SA	12.4	12.5	13.7	10.3	− 3.4
WA	7.0	7.0	10.2	9.0	− 1.2
Tasmania	7.0	3.0	2.0	3.0	+ 1.0
ACT	na	1.0	1.0	2.0	+ 1.0
NT	na	0.7	0.7	0.7	0.0
total*	100	100	100	100	–
n	49,850	51,948	58,620	55,610	− 3,010

Note: * Percentages may not add to total because of rounding off.
Legend: NSW = New South Wales; Qld = Queensland; SA = South Australia;
WA = Western Australia; ACT = Australian Capital Territory; NT = Northern
Territory.
Source: Computed by the author from ALP membership data published in Ward, I.
(1989: 166).

by 5.8 per cent in NSW while it declined by 3.7 per cent in Victoria
(table 4.2). Membership dropped in South Australia and Western
Australia and slightly improved in ACT and Northern Territories.
These figures indicate that NSW was the strongest state-branch and the
one with the fastest-growing membership as well.

The picture that emerges is that of three strategic groups within the
party competing against each other as parties would in the political
system. At one ideological extreme was the National Right[6] led by Bob
Hawke, and other prominent leaders of the New South Wales branch,
such as Paul Keating, Robert Ray and Graham Richardson. Right-
wingers were ideologically committed to the free market economy and
the minimalist state. At the other ideological extreme, the Socialist
Left controlled by Brian Howe, Gerry Hand and Bruce Childs em-
braced the socialist objectives of the ALP and rejected the capitalist
system. Between these two positions, the Centre-Left led by Bill Hayden, Peter Cook and Rosemary Crowley, appealed to socio-economic
equality through democratic means. The redistributive stance of each
faction set the factional boundaries and defined what differentiated

[6] Formally the National Right is called Centre Unity but in practice it is referred to as National
Right, or more simply Right.

Table 4.3. *ALP national factions: voting power expressed as a percentage of total members*

Party conference	ALP factions		
	Right	Centre-left	Left
National Conference 1984	30	28	41
National Conference 1986	41	19	39
Percentage change 1984–1986	+ 36	− 32	− 5

Source: Calculated and adapted by the author from Lloyd and Swan, 1987, table 1: 109.

one faction from another in the eyes of the electorate and the party members.

We should keep well in mind that whatever their ideological position, power games were always a primary consideration. In the words of Robert Ray, then Labor Minister of Defence, 'no matter how much ideological verbiage an ALP faction may produce, reality is that it seeks to advance its position relative to other contending factions' (Ray, 1991: 29). Factional identity legitimised the existence of the faction itself in that it gave factions their raison d'être over and above the mere pursuit of power.

The Centre-Left quickly acquired the position of power broker within the party. From table 4.3. we see that none of the factions was sufficiently predominant to impose its policy programme on the other two groups. Crucial was the pivotal position of the Centre-Left because it had the numbers to give victory to the Right or to the Left. Its vital support was immediately evident at the Annual Conference of 1984 when Keating sought to qualify the party's redistributive ambitions. When the Left proposed an amendment to establish redistribution as an unqualified objective, the Centre-Left supported it and the Treasurer eventually accepted it.[7] A similar process developed at the Annual Conference of 1986. As stated in the *Centre Left Report on the National Conference 1986* 'on negotiations the Right were determined never to be out-voted by a combination of the Centre-Left and the Left and therefore accepted most Centre-Left proposals' (p. 8). In Sartori's terms

---

[7] *Reason and Reform, 1984,* Centre-Left publication. I would like to thank Daniel Encel for providing me with the documentation.

Table 4.4. *Preference ordering of Labor factions with respect to income redistribution*

Factions	Left	Centre-left	Right
Most preferred	R	r	M
	r	R	r
Least preferred	M	M	R

(1976: 122–123), the Centre-Left was endowed with coalition potential, which it could deploy to hamper or facilitate policy decisions.

TWO-STAGE GAME OVER REDISTRIBUTIVE POLICIES

To spell out the dynamics of Labor redistributive policies a useful starting point is to describe the probable alternatives. For simplicity I shall illustrate three basic choices. Redistribute from rich to poor by increasing transfer spending and the progressivity of taxation (R); adapt to change through minor reforms (r); market-oriented policy based on regressive taxation and stiffer eligibility and entitlement rules (M). Labor factions had the preference ordering described in table 4.4. None of the factions coincided in their first preference. The Centre-Left and Left coincided in their least preferred alternative and their first- and second-most preferred alternatives were inverted. Each faction had therefore to enter into processes of exchange, concession and compromise with at least one of the other factions to achieve its goal.

A major shortcoming of the Centre-Left was its weak organisational and public identity. As Mick Young, a leading member of this new faction, emphasised at the first national Centre-Left meeting, 'it was necessary that the Centre-Left built a clear and strong public identity' so that the power brokers of the other two factions were compelled to take it into account (Minutes of the First National Centre Left Meeting, 19 February, 1984). But a weak organisational identity signified that the Centre-Left could rapidly change allegiance from one faction to the other, and thus turn its organisational vulnerability into strategic advantage.

It was not unusual for the Centre-Left to ally with the Right to defeat the Left (McAllister, 1991: 213). There are at least two reasons why the Centre-Left allied more often with the Right. Weak factions, like weak political parties, seek to avoid forging alliances with ideologically similar but stronger factions for fear of being absorbed by their ally (Colomer,

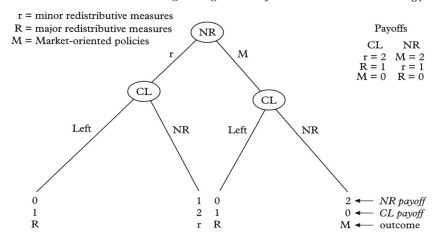

r = minor redistributive measures
R = major redistributive measures
M = Market-oriented policies

Payoffs

	CL	NR
	r = 2	M = 2
	R = 1	r = 1
	M = 0	R = 0

Figure 4.2. Two-stage redistributive game in the ALP

1991; Grøennings, 1970: 455). Coalescing with an essentially conservative faction enabled the Centre-Left to build a separate image from the Left.

Another reason is found in its membership. The Centre-Left faction drew its support from young Laborites who were more attracted to right-wingers' emphasis on the private sector. New party members were coming to the fore supporting free market principles and neoclassical economics (McAllister and Ascui, 1988: 220). The individual membership drive aimed at countering the increasing takeover of sub-branches by the Left and at undermining its traditional base in the union movement (Jaensch, 1989: 48). Pumping up the number of individual members in the party organisation was tantamount to attenuating the influence of state branches and trade unions – and correspondingly of the Left faction. These were good reasons for the Centre-Left and the Right to stipulate an alliance against the Left.

Labor's redistributive policies can thus largely be explained by focusing on the interactions between the Centre-Left and the Right.[8] A simplified account of the strategic moves between the two factions is provided by the backward induction argument, which proceeds from the second stage of the game, when the Centre-Left (CL) moves, and works out to the first (Figure 4.2.)[9]

[8] The focus on the Centre-Left and the National Right does not imply that the Left faction was ineffective. Had this been the case the Centre-Left would have lost its pivotal power.
[9] The backward induction argument was developed by Rubinstein (1982).

In deciding its moves the National Right (NR)[10] must take into account the Centre-Left's choices. Suppose in stage one the NR opts for market-oriented policies (M), then in stage two the CL could retaliate by coalescing with the Left in order to formulate less-stringent redistributive measures. The Centre-Left would be better off in allying with the Left where its payoff is 1. However, for the NR this is the worst solution because it undermines its chief article of faith, which is to reduce government intervention in the economy and devolve power to the individual. If the CL coalesces with the Left the payoff for the NR is 0.

The optimal strategy for the Centre-Left in stage two induces the NR to pre-empt this move by opting for *r* in stage one. The CL would then enter in alliance with the National Right with payoffs 2 to the CL and payoff 1 to the NR. Since both factions have no incentives to deviate from *(r,NR)* the equilibrium solution at the second stage of the game is the pair of strategies *(r,NR)*.

The two-stage game helps to distil the essence of the strategic manoeuvring which underpinned the pattern of redistributive policies under Hawke. Crucial was the role of the Centre-Left as veto player against market-oriented and regressive policies of the Right (Gruen and Grattan, 1993: 30–32). The coalition potential of the pivotal player was a powerful weapon against right-wing leanings towards radical social policies. In this manner, factional games acted as a brake, preventing the Labor government from pushing retrenchment policies too far.

Internal governance halts regressive taxation

The failure of the Tax Summit in 1985 is an excellent illustration of the impact intraparty games exerted on redistributive outputs. Had Keating succeeded in introducing regressive taxation policy, lower-income groups would probably have been worse off. Keating's taxation reform was essentially regressive since it was committed to shifting the tax burden from income to consumer goods. The provision was presented in the government's Draft Paper discussed at the Tax Summit in 1985, which included three options. Option C was prepared by Keating, endorsed by the Cabinet and strongly supported by the Treasury. It recommended a 30 per cent cut in personal income tax supplemented by a broad-based consumption tax of 12.5 per cent on almost all

---

[10] I introduce here the formal name of the Right faction, that is, National Right, in order to avoid confusion in the following discussion between Right intended as the faction and right intended as direction.

commodities. Option A proposed measures to broaden the tax base and introduce capital gains tax and cuts in income tax; Option B introduced a broad-based consumption tax at a rate of 5 per cent plus a wholesale tax of 10 per cent to apply to a range of goods. The three options had some support from different sections of the community. Option C was endorsed by the government and by significant sections of the business community. Welfare lobbies and trade unions accepted the general thrust of option A.

Yet no agreement was reached and the consumption tax was abandoned. Most analysts attribute the eventual demise of the taxation reform to mounting pressures from within the party and among ACTU leaders (Jaensch, 1989; Singleton, 1990). Hawke makes a strong case for this view in his memoirs:

On Thursday morning, 4th July, Paul and I met the Labor Premiers (Neville Wran, New South Wales; John Cain, Victoria; Brian Burke, Western Australia; and John Bannon, South Australia) in my office... They unanimously reiterated that they could not and would not support [the consumption tax] ... after lunch I formally announced the death of [the tax]. (Hawke, 1994: 310)

This description points to the narrow margin of manoeuvre enjoyed by the Labor Prime Minister with respect to the other centres of power within the party organisation. It suggests that the negotiations between leaders and subleaders were the key for rejecting regressive taxation. I find this view rather unconvincing because other policies, notably financial deregulation and privatisation, had been carried out despite bitter internal conflict.

Another view holds that the Tax Summit was a disguised power play, an early test of strength between Keating and Hawke (Gruen and Grattan, 1993: xiii). For Kelly, the Tax Summit was 'an exposure of the ultimate issue between them – the leadership' (1992: 173). Maddox reinforces this point by arguing that holding a summit on such a visible issue ensured taxation reform would not be implemented (1989: 131). Anticipating this result, Keating had been reluctant to call a summit and eventually perceived the abandonment of the consumption tax as a betrayal (Gordon, 1993: 127).

The outcome of the Tax Summit constituted the first breach of trust in the Hawke–Keating relationship. Hawke derided Keating's protest of betrayal by portraying him as a good actor who 'played the injured party whose pride of authorship had been spiked by a Prime Minister who has abandoned his most cherished reform' (Hawke, 1994: 311).

Such abrasive wording may lead us to believe that internal warfare was fuelled by the confrontational personalities of Keating and Hawke. However, I have already argued in the British chapter that explanations couched in terms of personalities side-step the crucial question regarding the distribution of power within the party, which is the central concern of this book. Keating was the leader of the most powerful faction and it is reasonable to assume that the issue at stake was control over key posts, such as the party leadership, rather than questions of personality.

There is little doubt that the failure of the Tax Summit mitigated the regressive impact of Labor's redistributive policies. Research on the Australian taxation system shows that a significant shift towards a broad base consumption tax has potentially damaging effects on household savings (Apps, 1997b).

THE ACQUIESCENCE OF TRADE UNIONS: CONSENSUS OR IMBALANCE?

Few accounts of Labor redistributive policies can get away without examining the influence of trade unions. Historically, the Federal Parliamentary Labor Party was created to represent and strive for the interests of the union movement (Jaensch, 1983, ch 5). Consequently, the legislative actions of Labor members of parliament should in principle have echoed the wishes of the extraparliamentary organisation. Trade unions had been the main source of legitimacy for the party organisation because they provided both the funding and the loyalty of affiliated members. Moreover, unions wielded considerable control of the decisionmaking process through the preselection of parliamentary candidates.

This distribution of power signified that tensions between the party subunits constantly surfaced throughout Labor history (McIntyre, 1991: 21). Friction between the ACTU and the ALP often erupted when Labor took office because the interests of the two Labor wings typically diverged. Policy and public antagonism between the political and industrial wings of the labour movement were conspicuous under the Whitlam government.

A remarkable feature of the 1980s was that unions raised little or no opposition to Hawke's departure from traditional Labor redistributive goals. Over the 1980s the ALP–ACTU relationship was unexpectedly smooth and largely constructive (Kelly, 1992). Partly this partnership was the result of Hawke's personal ties with the ACTU. He had been president of the ACTU during the Whitlam government and was Labor's first federal parliamentary leader to have held high office within the trade unions. His grasp of the unions and the wage system was far superior to that of any of his predecessors. Hawke's understanding of the arbitration system was one reason why ACTU leaders supported him against Hayden as leader in early 1983, and why they were prepared to display a type of restraint which Hawke as ACTU leader had never offered Whitlam. The reforming ideas of Hawke and Keating were shared by the ACTU new men, Kelty, the head of the ACTU and his associate, Simon Crean (Gruen and Grattan, 1993: 111–134).

Most analysts believe that the roots of this harmony lay in the recognition of mutual dependence sanctioned by the Accord (Manning, 1995; Singleton, 1990; Stutchbury, 1990: 58). Robert Ray, then Minister of Defence, makes a strong case for this argument. In his words, Hawke's strategic manoeuvring ensured that 'many prominent left-wing union officials ... enjoyed a new enhanced status in renegotiating, redefining and reassessing the ALP-ACTU Accord' (1991: 32). Central to this approach was the interdependence between the political and the industrial wing of the Labor Party.

A different view is expressed by Lindsay Tanner, the Victorian secretary of the Federated Clerks Unions, who claims that the 'gap between the interests and obligations of the two wings of the movement has progressively widened' (1991: 76). Tanner describes the looser ties between unions and ALP as 'the soft underbelly of the Labor movement' (1991: 76). In this light, interpretations stressing consensus and convergence perhaps pay insufficient attention to the growing *asymmetry* between trade unions and the Labor Party.

One expression of this asymmetry was the incipient organisational decline of trade unions, on the one hand, and the string of electoral successes accumulated by the ALP, on the other. This divergence was reflected in the growing percentage of votes gained by the Labor Party and the declining percentage of trade union officials in parliament. Between 1971 and 1983 the proportion of union officials in parliament almost halved, falling from 20.9 per cent to 10.5 per cent (Kemp, 1988: 344).

Under Labor rule union membership as a proportion of the labour force dropped by 8 per cent (see table 4.5). Several factors affected union density rates, most notably the expansion of jobs in traditional non-unionised sectors, such as non-manual service, female employment and

Table 4.5. *Trade union density rates and collective bargaining coverage rates in selected OECD countries*

Country	Data*	Trade union density rates			Bargaining coverage rates		
		1980	1990	Absolute change	1980	1990	Absolute change
Portugal	R	61[e]	32	− 31	70	79	+ 9
Spain	E	25	11	− 14	67[c]	68	+ 1
United Kingdom	E	50	39	− 11	70[d]	47	− 23
Netherlands	E	35	25	− 10	76	71	− 5
Australia	E	48[g]	40	− 8	88[f]	80	− 8
France	E	17	10	− 7	85	92[b]	+ 7
Japan	E	31	25	− 6	28	23	− 5
West Germany	E	36	33	− 3	91	90	− 1
Norway	E	57	56	− 1	n/a	n/a	n/a
Canada	R	36	36	0	37[a]	38	+ 1
Finland	E	70	72	+ 2	95	95	0
Sweden	E	80	83	+ 3	n/a	n/a	n/a

Notes: *E = based on employed members only.
R = based on recorded membership, not corrected for retired, unemployed and self-employed members.
[a] 1985; [b] 1985; [c] 1985; [d] Great Britain; [e] 1984; [f] 1974; [g] 1982.
Source: Calculated and adapted by the author from OECD *Employment Outlook*, 1994, Tables 5.7 and 5.8. Countries are ordered according to the absolute change in trade union density rates.

part-time work. Union apathy is particularly high among individuals employed in casual and part-time work (Peetz, 1997).

Lower trade union density rates, however, were not a universal trend. In the Scandinavian countries there were gains in unionisation, while in Canada the trend was stable. Not only did trade union density rates drop in Australia, but also collective bargaining coverage rates declined. By contrast, in Portugal, Spain and France, de-unionisation was associated with rising collective bargaining coverage rates. Only in the United Kingdom did trade union coverage rates fall more sharply than in Australia.

Apart from structural shifts, wider earning differentials induced by the Accord contributed to de-unionisation (Kenyon and Lewis, 1992). Between 1980 and 1988 the real value of the federal minimum wage declined by 23 per cent, mainly because the ACTU had agreed on wage de-indexation (King, Rimmer and Rimmer, 1992). De-unionisation, moreover, was a protest act against the economic consequences of the Accord. Lower trade union density rates offered compelling evidence

Table 4.6. *The preferences of ALP and ACTU*

ALP	ACTU	
	Moderate	Aggressive
Generous	(a) 2,2	(b) 4,1
Stiff	(c) 1,3	(d) 3,4

that unions were losing the monopoly of workers' representation, the most powerful resource they could deploy in bargaining games with the ALP. All in all, the growing asymmetry in the resources of power controlled by the ACTU and the ALP played a significant part in the acquiescence of trade unions to Labor's redistributive policies.

ASYMMETRIC BARGAINING AND SOCIAL SECURITY REFORMS

To clarify the dynamics that led unions to acquiesce in Labor social security reforms I use a simple game-theoretic model in normal form where players move simultaneously.[11] The left-hand column of table 4.6 describes the redistributive choices of the ALP, generous or stiff entitlement and eligibility rules. The top right-hand side of the figure illustrates two strategies of wage policy pursued by the unions, moderate or aggressive; while the numbers in the cells indicate the preferences of the two players in rank order from 1 to 4.

From the unions' point of view the best solution would have been cell (b) where the combination of aggressive wage policy and generous social security benefits increase real wages, abate de-unionisation and reduce poverty. From the ALP point of view cell (b) would have been the worst outcome because it undermines its strategy of promoting an image of financial discipline as opposed to Whitlam's profligacy. It would, therefore, have preferred to have chosen cell (d)[12] in which the

---

[11] This model is a variation of Fritz Scharpf's (1997) monetarist coordination game. It differs form Sharpf's model in that the key for the bargaining outcome is the organisational decline of the trade unions.

[12] The ALP preference ordering represents the Hawke–Keating ordering rather than the Centre-Left's ordering. At first sight, this ordering is puzzling. In the previous pages I argued that the Centre-Left was pivotal and therefore its preference ordering should have dictated Labor policy with the trade unions. The reason why the Centre-Left was relatively ineffective may be related to its very weak links with the trade unions.

unions end up with the worst possible outcome because the reputation of fiscal responsibility the ALP seeks to build and defend translates aggressive wage policy and stiffer entitlement rules into higher unemployment, poverty and wage dispersion, thus fuelling de-unionisation. Unions would be better off by shifting to wage restraint in order to mitigate job losses, ending up in cell (c). Since the last is the best outcome for the economic beliefs underpinning the Hawke–Keating partnership, the government has no reason to deviate. Thus cell (c) represents the bargaining equilibrium, being a point of stability for both partners.

This analysis suggests that Hawke had restored a workable balance to the complex relationship between ACTU–ALP, but the fulcrum of that balance was the asymmetry of power. Labor leaders had a dominant strategy, that is a strategy preferred irrespective of the choices of the ACTU, which induced unions to accept the government's social reforms as the least-worst solution. In the mid 1980s the choices of union leaders were a function of ALP policies.

Needless to say, asymmetry meant that the power of the unions was lessening not subsiding. Comparative research shows that the pace of social reform was slower in Australia than in New Zealand over the 1980s, chiefly because of the different relationships between the two Labour governments and trade unions (Bray and Neilson, 1996). In New Zealand the virtual exclusion of a union role in policy formation yielded much more radical social policies. This says that the relative influence of trade unions on the Labor Party mattered for policy making.

In Australia, Labor leaders paid off the cooperation of trade unions with the tax cut concessions reviewed in the previous sections. In the Federal Budget of 1984 trade unions had received virtually what its moderate Australian Council of Trade Unions (ACTU) leadership demanded. ACTU president Cliff Dolan denied that this was 'A Dolan or an ACTU document' but admitted '... it is one that the ACTU has had the most influence in' (Galligan, 1984a: 429). Labor leaders were responding to the ACTU's concern regarding membership decline by protecting unionised members. Over the 1980s the alliance stipulated between ACTU and ALP was a manifestation of a twin process: changing patterns of allegiance for the two wings of the Labor movement and the loosening of organisational ties between them (Hagan and Turner, 1991). Trade unions raised little opposition to Hawke's social reforms, because the ACTU–ALP alliance was increasingly lopsided.

My approach qualifies the conventional view that the ACTU–ALP cohesion under Hawke was the outcome of a balanced, mutually supportive relationship. During the Labor decade the relationship between the two wings of the Labor movement was turned on its head. The pervasive rethoric of consensus masked a growing imbalance between the two partners in which trade unions played a subordinate role. As Manning put it, the 'creator of the Labor Party faced a less than certain future due to the cancer of membership decline' (Manning, 1995: 3). Union leaders accepted the retrenchment of redistributive policies partly because of their organisational weakness. In turn, agreements between Labor and trade unions were a factor that partially defused labour movement militancy concerning declining standards of living (Castles and Shirley, 1996: 102).

Finally, any residual hostility unions nourished towards the Labor government was assuaged by the aggressive policy proposals of the Coalition parties, aimed at either decollectivising employment relations, promoting individual contracts or abolishing compulsory unionism. As mentioned earlier, this shift to the right of the Coalition partners endowed the Labor government with greater margins of discretion. My account supports the contention that the triumph of economic rationalism over the Labor government was more an exercise of strategic political choice than the inevitable outcome of international pressures (Painter, 1996).

INCOME INEQUALITY: DEMOGRAPHY, MARKETS AND TRANSFER POLICIES

The discussion regarding income inequality trends follows the structure outlined in the chapters on Canada and Britain. A comprehensive assessment of the redistributive impact of Labor can only be reached after examining the trends in income inequality and poverty. We have seen that specific policy initiatives were undertaken on key client groups, such as pensioners and low-income families, traditionally linked to the Left faction (Jennet and Stewart, 1990: 9). Since 1983 there was increased targeting of income maintenance on the aged pension through the re-introduction of the income test for those over 70 years old and the re-introduction in 1985 of the assets tests (both abolished by the Whitlam government). The result was a decline in the proportion of the aged population receiving benefits from 85.6 per cent in 1983 to 75.6 per cent in 1991 (Gruen and Grattan, 1993: 192).

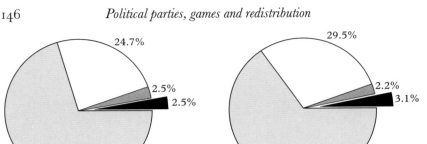

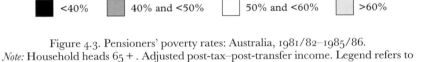

Figure 4.3. Pensioners' poverty rates: Australia, 1981/82–1985/86.
Note: Household heads 65 + . Adjusted post-tax–post-transfer income. Legend refers to income as a percentage of median income

Figure 4.3 shows the percentage of pensioners below or above three poverty lines. While the proportion of elderly below the 50 per cent poverty line grew slightly from 5 per cent in 1981/82 to 5.3 per cent in 1985/86, the proportion below 60 per cent of the median climbed by 4.8 percentage points.

A similar picture is offered by figure 4.6 which shows the proportion of the population living in households consisting of couples with children with income above or below three different poverty lines. When the poverty line was set at 40 per cent of the median, the proportion was exactly the same in both years. If one limits the analysis to the 50 per cent poverty line one reaches the mistaken conclusion that poverty rates declined by 0.4 per cent. On the contrary, the proportion of couples with children with income just above the 50 per cent poverty line grew from 6.3 per cent in 1981/82 to 7.8 per cent in 1985/86. It is evident from figure 4.4 that under the first term of the Labor government poverty rates increased.

Rising poverty rates meant that by early 1985 several issues of concern regarding the Family Income Supplement (FIS), the benefit for all low-income families, had emerged. Partly as a consequence of narrow targeting on very low-income working families and partly because of low take-up rates, there was evidence that many families entitled to FIS

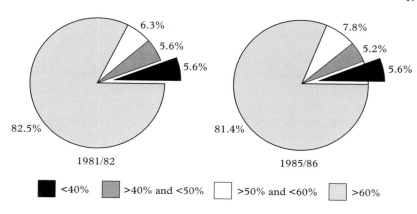

Figure 4.4. Family poverty rates: Australia, 1981/82–1985/86.
Note: Household heads < 65. Adjusted post-tax–post-transfer income. Legend refers to income as a percentage of median income

were not claiming it (Pech, 1986: 3). The take-up rate, which is the proportion of eligible families receiving the payment, was almost less than half. If take-up rates fall with increased targeting 'then the success of targeting as an overall strategy is brought into question' (Saunders, 1991: 311).

The data presented in this section indicate that Labor was actively engaging in social engineering by changing the categories identified as needy. A telling example of this strategy was the severe attack on youth welfare. In 1986 the government introduced the Young Homeless Allowance of $76 which was well below the poverty line and so strictly targeted as to be received by less than 10 per cent of the young homeless in 1988 (Gibson, 1990: 196). Unemployment benefits for young unemployed aged 16–17 were abolished and the waiting period for school leavers under age 21 was extended from 6 to 13 weeks (Carson, Fitzgerald and Jordan, 1989). This policy exacerbated the plight of low-income families because over 50 per cent of young unemployed were living in households with at least one other person who was also dependent on social security (Frey, 1986).

Labor leaders, however, were particularly careful not to alienate completely their core constituency. The redistributive strategy was to 'check the growth in [social security recipient] numbers in order to

Table 4.7. *Trends in income inequality in Australia, 1981/82–1993/94*
(adjusted household post-tax–post-transfer income)

Year	Coefficient of variation	Gini	Theil
1981/82	56.1	30.2	15.0
1985/86	59.9	30.9	16.1
1989/90	65.3	32.2	17.8
1993/94	67.4	33.6	19.5
Percentage change			
1981/82–1985/86	6.7	2.3	7.3
1985/86–1989/90	9.6	4.2	10.5
1989/90–1993/94	3.2	4.3	9.5
1981/82–1993/94	20.1	11.2	3.0

sustain real benefit increases' (Saunders, 1991: 324). A good illustration of this twin goal was the means testing of all social security benefits, except those for the disabled. Brian Howe, then Minister of Social Security, summarised the effectiveness of this policy as follows:

Labor's efforts in achieving social justice for people with disabilities represent our progress as a party committed to improving the quality of life for all people. The struggle for disability reform has epitomised the broader struggle for fairness, for expanded opportunities, and for better communities. (Howe, 1992: 39)

The emphasis on disability signalled that New Labor was willing to protect only those social categories marginalised by the private market for their alleged inefficiency.

In a similar manner, after the report of the Social Security Review in 1986 highlighted poverty trends, the government sharply increased some social security payments, including the Family Allowance Supplement and the Family Assistance Plan, but partly financed these increases through tighter income tests and stiffer eligibility requirements (Harding and Mitchell, 1992). The redistributive effect of these measures was offset by the slow demise of progressive income tax with significant cuts to the marginal tax rate (Krever, 1991: 152–153; Saunders and Hobbes, 1988).

Thus, Hawke could claim at once to defend market freedom and protect the most disadvantaged social categories. Redistributive policies were effectively deployed to project the Australian Labor Party as the

Table 4.8. *Quintile income share: Australia, 1981/82–1993/94*
(adjusted household post-tax–post-transfer income)

Population quintile	1981/82	1985/86	1989/90	1993/94
bottom	7.7	7.7	7.4	6.0
second	12.7	12.3	12.2	12.0
third	17.8	17.5	17.3	17.6
fourth	24.5	24.3	24.2	24.9
fifth	37.3	38.1	39	39.6

party still committed to social fairness with an appreciation of competition, market efficiency and high saving economy.

The problem was that social policy changes coincided with upward inequality movements. Comparative research on income distribution showed that during the 1970s, the Gini index for Australia was consistently amongst the lowest of the countries studied (Gruen, 1979: 10–15). Yet under Labor income inequality rose (table 4.7). According to three inequality indices, there is less equality in 1993/94 than in 1981/82, the most substantial changes occurring after the mid 1980s.

Looking at the movements in the quintile shares we see that the richest people expanded their proportion of disposable income under Labor rule (table 4.8). Between 1981/82 and 1993/94 the income accruing to the fifth quintile rose from 37.3 per cent to 39.6 per cent. At the same time, the income share of the poorest group dropped from 7.7 per cent to 6.0 per cent. More generally, closer investigation of table 4.8 indicates that under Labor the rich disproportionately gained at the expense of all other income groups.

Widening income differentials were compounded by greater dispersion in the distribution of wealth. Eaton and Stilwell (1991: 3) find that the 'prosperity of the wealthiest Australians during this period was truly spectacular'. In a comment reported by the British press, the former Australian Liberal Prime Minister, Malcom Fraser, ironically noted:

At the beginning of the decade the top 1 per cent of the population owned as much as the bottom 10 per cent. Now that 1 per cent owns as much as the bottom 20 per cent. What an epitaph for a Labour government, for any government. (*The Guardian*, 20 December 1991)

For Fraser growing income disparity between rich and poor was the outcome of Labor redistributive policies. This blunt statement ignores

Table 4.9. *Contributions of changes in within- and between-age-groups to the trend in total inequality: Australia, 1981/82–1993/94 (adjusted household post-tax–post-transfer income. Theil inequality index)*

Year	Total inequality	Within-age-group inequality	Age effect (between-group inequality)
1981/82	15.1	14.4	0.7
1985/86	16.1	15.0	1.1
1989/90	17.9	16.9	1.0
1993/94	19.5	17.0	2.5

that a variety of factors not directly connected to government policies may have influenced the distribution of household income. We have seen that the age structure of the population or the household composition could have altered the income distribution by changing the number of people in upper or lower income groups. Other factors, such as wage differentials, could have affected income *per se*. As in previous chapters, a fair assessment of the redistributive impact of the Hawke governments requires an examination of alternative explanations of inequality trends.

Demographic effects

Demographic variables in Australia over the 1970s and 1980s followed the general pattern described in the UK chapter, with an ageing population and a slowdown in birth rates (Cass, 1988). Demographic movements altered aggregate distribution and this may have given the appearance that inequality increased if measured with unsophisticated techniques (Harding and Landt, 1992).

Table 4.9 describes the contribution of inequality changes in within-group and between-age-group to total inequality. The age effect is stable throughout the 1980s but there is an ascending movement in the early 1990s, which means that the ageing of the population might have had some distributional consequences. However, the within-group component dominates the between-group one for each year. Changes in within-group inequality seemingly account for most of the changes in aggregate inequality, implying that other factors unrelated to the age structure had important distributional effects. In the period under examination the rate of change of the age effect was faster, confirming the findings in the previous two chapters. But the important point is that

Table 4.10. *Contribution of changes in within- and between-household types to the trend in total inequality: Australia 1981/82–1993/94 (adjusted household post-tax–post-transfer income. Theil inequality index)*

Year	Total inequality	Within-household inequality	Between-household inequality
1981/82	15.1	12.1	3.0
1985/86	16.1	12.7	3.4
1989/90	17.9	14.8	3.1
1993/94	19.5	17.0	2.5

their contribution to the level of income inequality is marginal. Explanations of aggregate inequality founded on the ageing of the population are therefore called into question.

We know that demographic movements may be sensitive to changes in household size and composition. The trend towards smaller households in Australia may give the mistaken impression that inequality has increased because there is less income pooling. Table 4.10 presents the results of inequality decomposition when the grouping variable is household size. The growing proportion of smaller household sizes had a slight impact on inequality, as revealed by the growth in the values of the Theil index for the grouping factor (between-household) inequality, from 3.0 per cent in 1981/82 to 2.5 per cent in 1993/94. Yet it was growth in the 'within-household' component of inequality, from 12.1 per cent in 1981/82 to 17.0 per cent in 1989/90 which exerted the strongest influence. Since the proportion of aggregate inequality attributable to the between-group component was negligible, the main conclusion is that the distributional impact of household size and composition was remarkably low. The growing proportion of elderly and the trend towards smaller households seem to have had almost no impact at all.

Market effects

If the demographic profile of the Australian population had negligible distributional consequences perhaps the market sphere played a more prominent role. Under Hawke wages were regulated by an incomes policy known as the Accord. Its main achievement was the reduction in long-term unemployment, which had been a major concern in the mid 1980s. The economics of the Accord was in sharp contrast to the previous monetarist experiment of the Fraser Liberal government

Table 4.11. *Proportion of the population with gross and net adjusted household income below different poverty lines: Australia 1981/82–1989/1990*

					absolute change		
year	income	1981/82	1985/86	1989/90	1981/82– 1985/86	1985/86– 1989/90	1981/82– 1989/90
Gross	< 40%	18.6	18.3	18.6	− 0.3	+ 0.3	0.0
Income	< 50%	25.5	25.9	25.7	+ 0.4	− 0.2	+ 0.2
	< 60%	30.1	31.5	31.2	+ 1.5	− 0.3	+ 1.1
Net	< 40%	17.3	17.3	18.9	0.0	+ 1.6	+ 1.6
Income	< 50%	24.9	25.9	26.3	+ 1.0	+ 0.4	+ 1.4
	< 60%	31.2	32.9	32.7	+ 1.7	− 0.2	+ 1.5

(Stutchbury, 1990: 55). It guaranteed wage restraint by the ACTU in exchange for increases in the social wage and commitment to tax reform to achieve greater vertical and horizontal equity. As written in the *Statement of the Accord*, a central tenet of the incomes policy was improved support for low-income groups:

> The parties have reached the agreement that the objectives of such an approach should be to protect the living standards of Australians including wage and salary earners and non-income earning groups. (*Statement of the Accord*, 1983: 5)

Underpinning the Accord were redistributive concerns aimed at improving the relative position of the most disadvantaged. Contrary to these expectations, table 4.11 shows that over the 1980s poverty rates steadily rose. The table also confirms our previous findings that poverty mainly increased in the second half of the 1980s during the economic recovery. It is possible, however, that unions were less worried about poverty as such and more narrowly preoccupied with the living standards of unionised workers.

In this view, the ACTU–ALP partnership stemmed from redistribution amongst wage-earners, between skilled (unionised) and unskilled (non-unionised) workers, rather than from redistribution from capital to labour. Stilwell estimated that about 10 per cent of national income was redistributed from labour to capital between 1983 and 1989 (Stilwell, 1993: 19).

In principle the Accord should have restrained wage dispersion but in practice over the 1980s and early 1990s the distribution of market income was more spread away from the middle (figure 4.5). Higher

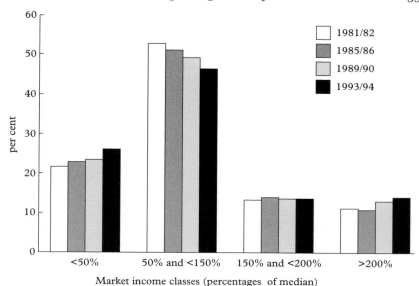

Figure 4.5. Proportion of the population in different market income classes: Australia, 1981/82– 1993/94 (head of household aged 20–64)

earners improved their position while the lower paid lost ground. The proportion of households earning less than 50 per cent of the median grew by 4.4 percentage points between 1981/82 and 1993/94 and those earning over 200 per cent of the median increased by 2.8 points. In the same period, the proportion of households earning between 50 and 150 per cent of median market income declined by 6.4 percentage points. Reduction in the number of workers with middle-range incomes was associated with growth in the lower and upper tails of the distribution.

Income polarisation in the market sphere mainly reflected structural and technological changes. Approximately one in three middle-earning jobs disappeared during the 1980s and most new jobs created were at the low earnings level (Gregory, 1993). There was an expansion of the secondary labour market, with an increase in temporary and part-time workers employed in low-skilled jobs. New jobs were largely taken up by married women, and the earnings of women partially offset inequality growth between male earnings, and reduced inequality in family income (Harding, 1995). On the whole, market income inequality was a significant factor in the trend towards wider income differentials. As in other industrialised countries income polarisation in Australia was associated with a shrinking middle class.

Table 4.12. *Gini coefficient (per cent) for selected adjusted income definitions:*
Australia 1981/82–1993/94

Year	Market income (1)	Post-transfer income (2)	Reduction from transfers (1)–(2)
1981/82	45.7	35.4	10.3
1985/86	47.5	37.0	10.5
1989/90	48.4	37.8	10.6
1993/94	50.8	38.8	12.0
Percentage change			
1981/82–1985/86	+3.9	+4.5	–
1985/86–1989/90	+1.8	+2.1	–
1989/90–1993/94	+3.0	+2.6	–
1981/82–1993/94	+4.9	+9.6	–

Transfer policies

The Labor governments improved the so-called social wage to offset some of the unfavourable effects on income distribution induced by the Accord and the freeing up of private markets. Labor expanded social services and the principal forms of assistance in-kind, covering education, child care and housing, to ameliorate the so-called social income (Harding, 1997; Johnson, Manning and Hellwig, 1995). Evaluations of the social wage raise formidable methodological and conceptual problems, which go beyond the scope of this work (see Saunders,1994b, chapter 6). Suffice it to note that since market income inequality had risen, government tax and transfers should have become more directly redistributive just to keep the distribution of post-tax–post-transfer income constant. Yet over the 1980s income inequality in post-transfer income rose at a much faster pace than market income inequality, and slightly decelerated in the 1990s (table 4.12); the former climbed by 9.6 per cent compared to a rise of 4.9 per cent in the latter. The data show that the drop in the Gini coefficient produced by income transfers remained fairly stable under Labor, despite the rise in wage dispersion. These findings support the argument that government policies contributed to the polarisation of income distribution in Australia (Apps, 1997a).

CONCLUSIONS

Labor leaders deliberately pursued a policy of greater reliance on means-testing with tighter eligibility criteria, which inevitably reduced the number of eligible people. Such policies included the abolition of youth unemployment benefit and stiffer entitlement rules for pensioners and low-income families. Electoral motives probably affected redistributive policies, but available explanations proved insufficient to understand Labor's choices. Other interpretations based on demographic variables did not withstand close scrutiny.

My analysis shows that different factors were at work. It points to the ascendency of Labor right-wingers, the role of a pivotal player and the asymmetry of power between trade unions and ALP leaders. Right-wingers aimed at shedding the old Labor image associated with income redistribution and Labor left-wingers. This rebranding of the ALP is consistent with theoretical developments in the party politics literature which indicate that, when circumstances trigger a profound change of a party's dominant coalition, the first target of the new elite is usually effacing the party image connected to the dislodged leadership (Harmel and Janda, 1994).

In order to project a new party vision, right-wingers could rely on a well-established tradition in the Australian welfare state of means testing and selectivity. A potential difficulty with a non-contributory scheme is that it may have less legitimacy than unemployment insurance, because there is no explicit perception of the employees having 'earned' their benefit through their years in the labour force (Cass, 1988: 37). The overall direction of social policymaking was driven by a belief in the ability of the free market to deliver prosperity associated with pressures for reduced taxes and the end of the assumption of full employment (Dalton *et al.*, 1996). Such changes did not amount to a wholesale replacement of Labor's tradition, but to an adjustment that blended existing symbols with new purposive incentives.

The newly established system of national factions attenuated the pull towards welfare retrenchment because it compelled right-wingers to enter into a process of compromise and exchange with a new faction, the Centre-Left, that became a pivotal player. The Centre-Left could deploy its coalition potential to tilt the balance of power in favour of the Left or the Right faction. One implication was that the institutionalisation of party factions ruled out the sudden introduction of undebated radical policies, and this may have saved the ALP from the fate of the

Lange–Palmer–Moore government in New Zealand (Vowles and McAllister, 1996: 208–209).

The balancing influence of national factions is a crucial difference with the Canadian case. Like previous leaders of the Liberal Party of Canada, Trudeau controlled key levers of power and was much less constrained by binding party platforms than Hawke. In one of the very few studies comparing political parties in Canada and Australia, Smiley (1980) captures this difference by describing the Liberal Party as a confederal party and the ALP as an integrated party. In confederal parties the national and state/provincial organisations rely on different groups for electoral allegiance, maintain autonomous bureaucracies and the ideology of the party at each level is often distinct. The autonomy of the national party from state organisations will give the leader of a confederal party greater intraparty authority. These organisational features go a long way in explaining Trudeau's ample margin of manoeuvre.

By contrast, the Australian Labor Party is an example of an integrated party where the national and state parties draw on the same electoral constituency, use the same organisational machinery, share a common ideology and compete at both levels. The ALP has several centres of power in the state branches, each with its own resources of power and its own legitimacy, but all needing to cooperate within the same party structure. State and national parties are thus fully integrated. This connected structure means that a Labor prime minister must always take into account the likely reactions of state premiers and consult them before reaching any decision that affects their interests (Weller, 1985: 23). Another major difference with Canada and Britain was the greater influence of trade unions in policymaking. Close collaboration between union leaders and ALP leaders enabled the government to show that Labor could handle industrial relations and ensure a minimum of industrial disturbance, thus withering the disastrous legacy of the Whitlam government.

This alliance was made possible by Hawke's personal ties with leading trade union officials and his deep knowledge of union institutions and practices derived from his experience as former president of the ACTU. Such an harmonious relationship, however, disguised an asymmetry in the resources of power controlled by the social partners. While the unions were losing the monopoly of workers' representation, manifested in declining trade union density rates and coverage rates, the ALP was accumulating a string of electoral successes. My account demonstrates that weak union opposition to Labor's redistributive policies partly rested on asymmetric power between the two players. The ALP paid off the collaboration of trade unions with tax concessions. Any further hostility unions might have nourished towards the Labor government was assuaged by the aggressive policy stance of the Coalition parties, aimed at either decollectivising employment relations, promoting individual contracts or abolishing compulsory unionism. The extremism of the Coalition parties backfired because it made them electorally uncompetitive. Such weakness endowed the ALP with greater margins of discretion.

Labor leaders used discretionary powers to scale down redistributive policies at the same time as wage dispersion increased. In the early 1980s the economy slumped as the price of raw materials plummeted and Australia registered large monthly current account deficits, which precipitated the AU$ depreciation. Labor leaders responded to economic vulnerability with policies of adjustment and compensation in the labour market. This argument reinforces Katzenstein's (1985) point that countries with open economies are particularly exposed to external economic pressures and their position in the international political economy shapes the structure of domestic institutions and policies. By the same token, in Australia the adaptation of the economy to the changing fortunes of the world economy was not left entirely to the market but was based on the incorporation of interests in domestic economic policymaking. This chapter shows that a narrow focus on institutional arrangements and international economics downplays the strategic options available to elected representatives. Policies designed for low-income groups were more the outcome of strategic political choices than the inevitable product of institutional structures or international forces. When Labor took office, the pivotal strategies of the Centre-Left and the politics of compromise and collaboration with trade unions slowed the right-wing push down. The emphasis on strategic interaction is particularly appropriate to the Australian context where the attempt to reevaluate and monitor policymakers is at the centre of a lively debate on accountability and constitutional changes (Painter, 1998; Uhr, 1998).

CHAPTER 5

The demise of the federal social safety net under Clinton

POLITICAL BACKGROUND

This chapter examines the redistributive game that led to the demise of the Aid to Families with Dependent Children (AFDC) in 1996, the only US federal entitlement to the social safety net. For the first time since the New Deal no guaranteed help from the federal government exists for the poor, marking a break in the development of social legislation in the twentieth century (Weir, 1998). The Welfare Reform Act of 1996 was the culmination of the increasing polarisation of American politics around a left–right conflict. 'This conflict is basically over income redistribution. Other dimensions of conflict, particularly race, have largely vanished as distinct lines of conflict because they have been incorporated into left–right or liberal–conservative conflict' (McCarty, Poole and Howard, 1997: 1).

Redistributive issues were brought to centre stage in 1992 when Bill Clinton campaigned as a New Democrat and made welfare reform and comprehensive health reform the centrepiece of his political agenda. With this decision Clinton staked his domestic policy on two objectives which, in his strategic vision, would have crafted the new image of the Democratic Party. Work-for-welfare programmes could have helped President Clinton to establish credibility as someone willing to move beyond his party's New Deal socio-political coalition (Akard, 1998; Morley and Petras, 1998). Consequently, welfare reform became crucial for remoulding the party image. Under the catchy phrase of 'ending welfare as we know it' Clinton promised to reform the AFDC in ways that stressed work requirements, training and supportive services and improved child support enforcement. Health reform, on the other hand, had eluded the old Democrats since the New Deal. It was especially important to the New Democratic vision because it reconfirmed the federal government's crucial role in guaranteeing social security for all Americans.

There were good reasons for the Democrats to be hopeful of turning around more than a decade of antiwelfare state policymaking (Schwartz, 1998). In 1992 the Democratic control of the White House and Congress had heralded the end of divided government that had dominated American politics for twelve years of Republican rule. It was assumed that divided government produced gridlock, a situation in which the status quo cannot be changed by any new policy proposal, and that unified government would put an end to it (Sundquist, 1993). This view obviously ignored the institutional constraint of the filibuster that in the first two years of the Clinton presidency blocked the economic stimulus package designed to create new jobs as well as the health reform plans. Weak party bonds and multiple veto points are perhaps the main reason why gridlock may be as common under unified party government as it is under divided government (Brady and Volden, 1998).[1]

Institutional constraints and gridlock may explain the failure of health reform under the first Clinton term (Mintz, 1998; Peterson, 1998; Skocpol, 1996). We know much less, however, about the dynamics of welfare policy.[2] Efforts at a comprehensive overhaul of the AFDC had previously foundered because of greater costs in the short term compared with the status quo, and multiple veto points in the legislative process created a strong bias against change.

The central question addressed in this chapter is why US policymakers were able to surmount those long-standing barriers against welfare reform. I propose an answer rooted in two claims. The first, which I take to be uncontroversial, is that the distribution of congressional programmatic preferences shifted after 1994 in a decidedly more conservative direction. The second claim is less obvious. I contend that President Clinton was playing a nested game with strategic timing. As we have seen in the Canadian chapter, an approach based on nested games highlights the possibility that a suboptimal outcome in one game may turn out to be optimal when the whole set of games is considered. My argument here complements the nested game framework with a perspective based on strategic timing. In one of the very few attempts at a detailed analysis of timing as a political phenomenon, Box-Steffensmeier and her co-authors (1997) show that the more momentous the decision, the more important the issues of timing are likely to be.

---

[1] A major research agenda in US political science focuses on the causes and consequences of divided government (Alesina and Rosenthal, 1995; Krehbiel, 1996; Mayew, 1991).

[2] Except for Weaver (1998).

Strategic timing is particularly appropriate to analysing decisionmaking in presidential systems because the President's fixed term of office 'breaks the political process into discontinuous, rigidly demarcated periods, leaving no room for the continuous readjustment that events may demand' (Linz, 1992). In my view, such predictability prompted President Clinton and Congressional Democrats to postpone a public debate on welfare reform, which would have shattered the party publicly. This strategy carried costs and benefits; the cost was to concede more to Congressional Republicans over welfare reform, the benefit was to keep the Democratic Party united.

To be sure, there were also short-term electoral calculations that prompted Clinton's willingness to sign a bill that many Democratic moderates thought was an excessive concession to the right. The Congressional Quarterly Weekly Report cited Dole as the big loser from the splitting of the Medicaid proposal from the welfare bill. It noted, 'The biggest loser in this strategy [of separating Medicaid from welfare reform] would be former Senate Majority Leader Bob Dole ... The notion of Republican Congressional leaders joining Clinton at a White House signing ceremony for a welfare bill would leave Dole as an outsider to the process' (22 June 1996, p. 1761).[3] One interpretation of Clinton's behaviour, therefore, is that it closed off a whole possible avenue of attack from Dole during the forthcoming election campaign. In this light, the Welfare Reform Act was really a response to the particular electoral conditions of 1996 as much as a long-term strategy. The point is that both short-term and long-term considerations help understanding of the welfare reform.

Moreover, special features of the presidential system associated with divided government after 1996, allowed Clinton to cunningly shift a sizeable number of Democratic legislators to a more conservative redistributive stance, thus recrafting Democratic social policy. My argument draws on Weaver's contention that welfare reform reflected the 'impact of President Clinton's strategic vision for reorienting Democratic social policy and the party's image with the electorate' (1998: 361). However, I dispute his conclusion that the law was merely the outcome of unforeseen consequences of that vision. Although the Republican takeover of Congress in 1994 was probably difficult to foresee, it does not follow that Clinton succumbed to Republican whims. It is equally plausible that Clinton's desire to prevent Liberal Democrats from stymieing his New Democratic vision pushed him to sign the Welfare

---

[3] I would like to thank Alan Ware for pointing out this report to me.

Table 5.1. *Income share of population deciles in the United States, 1974–1994 (adjusted household post-tax–post-transfer income)*

Decile	1974	1979	1986	1991	1994
bottom	1.8	1.9	1.7	1.8	1.5
second	4.1	4.1	3.8	3.8	3.6
third	5.5	5.6	5.2	5.2	4.9
fourth	6.7	6.9	6.6	6.5	6.2
fifth	8.0	8.3	7.9	7.9	7.5
sixth	9.4	9.6	9.4	9.3	9.0
seventh	10.9	11.2	11.1	10.9	10.8
eighth	12.8	13.0	13.2	12.2	13.0
ninth	15.6	15.9	16.2	16.3	16.3
tenth	25.0	23.7	24.8	25.1	27.1

Reform Act. After all, the health reform plans had foundered under united government. In such circumstances Clinton might have feared that if Republicans lost their majority in the House a Democratic Congress would have sanctioned the failure of welfare reform as it had with health reform.

The complexity of the situation can be gauged by considering the fact that when Clinton took office in 1992 the two rival parties had initially presented significantly different welfare reform initiatives. Clinton's administration endorsed a combination of training, time limits on cash benefits and jobs at the end of a specified period. This approach to welfare reform offered Democrats some potentially important political advantages. Emphasis on work and individual responsibility shielded Democrats against charges that they protected the non-working poor. Pressing the ideals of making work pay resonated well with constituencies that had suffered declining standards of living in recent years.

The low-middle-income groups lost a sizeable proportion of their takings over the 1980s (table 5.1).[4] For this reason the Clinton administration was hoping to regain favour among low-middle-income groups by insisting on work for welfare programmes. The low-middle-income groups were not the only losers as the bottom 20 per cent of the population were also worse off in the mid 1990s, but the poor are an easy target for budget cutters because they tend not to vote in American elections (Piven and Cloward, 1989). However, proposals for eliminating the social safety net were not on the Democratic agenda.

[4] Consistent with the operational definition in this book, low-middle-income groups are located at the third, fourth and fifth decile.

The Republican welfare reform initiative was far less favourable to low-income families. It would have ended individual entitlements to AFDC benefits, it would have restricted benefits to women who have children outside marriage and it would have prohibited payments to mothers for children conceived while the mother was receiving AFDC (family caps). Furthermore, the Republican proposal placed time limits on receipt of AFDC benefits and it reduced AFDC funding to the states.

Clinton vetoed the Republican welfare proposal twice, in December 1995 and in January 1996, apparently because it was linked to unpopular Medicaid cuts. However, on 11 July Congressional Republicans proposed *The Personal Responsibility and Work Opportunity Reconciliation Act*, a welfare reform bill that met some of the President's objections and omitted Medicaid cuts. At that point, Clinton announced both that he would sign the bill and that he would work on revisions in the next Congress (mostly in non-AFDC provisions).

Clinton's decision to sign the Welfare Reform Act is puzzling. Over the 1980s the Democratic Party was considered the only nationally organised political force actively working to defend the lines of social provision launched in the New Deal (Skocpol, 1988: 307). I argue that the demise of the federal social safety net was the outcome of dramatic modifications in the electoral and institutional determinants of the New Deal Coalition. These modifications set the preconditions for the evolution of sophisticated redistributive games, which eventually produced the Welfare Reform Act.

THE EVOLUTION OF POLICIES TOWARDS LOW-INCOME GROUPS: ELECTORAL AND INSTITUTIONAL DETERMINANTS

Under the New Deal social policy was driven by an unusual alliance between northern labour and a southern planter-merchant oligarchy, which provided the political basis for the US system of income transfers (King, 1995a; Weir *et al.*, 1988).[5] At the centre of southern power in modern American social policy lay the fragmented and decentralised structure of the US political system. The insertion of southern agricultural interests into federal political arrangements meant that control over key Congressional committees allowed the southern wing of the Democratic Party to preserve ethnic inequality in the distribution of

---

[5] Michele Landis (1998) advances a different perspective suggesting that the key to understanding both historical and contemporary patterns of American social welfare legislation is found in the narratives of blame and fate that surfaced in eighteenth-century contests over 'disaster relief'.

transfers (Quadagno, 1994). It is also important to note, however, that this power stemmed in part from regional stalemate within the Democratic Party (Brady and Epstein, 1997; Cox and McCubbins, 1993).

Coupled with the committee system was the criterion of seniority for selecting committee chairmen. Southerners often ran unopposed and therefore gained the seniority necessary to control key Congressional committees until the mid 1960s. Committees had the power to obstruct legislation because a bill could not be brought to the floor of the full House or Senate without favourable committee action.

Nearly everyone who has studied welfare policy in the US agrees that the Civil Act of 1964 and the Voting Rights Act of 1965 fundamentally altered the nature of Southern politics. In this period, a flood of social and political reforms under President Johnson's Great Society contributed to identifying the Democratic Party with social spending and racial liberalism (Carmines and Stimson, 1989). Class-based Republicans began to appeal to white working-class southerners, resentful of the progress of black people (Jones, 1995). Widespread hostility among white southerners towards racial and social advancement and the perceived position of Democrats on these issues caused defections from the Democratic Party among union members, Catholics and lower-status white southerners (Petrocik, 1981).

Thus the antitransfer bias of American social programmes was historically rooted in ethnic and regional divisions which shaped the politics of social policy in the United States (Quadagno, 1994; Williams, 1998). Discrimination against Afro-Americans flourished in other spheres of society. Black employees in the federal civil service were likely to be relegated to lower positions (King, 1995b: 172–204). Recruitment procedures and consignment to segregated units would also disadvantage them.

During the 1960s welfare became politicised along racially charged lines, because black families were overrepresented among AFDC recipients relative to their share of the population. By the end of the 1960s the welfare rolls were over 40 per cent black. This coincided with the high visibility of the civil rights movement which amplified both anti-black and antiwelfare sentiments (Walters, 1998). The racial skewing of the AFDC caseload gave the programme a racial cast that contributed to its extreme unpopularity with large sectors of the electorate.

The AFDC programme that had been quite minor at the time it was brought into the Social Security Act of 1935 expanded enormously in response to unanticipated social and economic changes. Although it kept very uneven standards of eligibility, coverage and benefits across the states, by the 1960s AFDC became the visible embodiment of welfare understood in contrast to social security (Skocpol, 1995).

Support for welfare programmes among southern Democrats was progressively eroded and it was possible for Republicans to make inroads into the Democratic Party constituency by taking a more restrictive stance on social welfare programmes. The replacement of southern congressional Democrats with conservative Republicans pulled the Republican Party further to the right.

At the same time, party polarisation on welfare policies was heightened by important reforms in party organisation. Waves of party development followed the turbulent Democratic convention in 1968, the Republican post-Watergate landslide losses and the traumatic Democratic defeat in 1980 (Kamarck, 1990: 162–174; Polsby, 1983). These events generated a more cohesive party leadership, especially among the Democratic ranks. Historically, the Democratic Party had always been more ideologically fragmented than the Republican Party. Such diversity combined with strict adherence to proportional representation in Democratic primaries to foster internal divisiveness (Wattenberg, 1997). After the mid 1960s southern Democrats became more similar to northern Democrats and the House Democratic Party became considerably less ideologically heterogeneous (Ware, 1985).

These institutional reforms strengthened party leadership. Some indicators of party strength were the shift from a transitory to a permanent bureaucracy, the employment of an increasing number of professional staff, greater division of labour and specialisation within the headquarters and regularised fundraising programmes. Congressional Party leaders aggressively used national campaign organisations to recruit and finance candidates. As a result, American political parties became stronger, more influential and stable (Herrnson, 1998). Such transformation made welfare policy differences between Democrats and Republicans more clear-cut than ever before.

As party organisations were growing more homogeneous, Congressional reforms in the mid 1970s entrusted party leaders with more authority in the House (Ferejohn, 1998; Owens, 1997).[6] Legislative party

---

[6] The earliest of these changes was to permit the Speaker to control the Rules Committee; the most significant of later reforms was the requirement that chairs be selected in caucus by secret ballot. Other modifications included reducing the power of committee chairs to select members, leaders and staff and increasing the openness of internal committee proceedings by recording committee roll calls. However, other reforms had decentralising rather than centralising effects, and further complicated the already difficult relationship between the White House and Congress (Mervin, 1993).

caucuses were revived, met far more frequently and had a greater role in Congressional proceedings. One immediate consequence of stronger national organisations was that party leaders were getting more loyal members on relevant committees, implying that violations of the seniority system became more frequent (Cox and McCubbins, 1993).[7] Party leaders were thus able to shape the substance of legislation more often than did their predecessors (Coleman, 1997; Sinclair, 1998).

The cumulative effect of these institutional reforms on welfare policy was suddenly felt after the election of President Reagan. Reagan succeeded in focusing attention on welfare state programmes and in setting the stage for continuing debate. Conservative thinkers provided intellectual backing for Republican efforts to curb antipoverty programmes. In a major study entitled *Losing Ground* (1984), Murray argued that government intervention in alleviating poverty discouraged the poor from solving their own problems and therefore made the situation worse.

Such intense political attacks against social programmes were launched at a time when the United States became the paradigmatic case of the 'new inequality' (Myles, 1996).[8] More than anywhere else in the industrialised countries, the polarisation of market income and the shrinking middle class combined with high divorce rates and the growth of one parent families (Smeeding, 1997; O'Connor, Orloff and Shaver, 1998).

However, market and demographic effects were overpowered by the popularity of monetarist policies in the 1980s, which aided the downward drift of the already modest programmes of social protection. It is likely that this outcome was a by-product of the welfare state design of the 1960s, but the neoconservative revolution deepened the antitransfer bias of American social programmes. Under Reagan welfare became synonymous with single black American mothers and their children (Quadagno, 1994).

The social policy legacy of the Reagan administration was twofold. First, Reagan reduced the growth rate of many programmes for the poor. New restrictions against combining paid work and welfare benefits brought in during the early Reagan administration bolstered this

---

[7] The negative correlation between the strength of the seniority system and cohesion of the majority party adds weight to the contention that seniority in the US Congress and factional stalemate in the majority party are inversely related (Brady and Epstein, 1997).

[8] For some authors most changes under Reagan were a continuation of policy decisions previously made under Carter (Ferejohn, 1991; Pierson, 1994). Others have noted that under Reagan the slashing of anti-poverty programmes had devastating effects on the standards of living of low-income families (Alber, 1997; Danziger and Gottschalk, 1993).

trend (Blank, 1997). Though low-income public assistance accounted for less than 18 per cent of federal social outlays, these programmes took the brunt of the Reagan efforts to trim spending. Means-tested benefits suffered reductions in eligibility levels, and the targeted jobs and education programmes for the poor were hit hard.

The second legacy was an unprecedented budget deficit which would have hindered any future effort from turning around antiwelfare policy making and from alleviating income inequality (Pierson, 1994). Over the 1980s tax policy was dramatically modified generating long-term effects for government revenue. In 1981 income taxes were slashed and the Tax Reform Act in 1986 broadened the tax base. During fiscal year 1990 the government collected approximately $100 billion less in revenues than it would have collected if no changes had been made to the tax code during the 1980s (Stewart III, 1991). While revenues were significantly curtailed, spending policy proceeded on a relatively normal trajectory thus generating runaway deficits.

With the rise of budgetary politics, liberal and conservative camps became more divided on welfare policy. In Congress 'votes were more divisive after the Tax cut of 1981 – there were winners and losers, and liberals and conservatives became more strident because there was more at stake' (Brady and Volden, 1998: 54). Although welfare policy was an issue in which the pattern of partisan difference and change over time had been rather distinctive (Hibbs and Dennis, 1988), budgetary politics sharply widened the policy distance between Democrats and Republicans, and marked the resurgence of Congressional Party conflict (Coleman, 1997).

President Reagan identified himself with the conservative wing of the party on economic, social and foreign policy in order to present a clear set of policy alternatives to the traditional Democratic and Republican programmes. In doing so Reagan polarised the parties in Congress. Congressional Republicans were solidly in support of his welfare programmes and Congressional Democrats were in opposition.

In terms of party competition, Reagan had succeeded in associating the public's negative image of welfare with the Democratic Party. Such developments pushed Democrats steadily in the direction of revising the traditional focus on income maintenance to a much stronger version of workfare. To this end, in 1984 several moderate Democrats created the Democratic Leadership Council (DLC). Under the guidance of the then Governor Bill Clinton of Arkansas, Congressman Richard Gephardt of Missouri, Governor Lawton Chiles of Florida, Senators Charles Robb of Virginia, Sam Nunn of Georgia and others the DLC pledged vigorous welfare reform (Walters, 1998: 44). By the late 1980s the Democratic Party stance on welfare policy had firmly moved in the direction of work rather than cash assistance, and internal coalitions were more divided in support for poverty and social welfare programmes. A further shift towards reform was brought about by the Democratic presidential defeat of 1988 when Rev. Jesse Jackson campaigned on behalf of the poor; and the subsequent electoral débâcle of 1992 indicated that the brand of liberalism promoted by the Democrats since their New Deal was in jeopardy.

STRATEGIC DISAGREEMENT AND THE STALEMATE OF WELFARE REFORM, 1992–1994

When the Democratic Party eventually succeeded in recapturing the White House in 1992, the electoral results reflected a message of continuity rather than change. President Clinton won 43 per cent of votes, and most probably was able to do so only because Perot and Bush divided the opposition. Not surprisingly, what stood out about the behaviour of President Clinton during his first term of office was the intensity and openness with which he courted public opinion (Jacobs and Shapiro, 1998: 96).

A fairly weak electoral mandate fuelled intraparty dissent over welfare policy, thwarting Clinton's efforts to shape the New Democratic image. Liberal Democrats and New Democrats posed different diagnoses for the problem of the rising number of welfare recipients and suggested different solutions for those diagnoses. In Weaver's description (1998),[9] Liberal Democrats endorsed a rehabilitation approach which viewed low wages and insufficient opportunities as the key problem and consequently concentrated on removing disincentives to work, overcoming human capital deficiencies, and weakening poverty traps that made it difficult to leave welfare. On the other hand, Bill Clinton and the New Democrats backed a paternalistic approach, demanding more responsible behaviour by welfare recipients. Its centre piece was work requirements with sanctions for non-compliance. New Democrats included Senators David Boren, John Breaux, Bob Kerrey and House representatives like Charles Stenholm and Tim Penny, who became advocates of an ambitious agenda of deficit reduction. Standing tough

---

[9] The description in the following paragraphs draws heavily on Weaver (1998).

on the deficit was a way of signalling that one was a new kind of Democrat (Pierson, P. 1998: 136–137).

Old and New Democrats differed on the extent and degree of federal intervention for the reduction of economic inequalities and on the balance between free market principles versus social security (Walters, 1998; Williams, 1998). In these circumstances the fate of President Clinton rested on the power to bargain successfully. Liberal Democrats were unhappy with Clinton's handling of racially charged social policies. The potential punitive aspects of the Clinton administration's welfare proposals were abhorrent to Congressional Black Caucus. New Democrats expressed increasingly rancorous complaints about his reluctance in accepting subsidised job slots. They pushed for time limits on cash benefits without work requirement (soft time limits) and on subsidised job slots (hard time limits). The support of Democratic Liberals would have been necessary to pass the legislation but they opposed both kinds of time limits. Similar strains surfaced in traditional Democratic constituencies especially organised labour. Proposals to increase the scope of public service 'workfare' programmes risked alienating public service employee unions that feared that workfare recipients would replace their members. Liberals and the Congressional Black Caucus opposed provisions they feared would deprive many low-income families of cash benefits; the Hispanic caucus objected to the cutbacks to immigrant benefits.

Clearly a prolonged congressional debate on welfare reform risked shattering rather than strengthening the Democratic coalition in Congress and in the electorate (Weaver, 1998: 380). In Gilmour's terms (1995), it was rational for Congressional Democrats to pursue a strategy of disagreement which aimed at avoiding reaching an agreement when compromise could have damaged their prospects in up-coming elections.

Clinton's attempt to recraft the party image away from New Deal policies threatened the electoral gains of the Liberals who defended those policies. Liberals preferred disagreement to a compromise that would have hurt their standing with their constituents. Both Liberals and New Democrats had a dominant strategy to defect from cooperation, which brought the two groups to a stalemate. Such a stand-off threatened Clinton's grand strategic design to refashion the image of the Democratic Party. Since health reform had failed, his credibility as a New Democrat delicately hinged on the achievement of welfare reform.

Strategic disagreement also postponed the discussion over welfare policy for reasons related to the political environment. An early welfare reform announcement would have run the risk of mobilising the conservative 'pro family' organisations that opposed the proposal. Powerful pressure groups, such as the Christian Coalition, Family Research Council, Eagle Forum and Traditional Values Coalition, became engaged in the welfare issue and some of these groups had a mass base and links with leaders in the evangelical Christian community. The importance of the electoral coalition composed of conservative groups was mirrored in the initial Republican initiatives to reduce out-of-wedlock births. An early announcement would have magnified the potential costs of mobilising the Christian Right and the other conservative social groups, increasing the likelihood that opposition groups could be more damaging to Congressional Democrats and to President Clinton's electoral fortunes than supporting groups could be helpful.

Internal and external considerations motivated strategic disagreement within the Democratic ranks during the 103rd Congress. This situation meant that the House Ways and Means Committee held hearings on the Clinton proposal in the summer of 1994 but never proceeded to mark up the bill.

THE PATERNALISTIC-DETERRENCE GAME

When the 104th Congress convened in January 1995 it was the first Republican-controlled Congress in forty years. Republicans had captured 22 of 31 Democratic open-districts (the districts in which a Democrat had retired after the 103th Congress) and defeated 34 of the 225 Democratic incumbents seeking reelection. Republicans gained in contested districts, which were moderate or conservative to begin with. Even more significant were the Republican victories over incumbent Democrats, because the traditional incumbent advantage should have favoured Democrats (Alford and Brady, 1993; King and Gelman, 1991).

The Republican advance was especially pronounced in the South, confirming the long-term realignment of this region to the right. This development was particularly worrisome for Clinton's re-election prospects, because if the Republicans captured all of the southern electoral votes, then it would become virtually impossible for the Democrats to win the White House (Black and Black, 1992: 5). President Clinton's electoral vulnerability provided a powerful incentive to move beyond the status quo in welfare policies. Results from the 1992 National

Election Studies showed that the overall salience of welfare reform with respect to other policies was 45.6 per cent, the highest level any dimension reached in the previous eleven elections. By contrast the salience of class was 37.2 per cent and that of fiscal and monetary policy was 40.7 per cent (Lawrence, 1996: 151). The higher the saliency of an issue the stronger the signal sent by constituencies to legislators about expectations of their vote (Kingdon, 1989).

Much has been written about the impact of public opinion on welfare reform (Feldman and Zaller, 1992; Zaller, 1992). One conclusion is that a sizeable majority of voters were against the status quo but did not completely abandon their concern for the poor (Weaver, 1995). Another issue is that American cultural antipathies towards welfare and the poor are long standing, yet the zeal and stridency of the contemporary campaign for welfare reform are relatively new (Piven, 1998). Finally, there is little evidence to suggest that the public position on social policy had shifted dramatically (Keeter, 1997: 111; Lawrence, 1996: 102).

This relative stability of public opinion indicates that party polarisation was likely to be elite initiated. The increasing ideological polarisation of the Democratic and Republican leaders in the Reagan and post-Reagan eras made it easier for voters to recognise the differences between the parties' policy stands (Abramowitz and Saunders, 1998). Political divisions over social policy was not new in American politics; what distinguished the 1990s were the centrality of these divisions to party strategies and the extent of polarisation. Conflict over social policy became the flashpoint for debates about the fundamental principles that should guide the scope and premises of governmental activity for the next generation (Weir, 1998: 8). Policies for low-income families became the focal point of controversy.

The Republican takeover of both Houses of Congress in the 1994 election redefined the agenda for low-income families. 'The Contract with America', the House Republican electoral manifesto, contained harsh welfare provisions. The Contract with America would have capped and reduced AFDC funding to the states, ended individual entitlements to AFDC benefits, restricted benefits to women who had children outside marriage and placed time limits on receipt of AFDC benefits.

Party polarisation over welfare policy escalated with Clinton's espousal of the paternalistic approach. Its centrepiece on time limits with work requirements pressed Republicans in the direction of deterrence strategies – time limits with no work guarantee in order to differentiate themselves from the Democrats as tougher on welfare. Deterrence gravitated on preventing undesirable behaviour from occurring in the first place: out of wedlock birth should be addressed by family caps (prohibiting payments to mothers for children conceived while the mother was receiving AFDC) and banning cash benefits to teenage mothers. Long-term dependence should be prevented by setting a fixed period after which recipients would be denied benefits. Despite disagreement over diagnoses and solutions, none of the contending partners wanted a deadlock that would have preserved the status quo. Shortly after the 1994 election a revised Welfare Reform Bill passed the House of Representatives on a party line vote, reflecting both effective Republican leadership and strong incentives for House Republicans to show unity. Congressional Democrats stayed united in opposing the final passage of the Republican Bill and joined around a conservative Democratic alternative sponsored by Nathan Deal of Georgia (who eventually switched to the Republican ranks). Clinton had sustained the Deal bill although it contained hard time limits, something the administration had ultimately backed away from in its own welfare package the previous June. Thus the president took an important step to the right, giving the Republicans additional leverage to insist on hard time limits in a final welfare reform package (Weaver, 1998: 389). President Clinton had also changed his budget proposal from one in early 1995 that planned successive annual deficits of $200 billion, to a proposal a few months later that embraced the Republican plan for a seven-year balanced budget.

It is worth noting that the Republicans' effort to articulate a coherent public philosophy was not without tensions. Perhaps the greatest conflict among Republicans involved the amount of flexibility to be given to states in reforming welfare. Deterrence-oriented approaches to welfare reform energised a core group of Republican members of the House and Senate but they also increased the probability of friction in the Senate, where the moderate wing of the Republican Party was stronger. Senate Republicans wished to mitigate the radical nature of the proposed House Republican welfare reform. Partly because their electoral constituencies are more heterogenous than those of the House members and partly because their seats are more competitive, more Senate Republicans tend to take moderate stances than do House members.

Frictions among Republican leaders meant that the Republicans' welfare reform initiative did come close to collapsing in the Senate. Senate Majority Leader Robert Dole, the leading Republican

Table 5.2. *Paternalistic-Deterrence game*

Clinton	Republicans			
	C		I	
C	a	2,2	b	0,3
I	c	3,0	d	1,1

contender, needed to show that he was an effective leader in getting legislation passed. In order to do so, Dole had to solidify support among moderate Republicans and gain support from Republican governors. He therefore criticised the evolving House Republican bill on welfare reform as being overly radical. In 1995 Dole offered a package of amendments, including more money for child care, that welded a broad coalition of moderate Republicans and Democrats for his bill (Weaver, 1998: 390–391). In this way conservative Republicans were outvoted and the Senate was able to approve the package.

The passage of the Senate welfare reform bill had obvious implications for the nature of later bargaining over welfare reform. Clinton basically endorsed the Senate bill, and the support for this bill from an overwhelming majority of Democratic senators meant that Democrats would have problems in backing away from the Senate legislation. Passage of the Senate bill allowed Republicans to gain in bargaining leverage and to try to push welfare reform further to the right.

In the year that elapsed between Senate approval and Presidential signature of the welfare reform bill several amendments were introduced. In this period Clinton and Congressional Republicans entered into a bargaining game with a view to arriving at a converging strategy. Such interaction lends itself to be modelled as a two-phase cooperative game where the first game is non-cooperative.[10] In Phase I the partners act independently and choose a threat strategy; in the second phase they bid around the outcome of Phase I. The moves of the two players are illustrated in table 5.2. Ideally, Clinton would have preferred to cooperate with Congressional Republicans because his commitment to ending 'Welfare as we know it' raised the danger that the administration might

---

[10] This way of modelling cooperative games is suggested in Nash (1953). Some authors believe that non-cooperative models are more fundamental than cooperative models (Binmore, 1992). For a criticism to this view and a summary of the debate focused on cooperative games see Osborne and Rubinstein (1994, chapter 7).

not be able to keep its promises and therefore risked being politically hammered by the Republicans if it did not achieve any reform. But if Clinton had decided to cooperate and had chosen cell (a) Congressional Republicans would have been better off to be intransigent (I) and pursue the deterrence strategy by moving to cell (b). Pressing on deterrence offered a real opportunity for Republicans to solidify links with conservative pro-family groups; it also energised a core group of Republican members of the House and Senate, especially among the newer and more conservative members. The average age of House freshmen in 1994 was less than 45 and more than half of House Republicans were first or second termers. Many of these young, inexperienced and ideological committed Republicans shared a relative clarity of purpose which helped to cement party cohesion (Ferejohn, 1998).

Republicans had strong incentives to present a unified front against President Clinton because few Republicans had significant constituency interests in resisting the cutbacks to means-tested programmes. If Republicans had insisted on deterrence and opted for cell (b), Clinton would have been better off by moving to cell (d). This is the strategy best preferred by Congressional Republicans and therefore cell (d) is an equilibrium solution. Phase I of the paternalistic-deterrence game has a dominant strategy of mutual intransigence that invariably yields a suboptimal outcome. Tensions between the paternalistic and the deterrence approach marked the trajectory of welfare proposals up to the final stage. Republicans were oriented to provoking a veto in order to enact a blame-generating strategy (Weaver, 1998). By passing a bill they knew the president would veto, Republicans hoped to underscore the differences between the two parties.

But the imminence of the November presidential election precipitated the implementation of strategies towards convergence. To get re-elected Congressional Republicans would need to enact welfare reform so that they would not be vulnerable to charges of inaction. In a close vote it is likely that attention is focused on those members who cast an unpopular vote. A further point is that public opinion had shifted radically against Congressional Republicans, after they forced a prolonged confrontation over the budget in 1995 that produced two governmental shutdowns. Hence the blame-generating strategy they wished to activate backfired. Consequently if they were not to lose control of Congress in the autumn election they had to act quickly to reform welfare on Republican terms. However, as long as welfare reform and Medicaid reform were linked, the deadlock between House

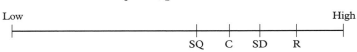

Figure 5.1. Credit claiming game

Republicans and Clinton was unlikely to be broken. Had House Republicans insisted on unpopular cuts on Medicaid, and thus rejected Clinton's proposal, they would have borne the responsibility of the failure of the Welfare Reform before the electorate.

These considerations eroded the Congressional Republican commitment to the linkage between welfare and Medicaid reform and shifted their strategies towards a cooperative game to cut deals with President Clinton and pull together a credible list of popular accomplishments. Phase II of the Paternalistic-Deterrence game is characterised by the replacement of a blame-generating strategy with a credit-claiming strategy where both partners make a bid for a point on the negotiation set.[11] In the end the bargaining game yielded what I shall define as soft deterrence provision.

In figure 5.1, I construct the spatial portrait of the interactions between Clinton (C) and Congressional Republicans (R). The preferences of the two players are located as points in the policy space, which represent their ideal points. The status quo (SQ) denotes the level of welfare generated by prevailing policies, and soft deterrence (SD) illustrates the policy output, which reflects the median position. As welfare could be increased by spending more money, the policy space can be cast in one dimension. Here the underlying dimension of welfare depicts the willingness to commit resources to reduce poverty.

In the event, the partners reached an agreement that reconciled the conservative political leanings of the New Democrats towards the welfare system while protecting Medicare, a policy popular with the party's traditional liberal constituency. Soft deterrence enabled Clinton to build the public and political coalitions needed to buttress the new

---

[11] Further evidence that Republicans and New Democrats were careful to credit claim for the Welfare Reform Act is provided by recent statements on the success of the bill in reducing the number of welfare caseloads. In searching for positive campaign issues for the November 1998 mid-term elections Republican John Boeher, chairman of the House Republican Conference, declared that 'Republicans welcome the president's cheerleading on the welfare issue. After decades of big government programs and failed welfare policies, it took a Republican-led Congress to forge a bipartisan approach to meet these critical problems' (Holland, Steve, *Washington Post*, Reuters, May 27).

programme initiatives in the field of welfare policy. His two vetoes in 1995 convinced Republicans that Clinton was prepared to threaten another veto.[12] President Clinton had already capitalised on the unique visibility of his office by exercising the distinctive power of 'going public' in order to monopolise public opinion and persuade Congress to cooperate (Kernell, 1997).

Congressional Democrats faced a political dilemma that revolved around avoiding blame. Liberal Democrats would have opposed any Republican bill and some moderate Democrats would have supported such a bill; many moderates were on the fence, they did not want to end up on the wrong side of a popular legislative initiative (Weaver, 1998). Clinton carefully gauged this strategy in order to profit from the situation through a triangulation game that positioned him ideologically between Congressional Republicans and Democrats (Jacobs and Shapiro, 1998: 109). He confronted the Republican majority on issues where the Democratic position had broad popular support (such as opposition to cuts in Medicare and Medicaid) and worked with the Republicans on issues where their positions were more popular (like balancing the budget).

The bill passed the House with solid Republican support and 30 Democrats defected to back it. Five days after House action, the Senate approved a slightly softer bill with near-unanimous Republican support and half the Democratic senators voting in favour. Both chambers passed the welfare bill by large margins, with Democrats strongly split. In the House the bill passed by a margin of 328–101, with Democrats split 98–98; in the Senate the bill obtained 78 votes in favour and 21 against, with Democrats split 25–21 in favour of passage. The statute put a fixed five-year time limit on cash assistance but no requirement for family cap or teenage mother exclusions, although states could impose those restrictions if they chose. Greater resources for childcare compared to the vetoed bill were included. Attention to women's issues may explain why in the 1996 election Clinton's biggest gain came from among women of lower-income groups, 56 per cent of their vote went to Clinton and 35 per cent to Dole.

Clinton signed the Welfare Reform Act and announced that he would introduce changes after the election. Hence he succeeded in campaigning with both a bill and an issue. Contrary to Gilmour's

---

[12] For a simple bargaining model between President and Congress based on the power of veto threats, see Mathews (1989). An empirical analysis of executive-legislative bargaining is offered in McCarty and Pool (1995).

contention that a typical strategic choice for legislators is whether to bargain over an issue or a bill, I argue that President Clinton achieved both at once. He passed welfare reform and prepared a declaration that he would strive to improve its quality once reelected. During his second term Clinton made a number of changes to the 1996 welfare reform statute in the Balanced Budget Act of 1997, which provided substantial additional funding for immigrant benefits and a little more for food stamps. However, the provisions regarding low-income families changed only modestly. Modifications focused on spending plans rather than on the statutory changes, such as loss of entitlement, time limits and work requirements.

'DESERVING AND UNDESERVING POOR'

AFDC served as a transitional safety net or as a kind of unemployment assistance in a labour market where jobs and child care arrangements were precarious, particularly for women of colour (O'Connor *et al.*, 1998). The new welfare law included harsh provisions that severely restricted the availability of food stamps for many unemployed individuals. Other major stipulations of the bill were that people on welfare were required to find work within two years or lose all their benefits; a lifetime maximum of five years on welfare was set. Significant cutbacks in other major social welfare programmes involved the food stamp provision and the Supplemental Security Income programme.

Welfare reform replaced individual entitlement to family assistance benefits with a block grant to the states called temporary assistance to needy families (TANF). TANF are fixed funds in nominal terms based on the total amount currently spent by the federal government on public assistance. They do not take inflation into account and will thus decline in real terms over time. About 40 per cent of the net savings in the bill were achieved by denying a wide range of benefits to immigrants, including poor immigrants who were very old. Illegal immigrants already were ineligible for most major means-tested entitlement benefits. When fully implemented this provision will terminate food stamps for over half a million poor jobless individuals who are willing to work but cannot find a job (US Congressional Budget Office, 1997).

The abolition of the federal social safety net took place at a time when the economy was performing less well in raising individuals out of poverty. The new Census data show that despite economic growth poverty remained significantly higher in 1996 than in 1989, before the

Table 5.3. *Trends in income inequality in the United States, 1974–1994
(adjusted household post-tax–post-transfer income)*

Year	Coefficient of variation	Gini index	Theil index
1974	70.7	34.6	20.8
1979	61.9	33.0	18.2
1986	69.6	35.5	21.3
1991	69.3	35.8	21.5
1994	78.9	38.3	25.4
Percentage change			
1974–1979	− 12.4	− 1.6	− 12.5
1979–1986	+ 12.4	+ 7.5	+ 1.7
1986–1991	− 0.9	+ 0.8	+ 0.9
1991–1994	+ 13.8	+ 6.9	+ 18.1
1974–1994	+ 27.4	+ 10.6	+ 22.1

recession of the early 1990s began ('Current Population Reports', 1997). Unemployment rates were nearly identical in 1996 and in 1989 but the US economy was richer in 1996 than in 1989. Moreover, while the income of the typical family rose modestly between 1995 and 1996, the average incomes of the bottom three-fifths of the US population stayed below pre-recession levels.

If we look at table 5.3 we see that income disparities rose substantially in the 1990s and that measured income inequality had been moving upwards almost consistently since the late 1970s. Estimates on the proportion of the population which actually saw their real income decline between the mid 1970s and the mid 1990s range from 35 per cent to 10 per cent (Burckhauser *et al.*, 1996; Duncan, Rogers and Smeeding, 1993).

Similarly to Canada, Britain and Australia, there is little evidence in the USA that the inequality drift is purely cyclical. The main causes of rising income inequality are attributable to the relative weakness of the American income support system for families with children and relatively low wages in the labour market (Gottschalk and Smeeding, 1997; Smeeding, Rainwater and Torrey, 1993). Table 5.4 illustrates that income gains from economic growth over the course of the business cycle since 1989 have disproportionately gone to those at high-income levels. Hence the role of the safety net in mitigating poverty should have taken on an added significance. Instead, the federal government abolished the automatic entitlement to benefits.

Table 5.4. *Poverty rates for one-parent families and for the elderly: United States 1974–1994 (adjusted household post-tax–post-transfer income)*

Per cent of median income	1974	1979	1986	1991	1994	percentage change		
						1974–1979	1979–1986	1974–1994
One-parent families								
Less than 40%	46	36	45	42	37	− 21	+ 25	− 19.5
Less than 50%	57	48	54	50	46	− 15	+ 12	− 19.2
Less than 60%	65	59	62	58	55	− 9	+ 5	− 15.3
*Elderly**								
Less than 40%	13	13	11	9	9	0	− 15	30
Less than 50%	22	24	20	18	17	+ 9	− 16	− 22
Less than 60%	33	34	31	28	27	18	− 8	− 18

*Note: *Household heads aged 65+.*

A popular explanation of the Welfare Reform Act of 1996 is the straightjacket imposed by the budget constraint. It argues that welfare provisions were intended to reduce spending levels in the short term and to ensure lower spending in the long term by putting a firm cap on spending for AFDC and a number of other means-tested programmes, rather than preserving them as an open-ended entitlement. But the elimination of the AFDC did nothing to balance the federal budget. As a programme that consumed only 1 per cent of federal spending its fiscal significance was minimal. Notably absent was any action on the three welfare state programmes that consume nearly half of the federal budget – social security, Medicare and Medicaid (Quadagno, 1998: 95). To realise the larger goals of debt reduction and a smaller role for the federal government as envisioned in the Republican 'Contract with America', attention should have turned to these large universal programmes. The problem was that these programmes enjoyed high public support, especially among the elderly, and were considered sacrosanct for electoral reasons (Page and Shapiro, 1992). The elderly are a powerful, large and cohesive pressure group, a fact that helps to make social security programmes politically untouchable. On the other hand programmes specifically aimed at the poor and the 'disreputable' are easy targets for budget cutters.

One crucial consequence is that state protection of dependent recipients has taken divergent paths. While single parents (mostly females) persistently suffered, the elderly clients of social security continued to improve their economic condition (see table 5.4). The implications of belonging to a state-protected or a risk-exposed group in the American transfer system are acutely evident in table 5.4. When I set the poverty line at 40 per cent of the median, the proportion of poor lone parents rises by 25 per cent and the proportion of poor elderly declines by 15 per cent between 1979 and 1986. My findings are corroborated by official reports which show that in 1996 government benefits lifted from poverty more than four of every five elderly people who otherwise would have been poor, but fewer than one in three children who would otherwise have been poor ('Centre on Budget and Policy Priorities', 1998). Means-tested benefit programmes removed 400,000 fewer children from poverty in 1996 than in 1995 ('Census', 1996).

CONCLUSIONS

The Welfare Reform Act of 1996 was the culmination of the rise of welfare politics in the late twentieth century, which stemmed from the ongoing realignment of the South and the resurgence of party government in the US political system. This chapter shows that the complexity of the US institutional setting helped generate sophisticated redistributive games, which eventually lowered the barriers for welfare reform.

The return of party government under Reagan polarised welfare policy in the 1980s. Yet the Welfare Reform Act of 1996 went far beyond Reagan's actions which were designed to restrict eligibility for welfare and cut spending costs but not to eliminate the programme altogether. A familiar explanation rests on electoral competition. Surely, the antipathy of a large section of the public towards the AFDC programme nourished party competition on social policy. Parties responded to the most prominent problems in the voters' agenda but they were less responsive in the actual formulation of social policies. Democrats and Republicans engaged in aggressive politicisation of public opinion and combined elements of accommodating and directing voters' demands (Jacobs and Shapiro, 1998: 85).

In particular, President Clinton and the New Democrats sought to eradicate the Democratic image that was associated with welfare state expansion. In the process, they were confronted with the New Deal tradition defended by liberal Democrats. This situation is similar to the ones encountered in the chapters on Canada, Britain and Australia, where an emerging faction attempted to dislodge the old guard by effacing the party image associated with the dominant group.

The distinctiveness of the US experience is that intraparty politics is enmeshed with cross-party blocs. Welfare reform relied on a triangulation game between Liberal Democrats, the President and Congressional Republicans. Clinton confronted the Republican majority on issues where the Democratic position had broad popular support and worked with the Republicans on issues where their positions were more popular.

Among the Democratic ranks a game of strategic disagreement postponed the debate on welfare reform until 1994 when Republicans seized Congress. At that stage Clinton entered into a paternalistic-deterrence game with Congressional Republicans that initially brought the negotiations to a standstill. This stalemate was followed by the replacement of a blame-generating strategy with a credit-claiming strategy that yielded a soft deterrence welfare provision.

This chapter demonstrates that a focus on the redistributive impact of factional politics is especially appropriate for the US institutional setting. Loose party organisations coupled with multiple veto points meant that shifting factional coalitions have been the core of welfare policy in the US. For once, American party politics is not an exception but a logical expectation.

CHAPTER 6

Conclusions

The foregoing analyses of redistributive actions and reactions in Canada, Britain, Australia and the US describe and explain how each governing party devised transfer programmes. Of course, these accounts are historically incomplete; like other works in comparative politics my aim is not detailed description but analytic narrative (Bates *et al.*, 1998). Rather than registering events I focus on those critical junctures that set the preconditions or saw the main battles taking place.

In this chapter I review the material presented from an explicitly comparative perspective in order to highlight similarities and differences among the four countries. On the basis of their historical experience, it is possible to outline a set of propositions about the incentives for income redistribution in a liberal democracy.

The story of why we observe differences in inequality movements is necessarily incomplete because of the confluence of market, social, demographic, institutional and policy forces combined with behavioural changes by individuals, families and households. My account concentrated primarily on actor-centred institutionalism and showed that interdependent strategic action within party organisations sheds considerable light on redistributive games. The game theoretic models obviously did not determine the outcomes. What differed among the countries were the institutional settings within which those games were played.

I analysed how party leaders of different ideological persuasions reacted to problems that arose from fundamental changes in international socio-economic conditions. But I was less concerned with similarities among the cases than with their differences, and less with governments' efforts to steer the economy than with their strategic options in redistributing burdens and benefits. I therefore concentrated on the factors that permitted the ruling parties of Canada, Britain, Australia and the United States to manipulate entitlement and eligibility rules. Policymakers in the four countries designed very different strategies to allocate redistributive costs and benefits.

In Canada, Trudeau initially expanded universal social security programmes but failed to sustain generous unemployment benefits later in the term. In Britain the Conservative government enacted redistributive policies which advantaged specific categories of the dependent population at the expense of other categories. The Australian Labor Party successfully implemented an incomes policy of wage stability to fight unemployment, but at the same time penalised the state-dependent population by increasing targeting and abolishing universal benefits. President Clinton, on the other hand, signed a landmark Welfare Reform Act that overturned 60 years of American social policy by eliminating the automatic entitlement to benefits.

Precisely because of the differences in the strategies adopted, neither declining nor rising inequality were unavoidable fates. If some country was nevertheless unable to avoid growing inequality, then the reasons must lie less in international trends than in national factors, and perhaps in the varying strategic options of party leaders. Before proceeding further, let us summarise briefly what the incentives are for redistribution in a liberal democracy.

THE REDISTRIBUTIVE LOGIC IN LIBERAL DEMOCRACIES

Scholars concerned with income redistribution have assumed that electoral politics and economic development have an inbuilt mechanism in favour of equality. Political sociologists see redistributive policies as the outcome of contrasting distributive goals that are consistent with the locations of the party's core constituencies in the hierarchy of income classes. The expectation is that, on the one hand, left-wing parties reduce income inequality by redistributing income from rich to poor and that, on the other hand, right-wing parties in a process of contagion from the left become less anti-egalitarian in order to appeal to low-income groups. Rational choice theorists believe vote-maximising parties redistribute income either to improve the economic position of median voters, or to achieve short-term electoral benefits.

Against this background, the upward inequality movement over the 1980s suggests that inequality had in some sense evolved counterintuitively. Yet, the wider the gap between rich and poor becomes, the less plausible it is to suppose that liberal democracies converge towards equality and the more important it becomes to examine the sources of inequality growth. Perhaps the best example of counterintuitive trends is Australia where inequality rose in prosperous times under the Labor government. Hawke placed redistribution of wealth second to wealth production and implemented redistributive policies more congruent with right-wing ideologies. The incomes policy protected unionised workers, but tighter eligibility and entitlement rules severely penalised the dependent population. The Australian experience points out that free market principles can be espoused by Labor parties as well as by Conservative parties.

In the US it was a Democratic President who agreed to abolish the federal social safety net. In Canada, the Liberal government actively engaged in both generous and stiffer social security benefits, thus contributing to both falling and rising inequality. Economic prosperity and expansionary redistributive policies in the early 1970s substantially reduced income differences. Poor people appeared to be better off in the mid 1970s, as measured by the share of equivalised disposable income accruing to the bottom deciles. But in the late 1970s, the Liberal government implemented contractionary redistributive programmes which exacerbated the plight of the poor during the economic recession.

That democracy has no inbuilt mechanism towards equality was clearly highlighted in Britain where inequality grew faster than in most other countries. Thatcher's redistributive policies, moreover, were marked by a curious asymmetry, whereby some risk categories were more protected than others. Neither political sociology nor demand-driven explanations appeared consistent with these facts.

Since established approaches seem incongruent with empirical evidence, it is important to stand back from the analytic narratives of the case studies and again raise the question of what the incentives are for income redistribution in a liberal democracy. The literature on the redistributive impact of parties has with good reason emphasised the role of demand-driven policies. Oriented towards the paradigm of representative democracy, exogenous preferences and interparty competition, this literature stresses the responsiveness of elected representatives to voters' demands. According to this thinking, party leaders represent the interests of the electorate by responding to their redistributive wishes.

Normatively speaking this argument is correct. In practice, however, its significance may be somewhat exaggerated because not all elected representatives may want to meet voters' expectations. Entitlement rules could change when politicians devise redistributive strategies

aimed at forging electoral alliances among protected voters. Redistributive policies are well-suited to trigger issues of inclusion and exclusion
because they define categories of privileged and less-privileged people.
By carving boundaries between risk-exposed voters and insured voters,
party elites can encourage shifting coalitions of supporters. Hence
rather than merely responding to voters' demands, party leaders actively engage in social engineering and public opinion formation.

What is more, contrary to the class politics view, which is based on the
assumption that redistribution occurs vertically from upper- to lower-
income classes, ruling parties also engage in *horizontal* redistribution
between social categories included in the same income class. Horizontal
redistribution may involve cutting benefits to one category of beneficiaries while increasing them to other recipients. Presumably because the
state-dependent population has been regarded as a homogeneous social
class, insufficient attention has been paid to the incentives for horizontal
redistribution in a liberal democracy.

A second limitation of established approaches seems more important
to me. Not all political parties act as cohesive groups. Discussion seems
to have focused too exclusively on the electoral logic of income redistribution, while paying little attention to strategic repositioning within
the governing party. By studying 'who wins, and in what combinations,
and who governs, and where, we have tended to shortchange the work
of examining the organisations that produce these fateful results' (Lawson, 1990: 107). One consequence is the paucity of studies on party
organisations, which unfortunately has imposed severe limits of preci-
sion in my account of all four countries.

Within these limits, I was able to show that incentives for redistribution may stem from internal feuding when a dominant faction is displaced by another one. For example, a newly established right-wing
faction of a Labor Party or Socialist Party may wish to project a new
party image in order to legitimise its leadership position; it may adopt
retrenchment policies to efface the party's previous identity. Alterna-
tively, credible threats by right-wing factions to the dominant position of
a centre-left faction can persuade the latter to endorsing right-wing
redistributive programmes. Stealing the clothes of the neighbour is a
familiar process in interparty competition, but its significance for intraparty strategies has not yet been sufficiently acknowledged.

Whilst some redistributive strategies may be beyond the manipulative
reach of governments, politicians can be unresponsive to voters' views
because they are entangled in internal strife. The formation, consolida-

tion and demise of party factions ushers in modifications to redistributive programmes.

Incentives for income redistribution, however, may also spring from the availability of external options to the bargaining partners. The appearance of new social cleavages, such as environmental politics, the feminist movement in the 1960s and 1970s, the end of the Cold War in 1989 and, more generally, rising electoral volatility may encroach on the internal balance of power. A turbulent electoral arena unleashes new social forces, offering unforeseen opportunities to party factions. Party leaders may avail themselves of these new conditions to redesign redistributive policies which adjust social relativities; or they may wish to reshape the party reputation to attract either previously unsympathetic or indifferent voters.

The mixture of objectives embedded in redistributive policies is more clearly detected if we relax the assumption of preference homogeneity within the ruling party and recognise that party organisations consist of a plurality of groups striving against each other to secure the leadership position. In this view variations in the allocation of social security benefits arise from shifting boundaries between party factions and social groups. Factions are better understood as distributive elites and subgroups of the electorate as social clienteles. Thus manipulations of eligibility and entitlement rules are regarded as attempts at moulding faction–voter alignments.

Keeping in mind these reasons for expansionary or contractionary redistributive policies in general, in the following sections I return to the case studies and review which incentives lay behind the redistributive strategies of the Liberal Party of Canada, the British Conservative Party, the Australian Labor Party and the Democratic Party in the United States. I then consider the role of demographic and market effects on inequality movements. Thereafter I turn to the broader implications of this analysis for understanding the party–policy link in the field of social security policies. Finally, I investigate inequality movements and transfer programme changes over the 1990s in selected OECD countries.

DISTRIBUTIVE ELITES, INSTITUTIONAL CONTEXT AND OPPOSITION EFFECTS

A major finding of this book is that ruling parties reallocated redistributive benefits and costs to forge new coalitions of voters. One implication is that electoral behaviour may be unstable because party elites are altering the boundaries of their core electorate in search of new alliances. In line with Director's Law of income redistribution, social groups may enter or exit electoral coalitions if redistributive policies alter their incentives to vote. For example, in Australia, the assets test on pensioners alienated the elderly from the ALP; under Trudeau expansionary transfer policies appealed to the NDP electorate; and in Britain the relative generosity of pension benefits compared to unemployment benefits presumably wooed some elderly voters. Demand-driven models overlook the fact that politics often implies the making and breaking of coalitions between party elites and voters, and that the plasticity of public opinion lends itself to being moulded by the redistribution of costs and benefits.

I examined the internal processes surrounding the selection of distinct social security programmes and I also explored how Opposition effects impinged on the internal balance of power. In the following sections I compare the processes within party organisations from three angles: the changing boundaries between factions and social clienteles, the constraints imposed by the institutional and organisational setting and, finally, Opposition effects on redistributive policies.

Distributive elites and social clienteles

A common feature of established approaches is that party leaders are assumed to act collectively to further their interests, or the interests of their core supporters. This argument did not withstand close scrutiny. In the four countries, party leaders pursued conflictual and contradictory goals, with some leaders joining pro-welfare alliances and others forming antiwelfare coalitions. Mostly, transfer policies evolved as a compromise between actors with heterogeneous preferences, suggesting that the assumption of preference homogeneity embedded in the unitary actor model is unwarranted.

By relaxing the unitary assumption, it was possible to disentangle the links between factions and social groups. In Australia, for example, the emphasis placed on means-tested benefits by the Labor Right aimed at reshaping the party image so as to secure the support of the business community and market-oriented voters. Because Labor Left had traditionally represented the interests of welfare recipients, the attack on cash benefits also discredited the role of left-wingers as leaders in the eyes of their constituency. The reason is that the Labor Left constituency did not see its interests represented and therefore the faction lost its legitimacy in the eyes of its core supporters. The displacement of the Left as dominant faction by the Right paved the way for the introduction of stiffer entitlement rules for pension benefits and unemployment compensation. Seen in this light, the urge to reshape the party image was a manifestation of the internal struggle for power.

Transfer policies in Britain also reflected shifting coalitions of distributive elites and social clienteles. The dries were able to reapportion redistributive costs and benefits at the expense of low-income families, who supported either the Opposition or the Tory wets. But it was not until the wets abandoned the internal battle that the Conservative government undertook the most radical departure from post-war social security policies, as expressed in the Fowler Report of 1984 and the 1988 social security bill.

In Canada, Trudeau initially expanded social security programmes to encourage closer ties between members of the prowelfare faction and voters worried with rising unemployment rates, including women, fishermen and teachers. By mobilising welfare recipients Trudeau reinforced his bargaining position with respect to the antiwelfare faction. Strategic repositioning of the Trudeauites and Turnites over the 1970s explained why specific social categories were either penalised or privileged by the reallocation of costs and benefits. The analysis of intraparty politics threw considerable light on both the expansion of family allowances and the contraction of unemployment benefits in the late 1970s. Redistributive outputs were partly the outcome of factional efforts to enhance their own position in the internal arena.

The US perhaps offers the clearest illustration of the connection between transfer policies and party image. Clinton's efforts to reorient the party's image with the electorate entailed the abandonment of Democratic social policy as represented in the New Deal tradition. This tradition was associated with Liberal Democrats and therefore in attempting to efface it New Democrats marginalised Liberals within the party.

In all four countries the evidence supports the theory of party goals which suggests that when a political party acquires a new image this testifies to the end of an era and to the success of those 'new faces' holding positions of responsibility in the internal hierarchy (Harmel and Janda, 1994).

When examining the organisational life of governing parties we see that relaxing the unitary assumption increases tremendously the explanatory power of our analysis. The unitary assumption prejudges the most interesting question – under what circumstances faction leaders develop and actively work towards redistributive goals. Understanding those circumstances and the effect of those circumstances on the manner in which redistributive goals are designed and attained seems to me the central task for anyone interested in the redistributive impact of ruling parties.

To some degree, of course, transfer policies were directed at representing the interests of party members and voters. Generally speaking parties would cease to be such if they did not muster votes. However, in the four countries, cash transfers were unevenly allocated partly because of changing boundaries between coalitions of distributive elites and social clienteles.

These redistributive policies built on the historical cleavages that shaped the politics of social policy in each country. In the US and Canada the historical development of the politics of region and ethnic division created a significantly different dynamics. Universal programmes in Canada cut across linguistic and regional divisions and reinforced the political legitimacy of the ruling party. The centralised system for income security was constructed around the 'politics of place' rather than the 'politics of class' as in Britain (Jenson, 1990). Canadian social reforms mitigated interregional disparities, in a very similar manner to developments in Australia, where the politics of equalisation helped to bridge the poverty gap between states. In the United States, by contrast, social policy was primarily driven by the politics of race. Ethnic and regional divisions and their intersection with the organisation of the state and political parties combined to produce and preserve the anti-transfer bias of American social programmes.

Institutional constraints and opportunities

What made redistributive games intelligible was the manner in which power was distributed within the party and in the institutional setting. In the Liberal Party of Canada the combination of a weak bureaucratic structure and the concentration of decisionmaking power in the hands of the leader, granted Trudeau the flexibility to adjust transfer policies to his advantage. Trudeau enjoyed both the freedom to expand social security benefits when external options changed in his favour between 1972 and 1974 and the readiness to curb them in order to pre-empt Turner's leadership threat.

Alterations in the distribution of power within the British Conservative Party showed another aspect of the party–policy link. Modifications in the selection and reselection rules for the party leader altered the nature of bargaining games between Conservative elites from implicit to explicit games. Looser internal coordination and potential threats to the leadership ensued. During the first Conservative term, explicit games raised Thatcher's awareness of her vulnerability and thus gave some leeway to the wets. Arguably, however, her major strength lay in the tradition of unity and cohesion in the Conservative Party and in the concentration of decisionmaking authority in the hands of the leader. The joint impact of internal centralisation and the wide margin of freedom conferred by Westminster systems on Prime Ministers, provided Thatcher with the requisite autonomy to depart from post-war consensus on social security legislation.

In Australia, as well, institutional reform triggered new strategic games. The introduction of proportional representation for party delegates spawned a national system of faction, marked by the formation of the Centre-Left. The new electoral system endowed the Centre-Left with a pivotal position which enabled it to act as a brake on Labor's shift to the right. Another organisational feature was the declining number of unionised workers and the rising number of individual members, which yielded a growing asymmetry between the ACTU and the ALP. Such organisational asymmetry strengthened the bargaining position of the ALP, so much so that despite a significant drop in real wages the unions refrained from practising an aggressive wages policy.

In the USA, redistributive games were more complex. US party leaders find it extremely difficult to maintain party unity and American social policy has always been underpinned by cross-party coalitions. Presiding over divided government, President Clinton was nevertheless able to exploit the fragmentation of US political parties to pass the welfare reform, avoiding charges of inaction.

Key importance is ascribed to the structure of power within governing parties because it enhances or undercuts strategic flexibility (Kitschelt, 1994). Thus in devising redistributive policies, leaders have to consider which proposals jeopardise their internal position by preventing them from fostering enduring alliances with actual or potential partners.

Opposition effects

We have seen how the internal life of ruling parties was significantly influenced by opposition effects. Cooperation or competition, or lack thereof, in the electoral and legislative arenas altered the options available to the bargaining partners. Redistributive strategies in the four countries made sense when we looked at the internal repercussions of interparty competition.

Canada provided compelling evidence of the distributional consequences of electoral competition. The distinctiveness of the Canadian experience rests on the role of an electoral rival. Entrance of the NDP into the electoral arena afforded Trudeau incentives to mobilise voters. In game-theoretic terms, expansionary policies were a dominant strategy in interparty competition: irrespective of the NDP's redistributive choices, generous social security benefits were Trudeau's optimal strategy, because they enabled him to expand his electoral support and at the same time to consolidate his internal position with respect to the Turnites; similarly, whatever the choices of the Liberal government, the pursuit of generous benefits was the NDP's optimal strategy to garner electoral support.

The challenge from the left of the political spectrum impinged on the outcome of bargaining games between the Liberal pro-welfare and antiwelfare coalitions. Trudeau availed himself of the opportunities offered by the blackmail potential of the NDP, turning vulnerability into an asset for the Liberal pro-welfare alliance.

The interplay between Opposition effects and factional manoeuvring was also evident in Britain. Neither the SDP nor the Labour Party were able to provide a credible threat to Conservative rule. This situation deprived the wets of fundamental ammunition in the struggle for relative dominance within the Conservative organisation – namely the electoral weakness of the leading elite. In contrast to Australia, Opposition effects in Britain were reinforced by the centralisation of power in the Conservative Party that hindered internal rivalry. Strong party leadership and weak interparty competition explained why the dries were able to radicalise their anti-progressive stance and to engage in vote mobilisation by capitalising on the geographical distribution of poverty.

The fact that in Australia the Opposition was in a shambles reduced the incentives for Labor right-wingers to reach a compromise with minority factions. Left-wingers could easily be marginalised in the decisionmaking process because unpopular redistributive strategies carried low electoral risks. The pivotal role of the Centre-Left, however, meant that an enduring alliance with the Right could only be stipulated if right-wingers tempered their market-oriented policies. Hence the decentralisation of power within the ALP limited the margin of freedom that feeble Opposition effects had conferred on Labor right-wingers.

The redistributive impact of a united Opposition was evident in the US after the Republican landslide victory of 1994 redefined the welfare reform agenda. The Republicans' initiatives were far less favourable to low-income families but their support was vital for passing the law so President Clinton accepted to sign a bill largely on Republican terms.

When examining the redistributive choices of ruling parties along the dimensions of faction–voter alignments, the organisational and institutional power, and Opposition effects we see that sudden u-turns in transfer policies, curious asymmetries in social security benefits, and counterintuitive allocations of costs and benefits to voters become more intelligible. The ways in which faction leaders engaged in vote mobilisation, shaped the party image or defined privileged and less-privileged groups, were partly a function of their freedom to manoeuvre. This freedom, in turn, was largely explicable in terms of the distribution of power within the party organisation, in the institutional setting and in the electoral arena.

COMPARING REDISTRIBUTIVE GAMES

Stripping party behaviour of all misleading monolithic assumptions reveals that issues of party image and strategies of conflict management often coexist. Thus we are able to reconcile some of the core insights of political sociology and rational choice approaches and to provide a more encompassing framework for analysing the redistributive impact of ruling parties. In seeking to maximise their internal power, faction leaders manipulate entitlement and eligibility rules to mould new social constituencies.

The analytical gains offered in this book may be grasped by comparing my perspective with conventional interpretations of the redistributive impact of parties. Contrary to the class politics view endorsed by Hibbs and Dennis (1988), my account suggests that the dominant coalition consolidates its position within the party organisation not by devising redistributive programmes that reflect social cleavages, but by constructing new social constituencies which support and legitimise its dominant position. Thus my account turns the class politics view on its head. It highlights the fact that social constituencies are not pre-given constructs and points to the independent role of party politics in the apportionment of costs and benefits.

The second difference is that Hibbs and Dennis (1988) neglect the pervasiveness of rational, self-interested behaviour which precludes them the possibility of detecting non-societal, elite induced cleavages. In this way the authors fall prey to what Wilson defines as the Marxian fallacy, the belief 'that every organisation represents the underlying objective interests or social condition of its members' (Wilson, 1995: 14). The retrenchment of redistributive policies in Australia warns against the limits of interpretations which discard elite-initiated redistributive outputs. Even more blatant is the US case where a Democratic administration overturned decades of American social policy.

To the extent that changes in cash income were the result of discretionary policy choices I checked conventional public choice explanations regarding the incentives for income redistribution. We saw that the median-voter hypothesis was partly supported in Canada where median-income groups slightly improved their takings. However, a detailed examination of population deciles also suggested that the poorest 10 per cent had gained from government intervention, thus questioning the redistributive emphasis on median groups.

Even less-supportive evidence was found in both Britain and Australia. In these countries the rich households disproportionately benefited from the distribution of post-tax–post-transfer income to the disadvantage of middle- and lower-income groups. Median-income voters were net losers in the redistributive process. Hence the LIS data provided insufficient evidence to support the median-voter model, at least with respect to the distribution of disposable income. In so doing my results confound formal theories of redistributive policies that are associated with Downsian spatial modelling.

Patchy evidence, however, may reflect shaky theoretical premises. Assuming that the median voter and the median-income citizen overlap is perhaps a touch too simple. It is likely that the median-voter will be richer than the median-income person because there are turnout differences between income deciles, with much lower participation rates among the less well-off.

Another issue regards the choice between an absolute or relative income hypothesis. Real standards of living have been increasing in developed countries and we may expect to see a shift to retrenchment policies as real incomes increase. On the other hand, a relative rather than an absolute approach to income emphasises the fact that it is peoples' comparisons with others that are important, and therefore even if absolute income is higher some groups may nonetheless believe that they are falling behind their peers, and thus become dissatisfied with the government. The relative approach makes explicit the view that poverty standards should reflect changes affecting the general standard of living of a given society (Korpi, 1980).

A third issue relates to the redistribution of individuals into different income deciles. Some low-middle-income manual workers may have become unemployed over the periods considered and therefore moved from the middle income to the lower decile. The composition of different income deciles may have changed, and there is evidence in Britain that this had been the case in the mid 1980s (Heath *et al.*, 1991: 161–162). It is hoped that the growing availability of panel data may help in overcoming these problems.[1] A final point to note is that in single plurality systems rather than the median it may be the marginal voter which makes the difference (Cox, 1997).

I also examined roughly nineteen alterations in transfer policies introduced before and after eight elections. The picture that emerged was rather more complex than the one depicted by the political business cycle. Approximately 50 per cent of the changes were congruent with the predictions of this model, suggesting that the timing of elections was but one of several factors which influenced transfer policies.

In some cases transfer policy changes were in stark contrast with the PBC. Most striking was Hawke's announcement of the 'harshest budget for decades' just one year before the 1987 elections. In Britain, the Conservative governments reduced the scope and level of benefits regardless of the timing of elections and introduced controversial social security policies, such as the taxation of unemployment benefits in 1982, just one year before the 1983 elections. In Canada, cutbacks in unemployment benefits and family allowances were suddenly implemented in 1978, again just one year before the 1979 general election.

Conventional rational choice interpretations of redistributive policies failed to explain asymmetries in the allocation of welfare benefits. Why were unemployment benefits in Britain visibly curtailed and their real value reduced while the real value of pension benefits was protected?

---

[1] With the exception of a few countries, at the moment panel data on income distribution are not readily available, but see Goodin *et al.*, 1999.

And why was means testing in Australia counterbalanced with the Family Plan that increased spending for very poor families. Or, why did Trudeau initially advocate and then oppose generous benefits? And, finally, why did Clinton sign the Personal Responsibility Act just a few months before the Presidential election. These questions suggest that redistributive processes are more articulated and multi-layered than is usually assumed by available rational choice models.

A similar critique can be levelled at the class politics view. This perspective was particularly ill suited to interpret transfer policies in Canada where the core–periphery cleavage was, and still appears to be, the dominant political conflict. Welfare spending in the late 1960s and early 1970s redressed long-lasting imbalances between rich and poor provinces, rather than between rich- and poor-income groups. Generous family allowances clearly benefited a greater proportion of the population in the Atlantic regions and in Quebec because there were higher poverty rates in those provinces. The Canadian case supports the contention that the potential of the welfare state as an instrument of national integration on a territorial basis is underexplored (Banting, 1995). Sophisticated interpretations of the salience of class politics in shaping the social role of the state do not fully capture the experience of large countries characterised by territorial conflicts.

In my account, the salience of the class cleavage in Canada was a result of interparty competition between 1970 and 1974. Liberal leaders engaged in vote mobilisation over class issues by advocating universal social security to insure low-income groups from the risk of poverty. Vote mobilisation aimed at capturing sections of the NDP's electorate by downplaying the core–periphery cleavage and magnifying the class cleavage.

In Britain, as well, the class politics view was incongruent with the peculiarities of redistribution. Transfer policies seemed to encourage electoral coalitions between sections of one income class, most notably pensioners, and people in work. The relative generosity of pension benefits as compared to unemployment benefits during the first two Conservative terms probably increased the traditional concentration of Conservative voters in the South, where pensioners constituted a sizeable minority of the population.

Perhaps the clearest refutation of the class politics view were Hawke's policy initiatives undertaken against low-income families. The Labor government passed social security legislation which doubtlessly damaged the economic position of some traditional Labor supporters.

These policies included the abolition of unemployment benefits for those aged 16–17, the means testing of family allowances and the asset test for the elderly. Labor's attack on targeted groups of the state-dependent population cannot be adequately explained in class politics terms.

The US is more difficult to assess in class politics terms because of the absence of strong Socialist or Labor parties. However, over the 1980s the Democratic Party was considered the only nationally organised political force actively working to defend the lines of social provision launched in the New Deal. The fact that a Democratic administration accepted the demise of the AFDC points to the limits of the class politics framework.

Evidence from the four countries contributes to general knowledge of redistributive strategies, but it also brings to the fore important questions disguised by demand-driven approaches. It indicates that party elites can manipulate transfer policies and activate or repress societal cleavages in order to mobilise commitments to particular projects for the future.

Arguably, the most fundamental criticism to demand-driven approaches of income redistribution is their unidirectional conceptualisation of elite-voter alignments. By insisting on exogenous determinants of redistributive policies, these models unduly neglect the fact that party elites may autonomously alter the distribution of costs and benefits to mould electoral constituencies.

My account lends credence to the view that party leaders are sometimes constrained in their redistributive options by the wishes of party members and voters. For instance, Thatcher's appeal to the party rank-and-file and the successful campaign for membership recruitment signalled to the wets that Conservative activists favoured a radical change from previous redistributive policies. Although Thatcher was the leader of a minority elite, her popularity among Conservative members and their readiness to identify with Thatcherite policies, assuaged the wets' internal opposition.

In Australia, the Centre-Left faction aimed at guarding Labor's image as a party concerned with redistributive issues. The Centre-Left availed itself of the opportunity offered by its pivotal position to allay the economic burden on traditional Labor voters. Strategies of conflict management and issues of identity again overlapped. Mixed interests resurfaced in the relationship between trade unions and ALP. The image of Labor as the party of the workers was guarded by the governments' commitment to a policy of full employment, despite Hawke's efforts to appeal to market-oriented voters. To be sure, the comparative resilience of welfare spending in Australia could be seen in terms of pragmatic electoral politics (Brett, 1999). Australia has compulsory voting and voter turn-out is always in excess of 90 per cent of the electorate; thus the poorer sections of the population do not fall out of electoral politics through apathy or alienation as is the case in the US. However, this book shows that strategic considerations regarding party members were equally important. In Canada and in the US, by contrast, the role of party members was less relevant, primarily because party organisations have never developed into fully fledged mass parties.

Another significant difference between conventional rational choice models and my perspective is the time dimension. I applied a two-stage analytical framework, which first considered the historical preconditions of factional manoeuvring and then examined the choice situation. Rational choice theorists typically analyse 'snapshots' of the redistributive process. In most cases, this book indicated that the driving forces behind income redistribution could not fully be understood by glimpsing a single instant, and that historical reconstructions were necessary to understand how the bargaining partners found themselves in that particular situation.

Advances in the theory of party politics have their strongest analytical bite where ruling parties have not chosen the strategies mandated by their ideologies or by vote-maximising accounts, but where internal processes of coalition building and factional strife can explain the actual outcome. While the definition of factions and tendencies may be difficult in comparative analyses (Harmel and Janda, 1993), my study shows that historical reconstructions of the choice situation throw considerable insight on internal divisions. Consistent with theoretical progress in actor-centred institutionalism this book stresses the importance of historical developments in narrowing the choice-set of institutional actors and in linking the stages of the decisionmaking process through time (North, 1990: 112–115).

REASSESSING THE PARTY–POLICY LINK

Three propositions can be derived from the historical reconstructions of factional politics and income redistribution in the four countries. First, new social policies are often sparked by the *formation* of party factions. Emerging factions need supporters – party members and voters – to legitimise their struggle for internal power. Since redistributive policies define the categories in need new redistributive programmes may forge new social constituencies. This statement is substantiated by evidence from the four countries.

In Canada, the evolution of the left-wing faction led by Gordon in the early 1960s confronted the business and financial community, which had traditionally backed the Liberal antiwelfare coalition. The new faction aimed at introducing progressive redistributive policy and wished to protect the economic welfare of the vulnerable people. This programmatic stance involved a reexamination of the redistributive goals of the Liberal Party.

In a similar vein, but with opposite effects, in Britain the real break with post-war consensus was marked by the anti-egalitarian drive of the dries. We have seen that the formation of the internal coalition led by Joseph and Thatcher in the mid 1970s was intimately connected to questions of income inequality and to the redefinition of categories in need through the stigmatisation of some welfare recipients. In Australia the Centre-Left faction was anchored to the defence of income redistribution. And in the US members of the DLC pledged for vigorous welfare reform. These developments corroborate my hypothesis that redistributive policies are an integral part of factional politics, for they trace the boundaries between included and excluded groups.

The second proposition is that the *consolidation* of specific factions in a dominant position sparks the refashioning of the party image. When the party organisation finds a new image it testifies to the end of an era and to the success of those 'new faces' holding positions of responsibility in the internal hierarchy. In Australia, the Hawke–Keating partnership aimed at recasting Labor as the party of fiscal responsibility and wealth production against the Left's legacy of profligacy and redistribution. Right-wingers appeared more concerned with establishing a new party image in order to estrange internal, rather than external, rivals. In Britain there is scholarly consensus that Thatcher's appeal to monetarism was not entirely guided by economic reasons, and that recrafting the party image was just as important. Throwing the burden of fiscal restraint on the shoulders of 'scroungers' was instrumental to internal disputes. It facilitated the forging of new symbols in order to reconstruct the party image. In Canada, Trudeau's consolidation at the top of the Liberal Party in the early 1970s was associated with generous transfer payments aimed at moulding the party as the protector of the less-privileged people. The US, again, represents a most vivid example of this proposition. Clinton campaigned as a New Democrat who made welfare reform the centrepiece of his policy agenda.

The third proposition is that the *demise* of party factions brings about a radicalisation of redistributive programmes if interparty competition is ineffective. Unconstrained by internal and external credible threats the dominant coalition enjoys ample margins of manoeuvre to undertake radical departures from previous redistributive commitments. Evidence from Australia and Britain suggests that the demise of left-wing factions and the concomitant rise of right-wingers bolstered market-oriented provisions, irrespective of the location of the governing party on the ideological *continuum*. Hawke was relatively insensitive to the core supporters of the defeated faction and simultaneously mobilised voters to sustain the new dominant coalition. Factional conflicts can ignite social conflicts by resetting the boundaries between social groups. Focusing on the formation, consolidation and demise of party factions sheds considerable light on the development and selection of social policies, enhancing our understanding of the driving forces behind income redistribution.

I began this book by raising the question of whether there was any relationship between income distribution and liberal democracy. The end product suggests that we should be sceptical in embracing any deterministic reply. If redistributive policies partly reflect the equilibrium solution of factional games then politicians may level or exacerbate income differences irrespective of their ideology or the distributive demands of their core constituencies.

It should be acknowledged that this book explores a relatively uncharted area. It offers a theoretical perspective that calls attention to processes that seem to explain a variety of redistributive policies. This perspective is quite different from the usual way of examining the redistributive impact of parties – namely by identifying their stated goals or their electoral interests. I have argued that advances in the theory of political parties provide important insights on the incentives for generous or stiffer cash benefits. A combination of game theory and institutionalist approaches helped understanding of the dynamics of redistributive policies in the four liberal welfare regimes.

Research on strategic interaction within parties is still in its infancy, and the development of a rigorous and realistic model of intraparty politics has proved a daunting task (Laver and Shepsle, 1996). However, we need not despair. This study demonstrates that developments in the literature of party goals, party competition and party organisations can profitably be integrated into a more comprehensive framework. Advances in the theory of party politics have demonstrated a strong analytical bite where the ruling party did not choose the strategies mandated by its ideology or by vote-maximising accounts, but where internal processes of factional realignment helped explain the actual outcome.

The picture presented in this book shows that the party–policy link in the field of redistributive policies is potentially affected by a plurality of other social and institutional factors. In these concluding remarks we should note the degree of independence of the central banks in affecting policymaking. In comparative terms, the US Federal Reserve is a strongly independent central bank where the financial community rather than industry provides the main basis of societal support (Jayasuriya, 1994). The anti-inflationary policies pursued by the Federal Reserve in the United States reflects the dominance of financial rather than industrial sectors. In Australia the Reserve Bank lacks the strong connection between finance and industry that appears to be an essential component of effective central bank autonomy (Jayasuriya, 1994). More generally, central banks might limit policymakers because in a sense they are at the core of the internationalisation of the state (Strange, 1996).

Evaluating the distributional impact of ruling parties requires the identification of non-institutional effects on income inequality. Before proceeding further a word of warning is in order. It is very difficult to disentangle governmental and non-governmental effects. Partly the problem rests on behavioural responses; individuals may alter their behaviour as a reaction to government policies. Moreover, for the most part, social sciences are non-experimental, and this book is undoubtedly a non-experimental research where the causal mechanisms can only be inferred and not proved.

Nonetheless, there are sophisticated analytical techniques that help to understand more precisely the structure of income inequality. Decomposition techniques brought to the fore the role of demographic forces. Whether the grouping variable was age or household type, the results invariably indicated that demographic effects had a low impact on the level of income inequality. In Australia the ageing of the population and the slowdown in birth rates had a negligible impact on aggregate inequality over the 1980s. I found a similar pattern in Britain where the ageing of the population appeared less significant, in contrast to earlier results. In Canada the expectation that the 'baby boom' of the 1960s had distributional effects in the 1970s was largely refuted by the much greater impact of the within-group component.

A largely unexpected result was the low distributional impact of household composition. The decline in the traditional family composed of a couple with children and the concomitant increase of one-parent families should have in principle amplified the upward drift. Smaller households usually have a negative distributional impact because they prevent income pooling. My findings, however, suggested that within-household inequality accounted for most of the inequality growth.

The amount of inequality explained by population characteristics was rather small, calling into question demographic explanations. This was a very interesting conclusion, because it implicity underlined the relevance of other sources of income inequality. The marginality of demographic forces meant that I could safely concentrate on wage differentials and cash transfers.

Wage dispersion presented significant differences in Canada, Britain and Australia primarily, but not exclusively, because the time-frame was different. International comparisons show that trends in inequality of earnings in the 1980s differed from those of the 1970s (OECD, *Employment Outlook*, 1993: 157). Over the 1970s the earning distribution was relatively stable, while in the 1980s it exhibited a wider spread; this variation in wage differentials was reflected in the three countries. In Canada over the 1970s the distribution of market income was more concentrated towards the middle, with both upper and lower tails decreasing constantly. As a consequence, the proportion of the population in the middle-income class grew, suggesting market effects behind the drop in inequality. The tendency towards depolarisation in Canada sharply contrasted with income polarisation in both Australia and Britain. In these countries market income differentials showed a widening gap between rich and poor. Furthermore, the association of income polarisation in the market sphere and inequality growth in both Australia and Britain adds weight to research findings which detect a clear link between inequality and wage dispersion (Wes, 1996).

There are significant differences between Canada, Britain and Australia. For a start, the economic climate was different. The early 1970s were a period of general growth and expansion of the welfare state, and therefore the distribution of market income in Canada inevitably presents a different picture. Market income inequality in Australia is less pronounced than in Britain primarily because of the historical role of the Australian arbitration system discussed previously. Moreover, immigrants in Australia usually fare better than in other settlement countries because the arbitration system ensures that immigration cannot be used to undercut wages. All workers are legally entitled to the same level of protection and this reduces the possibility that immigrants are exploited. Immigrants in Australia come as settlers whereas in the United States they often acquire the status of guest workers. Today all four countries have stronger anti-immigration policies than they used to and discrimination is sometimes disguised behind attacks on unproductive immigrants living on the dole. In Australia, Pauline Hanson, leader of the One Nation Party, is following the tradition of White Australian policy and in Canada the Reform Party is going in a similar direction.

The emphasis on market forces in formal distributional analyses has often meant that little or no attention has been paid to the impact of transfer payments. And yet widening wage differentials expand the ranks of the 'working poor' and demand for social transfers rises. This book took the investigation one step forward and raised the question regarding the role of cash income. The results yielded consistent answers: cash benefits acted as a brake on upward movements in income inequality.

THE FUTURE OF REDISTRIBUTION

In the past 20 years Canada, Britain, Australia and the United States and many other Western industrialised countries have experienced a rise in popularity of ideologies celebrating market liberalism. Income redistribution by means of cash transfers is now undergoing the most sustained analysis in a generation, and questions of selectivity versus universalism dominate the debate (Toso, 1997). Conservatives have been in the forefront of the major criticism but in some cases left-wingers also joined the discussion, with the British Labour government being the most recent addition. One important outcome has been dramatic changes in social policy, which may have significant consequences for the most vulnerable groups, such as lone mothers (Land and Lewis, 1997; O'Connor, Orloff and Shaver, 1998: 1–3; Orloff, 1996).

These changes are reflected in a slowdown in transfer spending growth over the 1980s. Since the 1960s income transfer spending directed at those of working age rose on average about 3.5 percentage points of GDP until 1980 (OECD, 1996). Expansion in the coverage and

Table 6.1. *Trends in income inequality in nine Western countries, 1970s–1990s*
(Gini coefficient per cent for adjusted household post-tax–post-transfer income)

	1970s		1980s		1990s	
US	1979	33.0	1986	35.5	1994	38.3
UK	1979	27.6	1986	30.3	1995	34.4
Israel	1979	33.7	1986	33.0	1992	33.8
Australia	1981	30.2	1986	30.9	1994	33.6
France	1979	30.8	1984	30.4	1989	33.5
Germany	1978	23.0	1984	26.4	1994	30.7
Canada	1981	31.1	1987	30.6	1994	29.8
Norway	1979	24.9	1986	24.3	1995	25.0
Sweden	1981	19.9	1987	22.9	1992	23.8

generosity of transfer programmes rather than changes in demographic factors, such as the share of the working population, explain the variation. By the same token, in the 1980s modifications in eligibility and entitlement rules were more important in explaining variations in spending than changes in the size of the target group (i.e., those potentially falling within the scope of each programme). A key feature appears to have been a tightening up of access to and benefits from transfer programmes, with the exception of disability and retirement programmes (OECD, 1996: 151).

It is worth contrasting these policy changes with inequality trends in industrialised countries over the past decade. Table 6.1 displays inequality outcomes between the late 1970s and the mid 1990s for nine Western countries. The evidence indicates that in some countries inequality consistently grows over the two decades, but in other countries it declines, supporting the argument that there is no inevitable tendency for income inequality to rise. Germany stands out as the country with the sharpest increase, with the Gini values rising by 7.7 percentage points and the United Kingdom follows suit with a surge of 6.8 points. Canada, however, continues a declining trend and in both Israel and Norway the variation is very modest. This variety of experiences adds weight to the contention that national factors are at work.

Among these national factors, this book has primarily explored the role of income transfer programmes. A closer look at the redistributive impact of these programmes in the 1990s can be gauged by inspecting table 6.2 which sets out the Gini index for market income (pre-transfer income) and post-transfer income. In all the nine countries market

Table 6.2. *Income inequality before and after transfer income in nine Western countries 1980s–1990s (Gini coefficient per cent for adjusted income)*

	1980s			1990s		
Country	Pre-transfer income	Post-transfer income	Reduction from transfers	Pre-transfer income	Post-transfer income	Reduction from transfers
US	47.8	40.1	7.7	51.3	43	8.3
Canada	44.2	34.5	9.7	47.5	34.6	12.9
Australia	47.5	37.0	10.5	50.8	38.8	12.0
France	56.2	35.5	24.4	58.0	35.5	22.5
Germany	52.2	31.8	20.4	54.5	36.6	17.9
UK	53.6	34.9	18.9	54.7	38.4	16.3
Norway	43.5	28.6	14.9	47.3	29.9	17.4
Sweden	47.3	27.5	19.8	52.3	27.2	25.1
IS	49.2	38.9	10.3	49.4	38.8	10.6

Notes: US86/ 94; CN87/ 94; AS 86/ 94; FR84/89; GE84/94; UK86/95; NW86/95; SW87/92; IS86/92

income inequality rose between the mid 1980s and the mid 1990s; the salient point is that post-transfer income inequality dropped in Norway, Sweden and Israel and was stable in Canada. These figures show that despite a general tendency towards retrenchment, the redistributive options of ruling parties can still make a considerable difference in the standard of living of many individuals. In the light of research findings reporting a widespread concern in industrialised countries for the rise of the 'new poverty' grown out of the late 1980s recession (Eardley *et al.*, 1996), it is reassuring that governments may actively seek to mitigate deprivation. However, because poverty is a culture which is transmitted across generations, the general contraction of entitlement and eligibility rules is alarming for future generations (O'Neill and Sweetman, 1995). Even granting that income mobility is greater in the 1990s than in the 1970s, this does not mean that we should stop worrying about poverty (Hills, 1998a).

When it comes to political representation the poor face special difficulties for they lack traditional political resources of money, education, information and organisation. If they are represented at all, the disadvantaged invariably depend, at least in part, on the efforts of advocates on their behalf. Inevitably these surrogates have concerns and priorities of their own. During the 1980s the traditional allies of the poor (unions and civil rights groups) were preoccupied with their own concerns, including their own organisational weakness (Imig, 1996).

This book shows that when policymakers are worried about the image they project to the voters, issues of social exclusion and income redistribution may overlap. We have seen that redistributive policies carve the boundaries between protected and risk-exposed groups, and that policymakers are willing to alter these boundaries when they wish to shed an old party image. In such circumstances, redistributive policies may fail to alleviate deprivation.

Such inadequacy of conventional policies to fight poverty has prompted some political philosophers to argue in favour of a basic income, an income unconditionally paid to all on an individual basis without means test or work requirement (Baker, 1992; van Parijs, 1995; van der Veen, 1998). Another solution is to expand needs-based government funding in education, health and housing (Hendry, 1998). This book indicates that normative accounts of income redistribution might benefit from explanations which bring into sharp focus political games and redistribution.

Technical addendum

THE EMPIRICAL ANALYSIS OF POVERTY AND INEQUALITY

A rigorous analysis of the redistributive impact of parties inevitably raises a number of long-lasting questions associated with empirical work on poverty and inequality. How sensitive are poverty estimates to where the poverty line is drawn? How confident can we be in the empirical results and how should these results be presented and interpreted? How can we analyse the constituent components of the structure of income inequality? Reduced to their essence, it may appear that these are purely formal problems. Yet, although the subject matter of the empirical analysis of poverty and inequality is largely technique, the techniques involved are an essential prerequisite for coping with the analysis of economic problems in a rigorous fashion (Cowell, 1995: 16).

Evaluating the redistributive impact of governing parties entails formidable difficulties of data collection, of identification and measurement of poverty, of choices between different principles of equality, etc. Whilst a comprehensive treatment of all these issues lies beyond the scope of this work, some attention must be paid to methodological problems – not least to evaluate the statistical reliability of my results. Furthermore, in the empirical analysis I identify demographic and market effects on inequality, I use several inequality indices, and I compare the relative economic position of sub-groups of the population at one datapoint and between different periods. The methodological and substantive complexity of this kind of work soon becomes unmanageable without the aid of analytical techniques.

POVERTY HEAD-COUNT

Two important methodological aspects of any empirical study of inequality and poverty are what are known as the identification and the aggregation issues (Abul Naga, 1994). The identification problem confronts the decision regarding who is poor, and sometimes it also deals with the question of how poor is that person. It emerges whenever income is not observed or when the data are subject to measurement error.[1] The aggregation problem is concerned with summarizing the individual poverty data into a measure of poverty.

This book deals with the problem of aggregation, comparing poverty cross-nationally between different years and different subgroups of the population. Such comparisons are obviously affected by what conception of poverty one has in mind. The literature on poverty typically distinguishes between the absolute and the relative approach to poverty. In the absolute approach to poverty, the poverty standard is defined in terms of consumption of specific goods, and is not influenced by the general living standards of the society. It takes into account basic needs for survival, such as nutritional requirements, clothing and housing.

The main problem with this perspective is that minimum cost diets vary widely among individuals and with the level of development of a society. For this reason I have opted for the relative approach to poverty, which makes explicit the view that poverty standards should reflect changes affecting the general standard of living of a given society (Korpi, 1980). In this manner, it is possible to evaluate whether ruling parties redesign entitlement rights to adjust the relative economic position of social groups.

One way of defining relative poverty is in terms of 'economic distance' from a specified average standard. The most widely used economic distance measure is one half of median income, which has the advantage of taking directly into account changes in society through changes in median income. As a measure of 'average' income the median is better than the mean because the income distribution is typically skewed to the right. In this situation the arithmetic mean would be always higher than the median as it is affected by extreme values.

Summary measures for the analysis of poverty are often presented in the form of head-counts, that is, the proportion of the population below a given poverty line. Estimates of poverty rates are very sensitive to where the poverty line is drawn. Head-counts can vary quite dramati-

---

[1] The income status of a family may be measured with error because it is systematically underreported. There is a vast array of reasons why household heads may have an incentive to understate their resources. Some authors believe that families may benefit from welfare programmes when their income is low (Glewwe, 1990). Others maintain that the identification of poverty can be impaired by the existence of market imperfections, such as imperfect information, discrimination, obstacles to trade, and suggest the adoption of multiple indicators of poverty as a solution (Abul Naga, 1994).

cally with a small variation in the poverty line. The most common reason for this sensitivity is the 'clustering' of income units around the poverty line. Clustering effects are problematic for assessing the redistributive impact of governing parties because they may significantly alter the estimates. For example, if we observe that the proportion of the population below 50 per cent of median income has dropped in the past ten years, we might be inclined to think that overall poverty has fallen. A closer look at the data, however, could show that the proportion of the population below 60 per cent of the median has sharply increased, implying that our previous impression of declining poverty was misguided.

To avoid clustering effects, I have handled the problem by using three poverty lines (Mitchell, 1991). In addition to setting the usual poverty line at 50 per cent of median income, one line was set slightly lower at 40 per cent and another line was set slightly higher, at 60 per cent of median income; I then reported poverty rates at each of these levels. This methodological rigour means that a more accurate assessment of the redistributive impact of ruling parties is possible. I am able to provide a more comprehensive picture of poverty rates among the state-dependent population; I am also able to identify and compare movements between different poverty lines and datapoints.

Equivalence scales

Problems of aggregation and reliability emerge from comparisons of economic well being among households with different 'needs'. A single person with disposable income of £300 per month will, for instance, enjoy a very different level of economic well being from that of a family with three children but with the same disposable income. It is therefore important for a sound distributional analysis to capture this difference.

In this book I 'equivalise' the income of households with different economic needs by taking into account their size and composition. The 'equivalent income' is the standard of living available to each member of the household unit, assuming income pooling. Cash income is adjusted by the number of adults in a family in order to construct a measure of the level of economic welfare available to the family. Equivalence scales are valuable tools in assessing the redistributive impact of ruling parties because they allow for fundamental differences in need between households. These differences in need define the social categories at risk, such as single-parents, families, the elderly, etc. As mentioned in the

Introduction, coalition building within the ruling party is enmeshed with shifting coalitions of risk categories. Thus in order to detect the role of transfer policies in connecting party factions to risk categories it is necessary to know the level of economic well-being enjoyed by these groups.

Several *equivalence scales* have been constructed to allow comparisons across households and their members. The use of a particular equivalence scale can greatly influence the distributional analysis of economic welfare within and between societies (Coulter, Cowell and Jenkins, 1992). Unfortunately, there is no scholarly consensus regarding the appropriate equivalence scale, although research findings show that inequality and poverty estimates are sensitive to changes in the incorporation of needs (Duclos and Mercader, 1993: 39–40). In this study I adopt the OECD equivalence scale which is one of the most commonly used in developed countries for distributional assessments. This scale was suggested in the 'OECD list of social indicators' (1982) and it distinguishes only between children and adults.

Research on income inequality thus involves several methodological choices: choices of scale relativities, of inequality measures and poverty indicators, of definitions of resources (e.g., money income, expenditures, market income, etc.) and the choice of the unit of analysis. The role of these factors is directly or indirectly affected by the use of a particular equivalence scale. This means that, while equivalence scales make it possible to take into account differences in economic needs, they only partially remove the sensitivity of distributional results to the choice of the income unit within which resources are shared.

Decomposing income inequality

The sensitivity of distributional estimates to scale choice suggests that an effort should be made to strengthen the robustness of our empirical results. This I have done by decomposing aggregate inequality into a series of subcomparisons of the distributions for specified population groups (e.g., household type, age group). As Cowell put it, a drop in inequality could be an optical illusion if we have not taken into consideration demographic movements, or how income varies between and within different age groups (1995: 130). Alterations to the age structure, such as lower birth rates or the growing number of elderly, may affect the distribution of income among individuals (von Weizächer, 1995). Elderly people are overrepresented in lower-income groups, and, therefore, the ageing of the population may widen income differentials. By the same token, rising inequality could be the outcome of changing household size and composition. In the post-war period the number of large families steadily declined, while the number of single households and lone parents gradually increased. Smaller households may have a negative distributional impact because they prevent income pooling.

To assess the impact of demographic variables I decompose distributional comparisons for age groups and household types into two main contributions, the 'between-group' and 'within-group' component. Disentangling the within-group and between-group inequality components enables us to study more precisely the redistributive impact of governing parties: the higher the contribution of the 'between-groups' components, i.e., the stronger the association of the grouping factor with aggregate inequality, the more negligible the distributional role of transfer policies.

Inequality aggregation results can be expressed in simple terms, because total inequality is an additive function of between-group and within-group inequality. The between-group component of inequality is found by assuming that everyone within a group receives that group's mean income: it is independent of redistribution within any of the groups. Within-group inequality is a weighted average of inequality in each subgroup. By using decomposition techniques, I can detect the impact of three main components on the inequality trend: changes in the size of selected demographic groups (e.g., elderly, young, single households, families, etc.); shifts in the level of inequality within each group; relative variations in the groups' mean incomes. The decomposition is consistent in the sense that the sum of these three factors is equal to the change in overall inequality.

MEASURING INCOME INEQUALITY

Several other methodological choices need to be made when comparing income distributions between and within subgroups of the population, or within and between countries (Atkinson and Micklewright, 1992; van Ginneken and Park, 1984). The first choice to be made is related to the concept of income: inequality of what? In the three case studies, I use several income concepts according to the question posed.[2] Market income, for instance, is more appropriate when I discuss market effects

---

[2] Other individual resources, such as health and education, are important in assessing inequality. Their potential distributional impact, however, is outside the scope of this work.

Table A.1. *Ranking of ten OECD*
countries according to the bottom sensitive
Theil index (adjusted household
post-tax–post-transfer income)

Country	Theil index (%)
United States	21.3
France	17.9
Italy	16.6
United Kingdom	16.5
Australia	16.1
Canada	15.8
Netherlands	15.7
West Germany	13.5
Sweden	10.0
Norway	9.8

Note: The countries datasets are the following:
US, 1986; Australia, 1985–86; Italy 1986;
Canada, 1981; France 1984; United Kingdom
1986; Netherlands 1983; West Germany, 1984;
Sweden, 1987; Norway 1986.

on overall inequality. Net cash income, on the other hand, is the most accurate measure available in the LIS datasets for 'spendable income'. This measure includes all income from employment and self-employment, property income, occupational pensions and private cash transfers, as well as other cash income minus direct taxes. A broader definition of income would take into account non-cash transfers, such as social services,[3] as well as indirect taxes, capital gains and imputed rent, which are not considered in most national surveys.

The second choice refers to the problem of the time-span, inequality when? The time period considered affects the measurement of inequality. Life-time income, for instance, reduces the dispersion observed across the population. Since information on life-time income is seldom available I follow the convention to identify the contribution of age differences on overall inequality by using income decomposition methods (Jenkins, 1995).

Another set of questions is related to the thorny issue of whether one can unambiguously say that one distribution is more equal than an-

---

[3] The inclusion of non-cash transfers, however, would not necessarily reduce measured inequality. Le Grand and Winter (1987), for instance, find that almost all expenditure in social services in Britain benefits the better off to a greater extent than the poor.

Table A.2. *Ranking of ten OECD countries according to the middle-sensitive Gini coefficient*

Country	Gini coefficient (%)
United States	35.5
Australia	30.9
Italy	30.7
Canada	30.6
France	30.4
United Kingdom	30.3
Netherlands	29.4
West Germany	26.4
Norway	24.3
Sweden	22.9

other. The construction of inequality indices involves value judgements that are not necessarily desirable (Atkinson, 1989; Cowell, 1995: 60–65). Some indices, for instance, are bottom-sensitive, that is, transfers among lower-income groups yield larger effects on the index. Others are top sensitive, which means that it is transfers among upper-income groups which generate larger effects on the index. Thus the differing sensitivity of each index may reflect different rank orderings. Table A.1 ranks ten OECD countries according to the bottom-sensitive Their index. The table shows that in the mid 1980s the United States was the most unequal country, followed by France and Italy; West Germany and the Scandinavian countries were the most equal, with much lower Theil values. The United Kingdom, Australia and Canada were located in the middle of the ranking.

Table A.2. sets out the inequality ranking among these ten OECD countries when inequality is measured by the Gini coefficient, which is a middle- (modal) sensitive index. Interestingly, some countries change their position quite dramatically, including Australia which moves from fifth position in table A.1 to second in table A.2; Canada also shifts from the sixth to the fourth position. Hence the distribution of income in both countries appears less equal when inequality is measured by the Gini coefficient. The differences between table A.1 and table A.2 derive from the construction of the inequality measures: the Theil index is bottom-sensitive and the Gini coefficient is sensitive to transfers at the mode of the distribution. Assuming that modal-income groups overlap with

Table A.3. *Ranking of ten OECD countries
according to the top sensitive coefficient of variation*

Country	Coefficient of variation (%)
France	148.0
Italy	74.4
West Germany	72.9
United States	69.9
United Kingdom	64.7
Canada	62.5
Australia	59.9
Sweden	57.0
Netherlands	54.6
Norway	44.3

middle-income groups, the latter fall behind when Gini is higher; in contrast, the poor are worse off when Theil increases.

In order to provide a more complete picture of the sensitivity of inequality indices used in the three countries, table A.3. sets out the values for a top-sensitive measure, the coefficient of variation. The first point to note about this table is the remarkable change in the rank ordering. France ranked fifth when inequality was measured with the Gini coefficient but now ranks first, replacing the United States as the most unequal country. West Germany undergoes a similar, albeit less dramatic, shift in the ranking. According to the values of the coefficient of variation, the living standards of upper-income groups slipped in France and West Germany. Other countries, such as Canada and the Netherlands, maintained a stable position in the middle, while the Scandinavian countries invariably were the most equal countries.

The examples above highlight the limits and the risks of choosing only one summary measure of inequality, because it inevitably embeds views regarding distributional justice.[4] Since results are sensitive to methodological choices, a carefully chosen small set of inequality measures is necessary. A reasonable choice is to use one bottom-sensitive index, another middle-sensitive and the third top-sensitive (Cowell, 1995: 54–65). If all measures agree on a comparison of two or more income distributions we can then be moderately sure of the results. If they disagree no unambiguous ranking is possible.

---

[4] Following Atkinson we could seek to parameterise differences of judgment, giving numerical measures of the degree of inequality conditional on the choice of a parameter which incorporates the distributional judgment (Atkinson, 1970).

Bibliography

Abramowitz, A. T. and Saunders, K. L. 1998. 'Party Polarization and Ideological Realignment', in Meisel, S., ed., *The Parties Respond*. Boulder, CO: Westview Press.

Abul Naga R. H. 1994. 'Identifying the Poor: A Multiple Indicator Approach', Distributional Analysis Research Programme, Discussion Paper No. DARP-9, London School of Economics, London.

Akard, P. 1998. 'Where Are All the Democrats? The Limits of Economic Policy Reform', in Lo, C. Y. H. and Schwartz, M. eds., *Social Policy and the Conservative Agenda*. Malden, MA: Blackwell.

Alber, J. 1997. 'Il ripensamento del welfare state in Germania e negli Stati Uniti', *Rivista Italiana di Scienza Politica*, 27: 49–99.

Aldrich, J. 1995. *Why Parties? The Origin and Transformation of Political Parties in America*. Chicago: University of Chicago Press.

Aldrich, J. and McGinnis, M. D. 1989. 'A Model of Party Constraints on Optimal Candidate Positions', in Johnson, P. E., ed., *Formal Theories of Politics: Mathematical Modelling in Political Science*. Oxford: Pergamon Press.

Alesina, A. 1989. 'Politics and Business Cycles in Industrial Democracies', *Economic Policy*, 8: 57–98.

Alesina, A. and Rosenthal, H. 1995. *Partisan Politics, Divided Government, and the Economy*. Cambridge: Cambridge University Press.

Alford, J. and Brady, D. 1993. 'Personal and Partisan Advantage in US Congressional Elections, 1846–1990', in Dodd, L. and Oppenheimer, B. I., eds., *Congress Reconsidered*. Washington, DC: Congressional Quarterly Press.

Angell, H. M. 1987. 'Duverger, Epstein and the Problem of the Mass Party: The Case of the Parti Québécois', *Canadian Journal of Political Science*, 20: 363–378.

Apps, P. 1997a. 'Income Distribution, Redistribution and Incentives', Centre for Economic Policy Research, Discussion Paper No. 379, Canberra, The Australian National University.

1997b. 'A Tax-Mix Change: Effects on Income Distribution, Labour Supply and Saving Behaviour', Centre for Economic Policy Research, Discussion Paper No. 371, Canberra, The Australian National University.

Aranson, P. and Ordeshook, P. 1972. 'Spatial Strategies for Sequential Elections', in Niemu, R. G. and Weisberg, H. F., eds., *Probability Models of Collective Decision-Making*. Columbus, Ohio: Charles E. Merrill.

Argy, V. 1992. *Australian Macroeconomic Policy in a Changing World Environment, 1973–90*. Sydney: Allen & Unwin.

van Arnhem, C. J. M. and Schotsman, G. 1982. 'Do Parties Affect the Distribution of Incomes? The Case of Advanced Capitalist Democracies', in Castles, F., ed., *The Impact of Parties*. London: Sage.

Atkeson, L. 1993. 'Moving Toward Unity', *American Political Quarterly*, 21: 272–289.

Atkinson, A. B. 1970. 'On the Measurement of Inequality', *Journal of Economic Theory*, 2: 244–263.

 1989. 'Measuring Inequality and Differing Social Judgments', Luxembourg Income Study Working Paper No. 27.

 1995a. 'Income Maintenance for the Unemployed in Britain and the Response to High Unemployment', in Atkinson, A. B., *Incomes and the Welfare State*. Cambridge: Cambridge University Press.

 1995b. *Incomes and the Welfare State*. Cambridge: Cambridge University Press.

 1995c. 'What is Happening to the Distribution of Income in the UK?', in Atkinson, A. B., *Incomes and the Welfare State*. Cambridge: Cambridge University Press.

 1996. 'Seeking to Explain the Distribution of Income', in Hills, J., ed., *New Inequalities*. Cambridge: Cambridge University Press.

 1997. 'Bringing Income Distribution in from the Cold', *Economic Journal*, 107: 297–321.

Atkinson, A. B. and Hills, J. 1998. 'Exclusion, Employment and Opportunity', eds. Centre for the Analysis of Social Exclusion, CASE paper 4, London School of Economics and Political Science, London.

Atkinson, A. B. and Micklewright, J. 1989. 'Turning the Screw: Benefits for the Unemployed 1979–1988', in Dilnot, A. and Walker, I. eds., *The Economics of Social Security*. Oxford: Oxford University Press.

 1992. *Economic Transformation and the Distribution of Income in Eastern Europe*. Cambridge: Cambridge University Press.

Atkinson A. B., Hills, J. and Le Grand, J. 1986. 'The Welfare State in Britain 1970–1985: extent and effectiveness', WSP/9, STICERD.

Atkinson, A. B., Rainwater, L. and Smeeding, T. M. 1995. *Income Distribution in European Countries. Evidence from the Luxembourg Income Study*. OECD.

Aughey, A. and Norton, P. 1981. *Conservative and Conservatism*. London: Temple Smith.

Axworthy, T. and Trudeau, P. 1990. *Towards a Just Society*. Ottawa: Penguin Books.

Azoulay, D. 1995. 'The Evolution of Party Organization in Canada since 1900', *The Journal of Commonwealth and Comparative Politics*, 33: 185–208.

Bacharach, S. B. and Lawler, E. J. 1981. *Bargaining: Power, Tactics and Outcomes*. San Francisco: Jossey-Bass.

Bailey, D. J. and Naemark, M. 1977. 'A Note on the Transfer Payment Implications of Benefit and Contribution Operations under the Unemployment Insurance Act', *Canadian Statistical Review*, November: 3–10.

Baker, D., Gamble, A. and Ludlam, S. 1994. 'Mapping Conservative Fault Lines: Problems of Typology', in Dunleavy, P. and Stanyer, J., eds., *Contemporary Political Studies*. Political Studies Association of the UK.

Baker, J. 1992. 'An Egalitarian Case for Basic Income', in Van Parijs, P., ed., *Arguing for Basic Income*. London: Verso.

Baldwin, P. 1990. *The Politics of Social Solidarity: Class Bases of the European Welfare State 1875–1975*. Cambridge: Cambridge University Press.

Banting, K. 1979. *Poverty, Politics and Policy*. London: Macmillan.

1987. *The Welfare State and Canadian Federalism*. Montreal: McGill-Queen's University Press.

1995. 'The Welfare State as Statecraft: Territorial Politics and Canadian Social Policy', in Leibfried, S. and Pierson, P., eds., *European Social Policy. Between Fragmentation and Integration*. Washington DC: The Brookings Institution.

1997. 'The Social Policy Divide: The Welfare State in Canada and the United States', in Banting, K., Hoberg, G. and Simeon, R., eds., *Degrees of Freedom: Canada and the United States in a Changing World*. Montreal: McGill-Queen's University Press.

Barrileaux, C. 1997. 'Estimating the Effects of Electoral Competition and Party Strength on Public Policy', *American Journal of Political Science*, 41: 1462–1466.

Barry, B. 1998. *Social Exclusion, Social Isolation and the Distribution of Income*. Centre for Analysis of Social Exclusion, London School of Economics and Political Science, London.

1989. *Democracy and Power*. Oxford: Clarendon Press.

Bartolini, S. 1993. 'On Time and Comparative Research', *Journal of Theoretical Politics*, 5: 131–167.

Bartolini, S. and Mair, P. 1990. *Identity, Competition and Electoral Volatility: The Stabilization of European Electorates, 1885–1985*. Cambridge: Cambridge University Press.

Bates, R. H., Greif, A., Levi, M., Rosenthal, J. -L. and Weingast, B. R. 1998. *Analytic Narratives*. Princeton: Princeton University Press.

Batty, S. and Vesna, D. 1997. 'Gorbachev's Strategy of Political Centrism: A Game-theoretic Interpretation', *Journal of Theoretical Politics*, 9: 89–106.

Beach, C. 1989. 'Dollars and Dreams: A Reduced Middle Class? – Alternative Hypotheses', *Journal of Human Resources*, 24: 162–193.

Bean, C. and Butler, D. 1991. 'Uniformity in Australian Electoral Pattern: The 1990 Federal Election in Perspective', *Australian Journal of Political Science*, 26: 127–136.

Bean, C. and McAllister, I. 1989. 'Factions and Tendencies in the Australian Political Party System', *Politics*, 24: 79–99.

Behrens, R. 1980. *The Conservative Party from Heath to Thatcher: Policies and Politics, 1974–1979*. Farnborough: Saxon House.

Beilharz, P. 1994. *Transforming Labor*. Cambridge: Cambridge University Press.

Belloni, F. P. and Beller, D. C. 1978. *Faction Politics: Political Parties and Factionalism in Comparative Perspectives*, Oxford and Santa Barbara: ABC-Clio.

Berry, W. D. and Canon, B. C. 1993. 'Explaining the Competitiveness of Gubernatorial Primaries', *Journal of Politics*, 55: 454–471.

Binmore, K. 1992. *Fun and Games: A Text on Game Theory*. Lexington: D. C. Heath.

Birchfield, V. and Crepaz, M. M. L. 1998. 'The Impact of Constitutional Structures and Collective and Competitive Veto Points on Income Inequality in Industrialized Democracies', *European Journal of Political Research*, 34: 175–200.

Bishop, J., Formby, J. P. and Smith, W. J. 1991. 'Incomplete Information, Income Redistribution and Risk Averse Median Voter Behaviour', *Public Choice*, 68: 41–55.

Black E. and Black, M. 1992. *The Virtual South: How Presidents Are Elected*. Cambridge, MA: Harvard University Press.

Blank, R. 1989. 'Disaggregating the Effect of the Business Cycle on the Distribution of Income', *Economica*, 56: 141–163.

1997. *It Takes a Nation*. Princeton: Princeton University Press.

Blau, F. and Khan, L. M. 1996. 'International Differences in Male Wage Inequality', *Journal of Political Economy*, 24: 104.

Blondel, J. 1995. 'Toward a Systematic Analysis of Government-Party Relationships', *International Political Science Review*, 16: 127–143.

Bogdanor, V. 1994. 'The Selection of the Party Leader', in Seldon, A. and Ball, S., eds., *The Conservative Century. The Conservative Party since 1900*. Oxford: Oxford University Press.

Boix, C. 1998. *Political Parties, Growth and Equality*. Cambridge: Cambridge University Press.

Borooah, V. K., McGregor, P. P. L. and McKee, P. M. 1991. *Regional Income Inequality and Poverty in the United Kingdom*. Aldershot: Dartmouth.

Box-Steffensmeier, J. M., Arnold, L. W. and Zorn, C. 1997. 'The Strategic Timing of Position Taking in Congress: A Study of the North American Free Trade Agreement', *American Political Science Review*, 91: 324–338.

Boyne, G. 1995. 'Party Competition and Local Spending', Paper presented at the Rational Choice Group, London, June.

Bradshaw, J. 1992. 'Social Security', in Marsh, D. and Rhodes, R. A. W., eds., *Implementing Thatcherite Policies*, Buckingham: Open University Press.

Brady, D. W. and Buckley, C. Z. 1998. 'Coalitions and Policy in the US Congress: Lessons from the 103rd and 104th Congresses', in Maisel, S., ed., *The Parties Respond*, Boulder, CO: Westview Press.

Brady, D. W. and Epstein, D. 1997. 'Intraparty Preferences, Heterogeneity, and the Origins of the Modern Congress: Progressive Reformers in the House and Senate, 1980–1920', *Journal of Law Economics and Organization*, 13: 26–49.

Brady, D. W. and Volden, C. 1998. *Revolving Gridlock*. Boulder, CO: Westview Press.

Brandolini, A. 1992. 'Nonlinear Dynamics, Entitlement Rules, and the Cyclical Behaviour of the Personal Income Distribution', Centre For Economic Performance, London School of Economics, Discussion Paper No. 84.

1998. *Pareto's Law and Kuznets' Curve: A Bird's-Eye view of Long-Run Changes in Income Inequality*. Banca D' Italia, Research Department, Rome, Italy.

Brawn, K. 1998. 'Congressional Party Leadership: Utilitarian versus Majoritarian Incentives', *Legislative Studies Quarterly*, 23: 219–243.

Bray, M. and Neilson, D. 1996. 'Industrial Relations Reform and the Relative Autonomy of the State', in Castles, F. G., Gerristen, R. and Vowles, J., eds., *The Great Experiment*, Sydney: Allen & Unwin.

Brett, J. 1999. 'Social Democracy, Conservatism and Neoliberal Economic Reform: The Australian Experience', Paper presented at the European Consortium for Political Research Joint Session Workshops, Mannheim, 26–31 March.

Brown, R. D. 1995. 'Party Cleavage and Welfare Effort in the American States', *American Political Science Review*, 89: 23–33.

Bryson, L. 1988. 'Welfare Issues of the Eighties', in Najman, J. M. and Western, J. S., eds., *A Sociology of Australian Society*. Melbourne: Macmillan.

Budge, I. 1994. 'A New Spatial Theory of Party Competition: Uncertainty, Ideology and Policy Equilibria Viewed Comparatively and Temporally', *British Journal of Political Science*, 24: 443–467.

Budge, I. and Laver, M. 1986. 'Office-seeking and Policy Pursuit in Coalition Theory', *Legislative Studies Quarterly*, 11: 485–506.

Budge, I., McKay, D., Rhodes, R., Robertson, D., Saunders, D., Slater, M. and Wilson, G. 1988. *The Changing British Political System: Into the 1990s*, 2nd edn. London: Longman.

Budge, I., Robertson, D. and Hearl, D. eds. 1987. *Ideology, Strategy and Party Change: Spatial Analyses of Post-war Election Programmes in 19 Democracies*. Cambridge: Cambridge University Press.

Buhmann, B., Rainwater, L., Schmaus, G. and Smeeding, T. 1988. 'Equivalence Scales, Well-Being, Inequality and Poverty: Sensitivity Estimates Across Ten Countries Using the Luxembourg Income Study (LIS) Database', *Review of Income and Wealth*, 34: 115–142.

Bulpitt, J. 1986. 'The Discipline of the New Democracy: Mrs Thatcher's Domestic Statecraft', *Political Studies*, 34: 19–39.

Burch, M. and Holliday, I. 1995. 'Party and the Central Executive', in Lovenduski, J. and Stanyer, J., eds., *Contemporary Political Studies*. York: Political Studies Association of the UK.

Burchell, D. and Mathews, R., eds., 1991. *Labor's Troubled Times*. Sydney: Pluto Press.

Burckhauser, R. V., Crews, A. D., Daly, M. C. and Jenkins, S. P. 1996. 'Where in the World is the Middle Class? A Cross-National Comparison of the Shrinking Middle Class Using Kernel Density Estimates. Cross-National Studies in Aging Program Project', Paper No. 26, All-University Gerontology Center, The Maxwell School, Syracuse University, Syracuse, NY.

Burkhart, R. E. 1997. 'Comparative Democracy and Income Distribution: Shape and Direction of Causal Arrow', *Journal of Politics*, 59: 148–164.

Cairn, J. 1995. *John Cairn's Years*. Melbourne: Melbourne University Press.

Cairns, A. 1968. 'The Electoral System and the Party System in Canada, 1921–1965', *Canadian Journal of Political Science*, 1: 55–80.

Calise, M. 1989. *Governo di Partito*. Bologna: Il Mulino.

Campbell, A., Converse, P. E., Miller, W. E. and Stokes, D. E. 1960. *The American Voter*. New York: Wiley & Sons.

Cansino, C. 1995. 'Party Government: The Search for a Theory. Introduction', *International Political Science Review*, 16: 123–126.

Carew, E. 1992. *Paul Keating. Prime Minister*. Sydney: Allen & Unwin.

Carmines, E. G. and Stimson, J. A. 1989. *Issue Evolution: Race and the Transformation of American Politics*. Princeton: Princeton University Press.

Carson, E., Fitzgerald, P. and Jordan, A. G. 1989. 'Discouraged Workers: A Study of Long-term Unemployment and Sickness Beneficiaries Aged 45–54', *Social Security Review*, Department of Social Security, Australia.

Cass, B. 1986. 'The Case for Review of Aspects of the Australian Social Security System', Department of Social Security, Australia.

　1988. 'Income Support for the Unemployed in Australia: Towards a More Active System', Department of Social Security, Australia.

Castles, F. G. 1988. *Australian Public Policy and Economic Vulnerability*. Sydney: Allen & Unwin.

　1993. 'Changing Course in Economic Policy: The English-Speaking Nations in the 1980s', in Castles, F. G., ed., *Families of Nations*, Aldershot: Dartmouth.

　1998. *Comparative Public Policy: Patterns of Post-war Transformation*. Aldershot: Edward Elgar.

Castles, F. G. ed., 1982. *The Impact of Parties*. London: Sage.

Castles, F. G. and Wildenmann, R., eds., 1986. *Visions and Realities of Party Government*. Berlin: Walter de Gruyter.

Castles, F. G., Gerristen, R. and Vowles, J., eds., 1996. *The Great Experiment*. Sydney: Allen & Unwin.

Castles, F. G. and Mitchell, D. 1993. 'Worlds of Welfare and Families of Nations', in Castles, F. G., eds., *Families of Nations*, Aldershot: Dartmouth.

Castles, F. G. and Shirley, I. F. 1996. 'Labour and Social Policy: Gravediggers or Refurbishers', in Castles, F. G., Gerristen, R. and Vowles, J., eds., *The Great Experiment*. Sydney: Allen & Unwin.

Castles, S. S. 1992. 'Australian Multiculturalism: Social Policy and Identity in a Changing Society', in Freeman, G. P. and Jupp, J. eds., *Nations of Immigrants*. Melbourne: Oxford University Press.

Champernowne, D. G. and Cowell, F. A. 1998. *Economic Inequality and Income Distribution*, Cambridge: Cambridge University Press.

Charmley, J. 1996. *A History of Conservative Politics: 1900–1996*. Keele: Keele University Press.

Charnock, D. 1994. 'Electoral Bias in Australia 1980–1993: The Impact of the 1983 Electoral Amendments', *Australian Journal of Political Science*, 29: 484–500.

Chrétien, J. 1985. *Straight from the Heart*. Toronto: Key Porters Books.

Clarke, H., Jenson, J., LeDuc, L. and Pammett, J. H. 1984. *Absent Mandate*. Toronto: Gage Publishing.

Colburn, C. B. 1990. 'A Public Choice Explanation for the Decline in Real Income Transfers', *Public Finance Quarterly*, 18: 123–134.

Coleman, J. 1997. 'The Decline and Resurgence of Congressional Party Conflict', *Journal of Politics*, 59: 165–184.

Coleman, J. S. 1971. 'Internal Processes Governing Party Positions in Elections', *Public Choice*, 11: 35–60.

Collier, D. and Mahon, J. E. 1993. 'Conceptual Stretching Revisited – Adapting Categories in Comparative Analysis', *American Political Science Review*, 87: 845–855.

Colomer, J. M. 1991. 'Transitions by Agreement: Modelling the Spanish Way', *American Political Science Review*, 85: 1283–1302.

Coulter, F., Cowell, F. and Jenkins, S. P. 1992. 'Equivalence Scales Relativities and the Extent of Inequality and Poverty', *Economic Journal*, 102: 1067–1082.

Courtney, J. 1973. *The Selection of National Party Leaders in Canada*. Toronto: Macmillan.

Cowell, F. 1995. *The Measurement of Inequality*, 2nd edn. Hemel Hempstead: Harvester Wheatsheaf.

Cowell, F., Jenkins, S. P. and Litchfield, J. A. 1996. The Changing Shape of the UK Income Distribution: Kernel Density Estimates', in Hills, J., ed., *New Inequalities*. Cambridge: Cambridge University Press.

Cox, G. 1997. *Making Votes Count*. Cambridge: Cambridge University Press.

Cox, G. and McCubbins, M. 1993. *Legislative Leviathan*. Berkeley: University of California Press.

1994. 'Bonding, Structure, and the Stability of Political Parties: Party Government in the House', *Legislative Studies Quarterly*, 19: 215–231.

Cox, G. and Rosenbluth, F. 1996. 'Factional Competition for the Party Endorsement: The Case of Japan's Liberal Democratic Party', *British Journal of Political Science*, 26: 259–269.

Crewe, I. and King, A. 1998. *SDP: The Birth, Life and Death*. Oxford: Oxford University Press.

Crewe, I. and Searing, D. D. 1988. 'Ideological Change in the British Conservative Party', *American Political Science Review*, 82: 361–384.

Curtin, J. and Sawer, M. 1996. 'Gender Equity in the Shrinking State: Women and the Great Experiment', in Castles, F. G., Gerristen, R. and Vowels, J. eds. *The Great Experiment*. Sydney: Allen & Unwin.

Cutler, D. M. and Katz, L. F. 1992. 'Rising Inequality? Changes in the Distribution of Income and Consumption in the 1980s', *American Economic Review. Papers and Proceedings*, 82: 546–551.

Cutright, P. 1966. 'Political Structure, Economic Development and National Security Programs', *American Journal of Sociology*, 70: 537–550.

Cyert, R. and March, J. 1992. *Behavioral Theory of the Firm*, 2nd edn. Oxford: Blackwell Business.

Dalton, T., Draper, M., Weeks, W. and Wiseman, J. 1996. *Making Social Policy in Australia*. Sydney: Allen & Unwin.

Danziger, S. and Gottschalk, P. 1993. 'Introduction', in Danziger, S. and Gottschalk, P., eds., *Uneven Tides*, New York: Russell Sage.

Danziger, S. and Smolensky, E. 1985. 'Income Transfer Policies and the Poor: A Cross-National Perspective', *Journal of Social Policy*, 14: 257–262.

Danziger, S., Gottschalk, P. and Smolensky, E. 1989. 'How the Rich have Fared, 1973–1987', *American Economic Review*, 79: 310–314.

Davis, O., Hinich, M. J. and Ordeshook, P. 1970. 'An Expository Development of a Mathematical Model of the Electoral Process', *American Political Science Review*, 64: 426–448.

Deakin, N. 1987. *The Politics of Welfare*. London: Methuen.

DeFreitas, G. 1998. 'Immigration, Inequality, and Policy Alternatives', in Baker, D., Epstein, G. and Pollin, R., eds., *Globalization and Progressive Economic Policy*. Cambridge: Cambridge University Press.

Denham, A. and Garnett, M. 1994. '"Conflicts of Loyalty": Cohesion and Division in Conservatism, 1975–1990', in Dunleavy, P. and Stanley, J., eds., *Contemporary Political Studies*. Political Studies Association of the UK.

Denters, B. 1993. 'The Politics of Redistribution in Local Government', *European Journal of Political Research*, 23: 323–342.

Dilnot, A. and Walker, I. 1989. *The Economics of Social Security*. Oxford: Oxford University Press.

Dilnot, A. W., Kay J. A. and Morris, C. N. 1984. *The Reform of Social Security*. Oxford: Clarendon Press.

Dodge, D. 1975. 'Impact of Tax, Transfer and Expenditure Policies of Government on the Distribution of Personal Income in Canada', *Review of Income and Wealth*, 2: 1–52.

Dogan, M. and Pelassy, D. 1990. *How to Compare Nations*, 2nd edn. Chatham, NJ: Chatham House.

Donnison, D. 1982. *The Politics of Poverty*. Oxford: Martin Robertson.

Douglas, J. 1989. 'Review Article: The Changing Tide – Some Recent Studies of Thatcherism', *British Journal of Political Science*, 19: 399–424.

Dowding, K. 1991. *Rational Choice and Political Power*. Aldershot: Edward Elgar.

Downs, A. 1957. *An Economic Theory of Democracy*. New York: Harper & Row.

Duclos, J. -Y. and Mercader, M. 1993. 'Household Composition and Classes of Equivalence Scales: With Application to Spain and the UK', The Microsimulation Unit, No. MU 9403, Department of Applied Economics, Cambridge.

Duncan, G. 1989. *The Australian Labor Party: A Model for Others*. London: The Fabian Society.

Duncan, G., Rodgers, W. and Smeeding, T. 1993. 'Whither the Middle Class? A Dynamic View', in Papadimitriou, D. and Wolff, E. eds., *Economic Inequality at the Close of the 20th Century*. New York: Macmillan.

Dunleavy, P. 1990. 'Government at the Centre', in Dunleavy, P., Gamble, A. and Peele, G., eds., *Developments in British Politics*. London: Macmillan.

1991. *Democracy, Bureaucracy and Public Choice*. London: Harvester Wheatsheaf.

1993. 'The Political Parties', in Dunleavy, P., Gamble, A., Holliday, I. and Peele, G., eds., *Developments in British Politics*. London: Macmillan.

Dunleavy, P. and Husbands, C. 1985. *British Democracy at the Crossroads*. London: Allen & Unwin.

Dunleavy, P., Gamble, A. and Peele, G., eds., 1990. *Developments in British Politics*. London: Macmillan.

Dunleavy, P. and Rhodes, R. A., eds. 1995. *Prime Minister, Cabinet and Core Executive*. London: Macmillan.

Duverger, M. 1959. *Political Parties*. New York: John Wiley.

Eardley, T., Bradshaw, J., Ditch, J., Gough, I. and Whiteford, P. 1996. 'Social Assistance in OECD Countries: Synthesis Report', Department of Social Security, Research Report No. 46, London: HMSO.

Easton, B. and Gerristen, R. 1996. 'Economic Reform: Parallels and Divergences', in Castles, F., Gerristen, R. and Vowles, J., eds., *The Great Experiment*. Sydney: Allen & Unwin.

Eaton, M. and Stilwell, F. 1991. 'The Super Rich in Australia', *Journal of Australian Political Economy*, 30: 141–147.

Elgie, R. 1997. 'Models of Executive Politics: A Framework for the Study of Executive Power Relations in Parliamentary and Semi-Presidential Regimes', *Political Studies*, 45: 217–231.

Elster, J. 1982. 'Marxism, Functionalism, and Game Theory: The Case for Methodological Individualism', *Theory and Society*, 11: 453–482.

Enelow, J. M. and Hinich, M. J. 1984. *The Spatial Theory of Voting. An Introduction*. Cambridge: Cambridge University Press.

Engelmann, F. C. and Schwartz, M. A. 1975. *Political Parties: Origin, Character, Impact*. Scarborough, Canada: Prentice-Hall.

Epstein, L. 1986. *Political Parties in the American Mold*. Madison, Wisconsin.

Erikson, R. S., Wright, G. C. and McIver, J. P. 1989. Political Parties, Public Opinion and State Policy in the United States', *American Political Science Review*, 83: 729–750.

Esping-Andersen, G., ed., 1990. *The Three Worlds of Welfare Capitalism*. Cambridge: Polity.

ed. 1996. *Welfare States in Transition: National Adaptations in Global Economies*. London: Sage.

Evans, M. 1996. 'Fairer or Fowler? The Effects of the 1986 Social Security Act on Family Incomes', in Hills, J., ed., *New Inequalities*. Cambridge: Cambridge University Press.

1998. 'Social Security: Dismantling the Pyramids?', in Glennerster, H. and Hills, J., eds., *The State of Welfare*. Oxford: Oxford University Press.

Feenberg, D. R. and Poterba, J. M. 1993. 'Income Inequality and the Income of Very High-Income Taxpayers: Evidence from Tax Returns', in Poterba, J. M., ed., *Tax Policy and the Economy*, vol. VII, Cambridge, MA: MIT Press.

Feldman, S. and Zaller, J. 1992. 'The Political Culture of Ambivalence: Ideological Responses to the Welfare State', *American Journal of Political Science*, 36: 268–307.

Ferejohn, J. 1998. 'A Tale of Two Congresses: Social Policy in the Clinton Years', in Weir, M., ed., *The Social Divide. Political Parties and the Future of Activist Government*. Washington, DC: Brookings Institution Press.

Ferejohn, J. 1991. 'Changes in Welfare Policy in the 1980s', in Alesina, A. and Carliner, G., eds., *Politics and Economics in the Eighties*. Chicago: University of Chicago Press.

Ferrera, M. 1993. *Modelli di Solidarietà*. Bologna: il Mulino.

Fieldhouse, E. 1995. 'Thatcherism and the Changing Geography of Political Attitudes, 1964–87', *Political Geography*, 14: 3–30.

Fligstein, N., 1999. 'Is Globalization the Cause of the Crises of Welfare States?', EUI Working Papers, SPS No. 98/5.

Flora, P. 1986. 'Introduction', in Flora, P., ed., *Growth to Limits: the Western European Welfare State Since World War II*. Berlin: Walter de Gruyter.

Flora, P. and Alber, J. 1981. 'Modernization, Democratization, and the Development of Welfare States in Western Europe', in Flora, P. and Heidenheimer, A., eds., *The Development of Welfare States in Europe and America*. New Brunswick: Transaction Books.

Franks, C. E. S. 1989. *The Parliament of Canada*. Toronto: University of Toronto Press.

Freeman, R. and Katz, L. F. 1995. *Differences and Changes in Wage Structures*. Chicago: University of Chicago Press.

Frendreis, J. P., Gibson, J. L. and Vertz, L. L. 1990. The Electoral Relevance of Local Party Organizations', *American Political Science Review*, 84: 225–235.

Frey, D. 1986. 'Young Unemployed People in Households Dependent on Social Security', *Social Security Journal*. Spring: 22–31.

Fritzell, J. 1993. 'Income Inequality Trends in the 1980s: A Five-Country Comparison', *Acta Sociologica*, 36: 47–62.

Frolich, N. and Oppenheimer, J. 1984. 'Post-election Redistributive Strategies of Representatives: A Partial Theory of the Politics of Redistribution', *Public Choice*, 42: 113–131.

Galbraith, J. K. 1993. *The Culture of Contentment*. London: Penguin.

Galligan, B. 1985a. 'Political Review for the Australian Quarterly', *Australian Quarterly*, 57: 400–415.

1985b. 'Political Review: The 1984 Australian election', *Australian Quarterly*, 57: 165–187.

Gamble A. 1989. 'Thatcherism and the New Politics', in Mohan, J., ed., *The Political Geography of Contemporary Britain*. London: Macmillan.

1995a. *The Free Economy and the Strong State*, 2nd edn. London: Macmillan.

1995b. 'The New Political Economy', *Political Studies*, 43: 516–530.

Gardiner, K. 1996. 'A Survey of Income Inequality Over the Last Twenty years. How Does the UK Compare?', in Gottschalk, P., Gustafsson, B. and Palmer, E., eds., *Changing Patterns in the Distribution of Economic Welfare. An International Perspective*. Cambridge: Cambridge University Press.

Garrett, G. and Mitchell, D. 1996. 'International Risk and Social Insurance: Reassessing the Globalization-Welfare State Nexus', Annual Meeting of the American Political Science Association, San Francisco, 28 August–1 September.

Garry, J. 1994. 'The Internal Politics of the British Conservative Party and Margaret Thatcher's Position as Leader', Unpublished MA Thesis, University of Galway.

Gibson, D. 1990. 'Social Policy', in Jennet, C. and Stewart, R. G. eds., *Hawke and Australian Public Policy*. Melbourne: Macmillan, 83–98.

Gillespie, I. W. 1978. *In Search of Robin Hood*. Toronto: CD Howe Research Institute.

Gilmour, I. 1992. *Dancing with Dogma*. London: Simon & Schuster.

Gilmour, J. B. 1995. *Strategic Disagreement. Stalemate in American Politics*. Pittsburgh: University of Pittsburgh Press.

van Ginneken, W. and Park, J. 1984. *Generating Internationally Comparable Income Distribution Estimates*. Geneva: ILO.

Glennerster, H. 1998. 'New Beginnings and Old Continuities', in Glennerster, H. and Hills, J., eds., *The State of Welfare*, 2nd edn. Oxford: Oxford University Press.

1995. *British Social Policy since 1945*. Cambridge: Blackwell.

Glennerster, H. and Hills, J., eds. 1998. *The State of Welfare*, 2nd edn. Oxford: Oxford University Press.

Glewwe, P. 1990. 'Efficient Allocation of Transfers to the Poor', LSMS, Working Paper, n. 79, World Bank.

Glyn, A. 1998. 'Internal and External Constraints', in Baker, D., Epstein, G. and Pollin, R., eds., *Globalization and Progressive Economic Policy*. Cambridge: Cambridge University Press.

Golden, M. 1997. *Heroic Defeats: The Politics of Job Loss*. Cambridge: Cambridge University Press.

Goodin, R. E. 1996. 'Inclusion and Exclusion', *Archive Europeene de Sociologie*, 2: 343–371.

Goodin, R. E. and Le Grand, J. 1987. *Not Only the Poor: The Middle Classes and the Welfare State*. London: Allen and Unwin.

Goodin, R. E., Headed, B., Muffles, R. and Driven, H. 1999. *The Real Worlds of Welfare Capitalism*. Cambridge: Cambridge University Press.

Goodman, A., Johnson, P. and Webb, S. 1997. *Inequality in the UK*. Oxford: Oxford University Press.

Gordon, C. 1994. *New Deal: Business, Labor and Politics in America, 1920–1935*. Cambridge: Cambridge University Press.

Gordon, M. 1993. *A Question of Leadership*. St Lucia: University of Queensland Press.

Gordon, M. 1988. *Social Security Policies in Industrial Countries*. Cambridge: Cambridge University Press.

Gottschalk, P. 1997. 'Policy Changes and Growing Earnings Inequality in the US and Six Other OECD Countries', in Gottschalk, P., Gustafsson, B. and Palmer, E., eds., *Changing Patterns in the Distribution of Economic Welfare: An International Perspective*. Cambridge: Cambridge University Press.

Gosling, A., Machin, S. and Waldfogel, J. 1996. 'Women's Pay and Family Incomes in Britain, 1979–91, in Hills, J., ed., *New Inequalities*. Cambridge: Cambridge University Press.

Gottschalk, P. and Danziger, S. 1985. 'A Framework for Evaluating the Effects of Economic Growth and Transfers on Poverty', *American Economic Review*, 73: 121–128.

Gottschalk, P. and Smeeding, T. 1997. 'Cross-National Comparisons of Earnings and Income Inequality', *Journal of Economic Literature*, 35: 633–687.

Gramlich, E. M., Kasten, R. and Sammartino, F. 1993. 'Growing Inequality in the 1980s: the Role of Federal Taxes and Cash Transfers', in Danziger, S. and Gottschalk, P., eds., *Uneven Tides*. New York: Russell Sage Foundation.

Green, A. E. 1996. 'Aspects of the Changing Geography of Poverty and Wealth', in Hills, J., ed., *New Inequalities*, Cambridge: Cambridge University Press.

Green, D. P. and Shapiro, I. 1994. *Pathologies of Rational Choice Theory*. New Haven: Yale University Press.

Gregory, R. G. 1993. 'Aspects of Australian and US Living Standards: The Disappointing Decades 1970–1990', *The Economic Record*, 69: 61–76.

Griffin, L. J. and Leicht, K. 1986. 'Politicizing Welfare Expenditures in the United States', in Furniss, N., ed., *Futures for the Welfare State*, Bloomington: Indiana University Press.

Grœnnings, S. 1970. *The Study of Coalition Behaviour: Theoretical Perspectives and Cases from Four Continents*. New York: Holt, Rinehart & Winston.

Gruen, F. H., ed., 1979. *Surveys of Australian Economics*. Sydney: Allen & Unwin.

Gruen, F. H. and Grattan, M. 1993. *Managing Government: Labor's Achievement and Failures*. Melbourne: Longman Cheshire.

Guérin, D. and Nadeau, R. 1998. 'Clivage linguistique et vote economique au Canada', *Canadian Journal of Political Science*, 31: 557–572.

Guest, D. 1997. *The Emergence of Social Security in Canada*, 2nd edn. Vancouver: University of British Columbia.

Haddow, R. 1993. *Poverty Reform in Canada, 1958–78: State and Class Influences on Policy-Making*. Montreal: McGill Queen's University Press.

Hagan, J. and Turner, K. 1991. *A History of the Labor Party in New South Wales 1891–1991*. Melbourne: Longman Cheshire.

Hall, P. 1986. *Governing the Economy: The Politics of State Intervention in Britain and France*. Cambridge: Polity.

1997. 'The Role of Interests, Institutions, and Ideas in the Comparative

Political Economy of the Industrialized Nations', in Lichbach, M. I. and Zuckerman, A., eds., *Comparative Politics. Rationality, Culture and Structure.* Cambridge: Cambridge University Press.

Harding, A. 1993. 'Lifetime vs Annual Tax-Transfer Incidence: How much Less Progressive?', *The Economic Record*, 69: 179–191.

1995. 'The Impact of Family, Demographic and Labour Force Change Upon Income Inequality in Australia, 1982–1993', *Australian Journal of Social Research*, 1: 47–70.

1997. 'The Suffering Middle: Trends in Income Inequality in Australia 1982 to 1993–94', Discussion Paper No. 21, NATSEM, University of Canberra.

Harding, A. and Landt, J. 1992. 'Policy and Poverty: Trends in Disposable Incomes', *Australian Quarterly*, 64: 19–48.

Harding, A. and Mitchell, D. 1992. 'The Efficiency and Effectiveness of the Tax-Transfer System in the 1980s', *Australian Tax Forum*, 9: 277–304.

Hargreaves, H. S. P. and Varoufakis, Y. 1995. *Game Theory. A Critical Introduction.* London: Routledge.

Harkness, S., Machin, S. and Waldfogel, J. 1996. 'Women's Pay and Family Incomes in Britain, 1979–91', in Hills, J., ed., *New Inequalities.* Cambridge: Cambridge University Press.

Harmel, R. and Janda, K. 1993. 'Performance, Leadership, Factions, and Party Change', Paper delivered at the APSA Meetings, 1993.

1994. 'An Integrated Theory of Party Goals and Party Change', *Journal of Theoretical Politics*, 6: 259–287.

Hart, J. 1994. 'The Presidency in the 1990s', in Peele, G., Bailey, J. C., Cain, B. and Peters, G. B., eds., *Developments in American Politics.* London: Macmillan.

Hauser, R. and Becker, I. 1997. 'The Development of the Income Distribution in the Federal Republic of Germany during the 1970s and 1980s', Gottschalk, P., Gustafsson, B. and Palmer, E., eds., *Changing Patterns in the Distribution of Economic Welfare. An International Perspective.* Cambridge: Cambridge University Press.

Hawke, B., 1994. *The Hawke Memoirs.* London: Heinemann.

Heath, A., ed., 1991. *Understanding Political Change.* Oxford: Pergamon Press.

Heath, A., Jowell, R., Curtice, J., Evans, G., Field, J. and Witherspoon, S. 1991. *Understanding Political Change: The British Voter 1964–1987.* Oxford: Pergamon.

Heidenheimer, A. J., Heclo, H. and Adams, C. T. 1990. *Comparative Public Policy: The Politics of Social Change*, 3rd edn. New York: St Martin's Press.

Hendry, R. 1998. 'Fair Shares for All? The Development of Needs Based Government Funding in Education, Health and Housing', Centre for Analysis of Social Exclusion, CASEpaper 18, London School of Economics and Political Science, London.

Herrnson, P. S. 1998. 'National Party Organizations at the Century's End', in Maisel, S., ed., *The Parties Respond. Changes in the American Party System.* Boulder, CO: Westview Press.

Herrnson, P. S. and Patterson, K. D. 1995. 'Toward a More Programmatic Democratic Party? Agenda Setting and Coalition Building in the House of Representatives', *Polity*, 27: 607–628.

Hibbs, D. and Dennis, C. 1988. 'Income Distribution in the United States', *American Political Science Review*, 82: 467–488.

Hill, M. 1990. *Social Security Policy in Britain*. Aldershot: Edward Elgar.

Hills, J. 1987. 'What Happened to Spending on the Welfare State?', in Walker, A., ed., *The Growing Divide – A Social Audit, 1979–1987.* CPAG.

1998a. 'Does Income Mobility Mean That We Do Not Need to Worry About Poverty?', in Atkinson, A. B. and Hills, J., eds., *Exclusion, Employment and Opportunity*, Centre for the Analysis of Social Exclusion, CASEpaper 4, London School of Economics and Political Science, London.

1998b. *Rowntree Inquiry into Income and Wealth Distribution in the UK. The Latest Evidence*. York: Joseph Rowntree Foundation.

Hills, J. ed. 1996. *New Inequalities*. Cambridge: Cambridge University Press.

Hinich, M. J. and Munger, M. C. 1997. *Analytical Politics*. New York: Cambridge University Press.

Hofferbert, R. 1966. 'The Relation Between Public Policy and Some Structural and Environmental Variables in the American States', *American Political Science Review*, 60: 73–82.

Hogg, B. 1991. 'Crisis Management', in Burchell, D. and Mathews, R., eds. *Labor's Troubled Times*. Sydney: Pluto Press.

Hoggart, K. 1987. 'Does Politics Matter'? Redistributive Policies in English Cities, 1949–1974', *British Journal of Political Science*, 17: 359–384.

Howe, B. 1992. 'Social Justice-Vision and Strategies', in Kerr, D., ed., *Reinventing Socialism*. Sydney: Pluto Press.

Huber, J. 1996. *Rationalizing Parliament*. Cambridge: Cambridge University Press.

Huber, J. and Inglehart, R. 1995. 'Expert Interpretations of Party Space and Party Locations in 42 Societies', *Party Politics*, 1: 73–112.

Hughes, C. A. 1994. 'The 1993 Election and the Changing Electoral Map', *Australian Journal of Political Science*, 29: 103–117.

Imig, L. 1996. *Poverty and Power: the Political Representation of Poor Americans*. University of Nebraska Press.

Iversen, T. 1994. 'The Logics of Electoral Politics', *Comparative Political Studies*, 27: 155–189.

Jackson, L. and Bozic, S. 1997. 'The Australian Social Security Model: Revisiting the International Debate', *Social Security Journal*, September: 32–55.

Jacobs, L. R. and Shapiro, R. Y. 1998. 'The Politicization of Public Opinion: The Fight for the Pulpit', in Weir, M., ed., *The Social Divide. Political Parties and the Future of Activist Government*. Washington, DC: Brookings Institution Press.

Jacobsen, K. 1995. 'Much Ado About Ideas: The Cognitive Factor in Economic Policy', *World Politics*, 47: 283–310.

Jaensch, D. 1983. *The Australian Party System*. Sydney: Allen & Unwin.

1989. *The Hawke-Keating Hijack*. Sydney: Allen & Unwin.

Janda, K., Harmel, R., Edens, C. and Goff, P. 1995. 'Changes in Party Identity', *Party Politics*, 1: 171–196.

Jantti, M., and Danziger, S. 1992. 'Does the Welfare State Work? Evidence on Antipoverty Effects from the Luxembourg Income Study', Working Paper 74, CEPS/INSTEAD.

Jayasuriya, K. 1994. 'Political Economy of Central Banks', *Australian Journal of Political Science*, 29: 115–134.

Jenkins, S. P. 1991. 'Income Inequality and Living Standards: Changes in the 1970s and 1980s', *Fiscal Studies*, 12: 1–28.

1995. 'Accounting for Inequality Trends: Decomposition Analyses for the UK. 1971–1986', *Economica*, 62: 29–63.

Jennet, C. and Stewart, R. G., eds., 1990. *Hawke and Australian Public Policy*. Melbourne: Macmillan.

Jenson, J. 1975. 'Party Loyalty in Canada: the Question of Party Identification', *Canadian Journal of Political Science*, 8: 543–553.

1990. 'Representations in Crisis: The Roots of Canada's Permeable Fordism', *Canadian Journal of Political Science*, 23: 653–683.

Jessop, B., Bonnett, K., Bromley, S. and Ling, T. 1988. *Thatcherism. A Tale of Two Nations*. Oxford: Polity Press.

Johnson, C. 1989. *The Labor Legacy*. Sydney: Allen & Unwin.

1996. 'Shaping the Social: Keating's Integration of Social and Economic Policy', *Just Policy*, 5: 9–15.

Johnson, P. and Webb, S. 1992. 'Explaining the Growth of UK Income Inequality 1979–1988', *Economic Journal*, 103: 429–435.

Johnston, D. 1986. *Up the Hill*. Montreal: OPTIUM Publishing International.

Johnston, E., Manning, I. and Hellwig, O. 1995. *Trends in the Distribution of Cash Income and Non-Cash Benefits: An Overview*. Canberra: Australian Government Printing Services.

Johnston, R. J. and Pattie, C. J. 1989. 'The Changing Electoral Geography of Great Britain', Mohan, J., ed., *The Political Geography of Contemporary Britain*, London: Macmillan.

Jones, C. O. 1995. *Separate But Equal Branches. Congress and the Presidency*. Chatham, NJ: Chatham House.

Jones, G. W. 1991. West European Prime Ministers in Perspective', *West European Politics*, 14: 163–182.

Jones, H. and Millar, J., eds. 1996. *The Politics of the Family*. Aldershot: Avebury.

Joseph, K. and Sumption, J. 1979. *Equality*. London: John Murray.

Jowell, R., Curtice, J., Park, A., Brook, L., Thompson, K. and Bryson, C. 1997. *British Social Attitudes. The 14th Report*. Aldershot: Ashgate.

Jupp, J. 1982. *Party Politics in Australia, 1966–81*. Sydney: Allen & Unwin.

1994. *Exile or Refuge?* Australia: Bureau of Immigration and Population Research.

Kamarck, E. C. 1990. 'Structure as Strategy: Presidential Nominating Politics in the Post-Reform Era', in Maisel, S. L., ed., *The Parties Respond*. Boulder, CO: Westview Press.

Karmis, D. 1996. 'Federalism et Identités Collectives au Canada et en Belgique: des itineraires différents, une fragmentation similaire', *Canadian Journal of Political Science*, 29: 435–468.

Katz, R. 1986. 'Party Government: A Rationalistic Conception', in Castles, F. G. and Wildenmann, R., eds., *Visions and Realities of Party Government*. Berlin: de Gruyter.

Katz, R. and Mair, P. 1992. Introduction, in Katz, R. and Mair, P., eds., *Party Organization: A Data Handbook*. London: Sage.

1995. 'Changing Models of Party Organization and Party Democracy: The Emergence of the Cartel Party', *Party Politics*, 1: 5–28.

Katz, R. and Mair, P., eds., 1994. *How Parties Organize*. London: Sage.

Katzenstein, P. 1985. *Small States in World Markets: Industrial Policy in Europe*. Ithaca: Cornell University Press.

Kavanagh, D. and Morris, P. 1994. *Consensus Politics from Attlee to Major*. Oxford: Blackwell.

Kawachi, I. and Kennedy, B. 1997. 'Socioeconomic Determinants of Health 2: Health and Social Cohesion: Why care About Income Inequality?', *British Medical Journal*, 314: 1037–1040.

Keating, P. 1985. 'Labor's Commitment to Smaller Government', *Institute of Public Affairs Review*, 39: 19–22.

Keegan, W. 1984. *Mrs. Thatcher's Economic Experiment*. Harmondsworth: Penguin.

Keeney, R. and Raiffa, H. 1993. *Decisions with Multiple Objectives: Preferences and Value Tradeoffs*. Cambridge: Cambridge University Press.

Keeter, S. 1997. 'Public Opinion and the Election', in Pomper, G. M., Burnham, W. D., Corrado, A., Hershey, M. R., Just, M. R., Keeter, S., McWilliams, W. C. and Mayer, W. G., eds., *The Election of 1996. Reports and Interpretations*, Chatham, NJ: Chatham House Publishers.

Kelly, J., McAllister, I. and Mughan, A. 1985. 'The Decline of Class Revisited: England, 1964–1979', *American Political Science Review*, 79: 719–737.

Kelly, P. 1992. *The End of Uncertainty*. Sydney: Allen & Unwin.

Kelly, R. 1989. *Conservative Party Conferences*. Manchester: Manchester University Press.

Keman, H. 1993. *Comparative Politics. New Directions in Theory and Method*. Amsterdam: VU University Press.

Kemp, D. 1988. 'Political Behaviour', in Najman, J. M. and Western, J. S., eds., *A Sociology of Australian Society*. Melbourne: Macmillan.

Kenyon, P. D. and Lewis, P. E. T. 1992. 'Trade Union Membership and the Accord', *Australian Economic Papers*, 31(59): 325–345.

Kernell, S. 1997. *Going Public: New Strategies of Presidential Leadership*, 3rd edn. Washington, DC: CQ Press.

Kiernan, K. E. 1995. 'Transition to Parenthood: Young Mothers, Young Fathers and Later Life Experiences', London, London School of Economics and Political Science: STICERD Welfare State Discussion Paper WSP/113.

King, A. 1991. 'The British Prime Ministership in the Age of the Career Politician', *West European Politics*, 14: 25–47.

King, D. S. 1987. *The New Right*. London: Macmillan.

1995a. *Actively Seeking Work? The Politics of Unemployment and Welfare in the United States and Great Britain*. Chicago: Chicago University Press.

1995b, *Separate and Unequal*. Oxford: Oxford University Press.

King, A. ed. *The British Prime Minister*, 2nd edn. London: Macmillan.

King, G. and Gelman, A. 1991. 'Systemic Consequences of Incumbency Advantage in US House Elections', *American Journal of Political Science*, 35: 110–138.

King, J. E., Rimmer, R. J. and Rimmer, S. M. 1992. 'The Law of the Shrinking Middle: Inequality of Earnings in Australia 1975–1989', *Scottish Journal of Political Economy*, 39: 391–412.

Kingdon, J. W. 1989. *Congressmen's Voting Decisions*. Ann Arbor: University of Michigan Press.

Kirchheimer, O. 1966. 'The Transformation of Western European Party Systems', in LaPalombara, J. and Weiner, M., eds., *Political Parties and Political Development*. Princeton: Princeton University Press.

Kitschelt, H. 1989. 'The Internal Politics of Parties: The Law of Curvilinear Disparity Revisited', *Political Studies*, 37: 400–421.

1994. *The Transformation of European Social Democracy*. Cambridge: Cambridge University Press.

Klein, R. 1995. *The New Politics of the National Health Service*. London: Longman.

Klingemann, H. -D., Hofferbert, R. I. and Budge, I. 1994. *Parties, Policies, and Democracy*. Oxford: Westview Press.

Koelble, T. 1996. 'Economic Theories of Organization and the Politics of Institutional Design in Political Parties', *Party Politics*, 2: 251–263.

Kornberg, A. and Clarke, H. 1992. *Citizens and Community*. Cambridge: Cambridge University Press.

Korpi, W. 1980. 'Approaches to the Study of Poverty in the United States', in Corello, V., ed., *Poverty and Public Policy*. Oxford: Oxford University Press.

Krehbiel, K. 1993. Where's the party?, *British Journal of Political Science*, 23: 235–266.

1996. 'Institutional and Partisan Sources of Gridlock: A Theory of Divided and Unified Government', *Journal of Theoretical Politics*, 8: 7–40.

Krever, R. 1991. 'The Slow Demise of Progressive Income Tax', O'Leary, J. and Sharp, R., eds., *Inequality in Australia*. Melbourne: Heinemann, 150–163.

Krieger, J. 1986. *Reagan, Thatcher and the Politics of Decline*. Cambridge: Polity Press.

Kudrle, R. T. and Marmor, T. R. 1981. 'The Development of Welfare States in North America', in Flora, P. and Heidenheimer, A., eds., *The Development of Welfare States in Europe and America*. New Bruinswick and London: Transaction Books.

Lalonde, M. 1971. 'The Changing Role of The Prime Minister Office', *Canadian Public Administration*, 14: 509–531.

Land, H. and Lewis, J. 1997. 'The Emergence of Lone Motherhood as a Problem in Late Twentieth Century Britain', Welfare State Programme, STICERD, Discussion Paper 134.

Landis, M. L. 1998. 'Let Me Next Time be "Tried by Fire"': Disaster Relief and the Origins of the American Welfare State 1789–1874', *Northwestern University Law Review*, 92: 969–1036.

Laver, M. and Schofield, N. 1990. *Multiparty Government: the Politics of Coalition in Europe*. Oxford: Oxford University Press.

Laver, M. and Shepsle, K. 1990. 'Government Coalitions and Intraparty Politics', *British Journal of Political Science*, 20: 489–507.

1996. *Making and Breaking Governments*. Cambridge: Cambridge University Press.

Lawrence, D. 1996. *The Collapse of the Democratic Presidential Majority*. Boulder, CO: Westview Press.

Lawson, K. 1990. 'Political Parties: Inside and Out', *Comparative Politics*, 23: 105–119.

Lawson, N. 1992. *The View from no 11: Memoirs of a Tory Radical*. London: Bantam Press.

LeDuc, L. 1981. 'The Dynamic Properties of Party Identification: A Four Nation Comparison', *European Journal of Political Research*, 9: 257–268.

Le Grand, J. and Winter, D. 1987. 'The Middle Classes and the Defence of the British Welfare State', in Goodin, R. E. and Le Grand, J., eds., *Not Only the Poor*. London: Allen & Unwin.

Leman, C. 1980. *The Collapse of the Welfare Reform*. Cambridge MA. : MIT Press.

Levi, M. 1997. 'A Model, a Method and a Map: Rational Choice in Comparative and Historical Analysis', in Lichbach, M. I. and Zuckerman, A. S., eds., *Comparative Politics. Rationality, Culture, and Structure*. Cambridge: Cambridge University Press.

Lijphart, A. 1971. 'Comparative Politics and the Comparative Method', *American Political Science Review*, 65: 682–693.

1984. *Democracies. Patterns of Majoritarian and Consensus Government in Twenty-One Countries*. New Haven: Yale University Press.

Lijphart, A., ed. 1992. *Parliamentary versus Presidential Government*. Oxford: Oxford University Press.

1994. *Electoral Systems and Party Systems*. Oxford: Oxford University Press.

Lindbeck, A. and Weibull, J. 1987. 'Balanced-budget Redistribution as the Outcome of Political Competition', *Public Choice*, 52: 273–297.

Lindenberg, S. 1988. 'Contractual Relations and Weak Solidarity: The Behavioral Basis of Restraints on Gain-maximization, *Journal of Institutional and Theoretical Economics*, 144: 39–58.

Linz, J. J. 1992. 'The Perils of Presidentialism', in Lijphart, A. ed., *Parliamentary versus Presidential Government*. Oxford: Oxford University Press.

Lipset, M. S. and Rokkan, S. 1967. *Party Systems and Voter Alignments: Cross-national Perspectives*. New York: Free Press.

Lister, R. 1991. 'Social Security in the 1980s', *Social Policy and Administration*, 25: 21–33.

Lloyd, C. 1983. 'The Federal ALP: Supreme or Secondary', in Parkin, A. and Warhurst, J. eds., *Machine Politics*. Sydney: Allen & Unwin.

Lloyd, C. and Swan, W. 1987. 'National Factions and the ALP', *Politics*, 22: 100–110.

Lo, C. and Schwartz, M., eds., 1998. *Social Policy and the Conservative Agenda*. Malden and Oxford: Blackwell.

Lowi, T. 1979. *The End of Liberalism: The Second Republic of the United States*, 2nd edn. : Norton.

Luebbert, G. 1986. *Comparative Democracy: Policy-making and Governing Coalitions in Europe and Israel*. New York: Columbia University Press.

MacDonald, S. E. and Rabinowitz, G. 1993. 'Direction and Uncertainty in a Model of Issue Voting', *Journal of Theoretical Politics*, 5: 61–87.

Mackie, T. and Marsh, D. 1995. 'The Comparative Method', in Marsh, D. and Stoker, G., eds., *Theory and Methods in Political Science*. London: Macmillan.

Maddox, G. 1989. *The Hawke Government and the Labor Tradition*. Victoria: Penguin Books.

Mair, P. 1994. 'Party Organizations: From Civil Society to the State', in Katz, R. and Mair, P. eds., *How Parties Organize*. London: Sage.

1997a. 'Comparative Politics: An Overview', in Goodin, R. E. and Klingemann, H. -D., eds., *A New Handbook of Political Science*. Oxford: Oxford University Press.

1997b. *Party System Change. Approaches and Interpretations*. Oxford: Clarendon Press.

Malloy, J. 1996. 'Reconciling Expectation and Reality in House of Commons Committees: the Case of the 1989 GST Inquiry', *Canadian Public Administration*, 39: 314–335.

Manning, H. 1995. 'Traditions in Transition: The Australian Labor Party and the Union Movement', Paper delivered at the conference on 'Party Politics in the Year 2000', Manchester, 14–15 January.

Maor, M. 1992. 'Intra-party Conflict and Coalition Behaviour in Denmark and Norway: The Case of 'Highly Instituionalized' Parties, *Scandinavian Political Studies*, 15: 99–116.

1997. *Political Parties and Party Systems. Comparative Approaches and the British Experience*. London: Routledge.

1998. *Parties, Conflicts, and Coalitions in Western Europe*. London: Routledge.

Marsh, M. 1993. 'Introduction: Selecting the Party Leader', *European Journal of Political Research*, 24: 229–231.

Mathews, S. A. 1989. 'Veto Threats: Rhetoric in a Bargaining Game', *Quarterly Journal of Economics*, 104: 347–369.

May, J. 1973. 'Opinion Structure of Political Parties: The Special Law of Curvilinear Disparity', *Political Studies*, 21: 135–151.

Mayer, W. G. 1996. *The Divided Democrats*. Boulder, CO: Westview Press.

Mayhew, D. R. 1991. *Divided We Govern*. New Haven: Yale University Press.

McAllister, I. 1991. 'Party Adaptation and Factionalism within the Australian Party System', *American Journal of Political Science*, 35: 206–227.

1992. *Political Behaviour*. Melbourne: Longman.

1997. 'Political Culture and National Identity', in Galligan, B., McAllister, I. and Ravenhill, J., eds., *New Developments in Australian Politics*. Melbourne: Macmillan Education.

McAllister, I. and Ascui, A. 1988. 'Voting Patterns', in McAllister, I. and Warhurst, J., eds., *Australia Votes*. Sydney: Longman.

McCall-Newman, C. 1982. *Grits. An Intimate Portrait of the Liberal Party*. Toronto: Macmillan.

McCarty, N. M. and Poole, K. T. 1995. 'Veto Power and Legislation: An Empirical Analysis of Executive and Legislative Bargaining from 1961 to 1986', *Journal of Law Economics and Organization*, 11: 282–312.

McCarty, N. M., Poole, K. T. and Rosenthal, H. 1997. *Income Redistribution and the Realignment of American Politics*. Washington, DC: AEI Press.

McCubbins, M. and Thies, M. F. 1997. 'As a Matter of Factions: The Budgetary Implications of Shifting Factional Control in Japan's LDP', *Legislative Studies Quarterly*, 3: 293–328.

McDowell, L. 1989. 'Women in Thatcher's Britain', in Mohan, J., ed., *The Political Geography of Contemporary Britain*. London: Macmillan.

McGillivray, F. 1997. 'Party Discipline as a Determinant of the Endogenous Formation of Tariffs', *American Journal of Political Science*, 41: 584–607.

McIntyre, S. 1991. 'Decline and Fall?', in Burchell, D. and Mathews, R., eds. *Labor's Troubled Times*. Sydney: Pluto Press.

McKenzie, R. 1963. *British Political Parties*, 2nd edn. London: Heinemann.

McRae, K. 1974. *Consociational Democracy*. Toronto: McClellan & Stewart.

Mervin, D. 1993. *The President of the United States*. London: Harvester Wheatsheaf.

Michels, R. 1959 [1915]. *Political Parties: A Sociological Study of the Oligarchical Tendencies of Modern Democracy*. New York: Dover.

Midlarsky, M., ed. 1997. *Inequality, Democracy and Economic Development*. Cambridge: Cambridge University Press.

Milkis, S. 1993. *The President and the Parties*. Oxford: Oxford University Press.

Mintz, B. 1998. 'The Failure of Health-Care Reform', in Lo, C. Y. H. and Schwartz, M., eds., *Social Policy and the Conservative Agenda*. Malden and Oxford: Blackwell.

Mishra, R. 1990. *The Welfare State in Capitalist Society: Policies of Retrenchment in Europe, North America and Australia*. London: Harvester Wheatsheaf.

Mitchell, D. 1991. *Income Transfers in Ten Welfare States*. Aldershot: Avebury.

Mitchell, D., Harding, A. and Gruen, F. 1994. 'Targeting Welfare', *The Economic Record*, 70: 315–340.

Mookherjee, D. and Shorrocks, A. 1982. 'A Decomposition Analysis of the Trend in UK Income Inequality', *Economic Journal*, 92: 886–902.

Morisette, R., Myles, J. and Picot, G. 1995. 'Earnings Polarization in Canada, 1969–1991', in Banting, K., ed. *Labour Market Polarization and Social Policy*. Kingston: Queen's University Press.

Morley, M. and Petras, J. 1998. 'Wealth and Poverty in the National Economy. The Domestic Foundations of Clinton's Global Policy', in Lo, C. Y. H. and Schwartz, M., eds., *Social Policy and the Conservative Agenda*. Malden, MA and Oxford: Blackwell.

Morton, D. 1986. *The New Democrats 1961–1986: The Politics of Change*. Toronto: Copp Clark Pitman.

Mulé, R. 1997. 'Understanding the Party-Policy Link: Established Approaches and Theoretical Developments', *Party Politics*, 3: 493–512.

1998a. 'Does Democracy Promote Equality?', *Democratization*, 5: 1–22.

1998b. 'Financial Uncertainties of Party Formation and Consolidation in Britain, Germany and Italy: A Theoretical Perspective on the Early Years', in Burnell, P. and Ware, A., eds., *Funding Democratization*. Manchester: Manchester University Press.

1999. 'New Institutionalism: Distilling Some "Hard Core" Propositions in the Works of Williamson and March and Olsen', *Politics*, 3: 141–145.

Muller, N. E. 1988. 'Democracy, Economic Development and Income Inequality', *American Sociological Review*, 53: 50–68.

Murray, C. 1984. *Loosing Ground*. New York: Basic Books.

Myles, J. 1996. 'When Markets Fail: Social Welfare in Canada and the United States', in Esping-Andersen, G., ed., *Welfare States in Transition*. London: Sage Publications.

Myles, J. and Pierson, P. 1997. 'Friedman's Revenge: The Reform of "Liberal" Welfare States in Canada and the Unites States', *Politics and Society*, 25: 443–472.

Nagel, J. H. 1993. 'Populism, Heresthetics and Political Stability: Richard Seddon and the Art of Majority Rule', *British Journal of Political Science*, 23: 139–197.

Narud, H. M. 1996. 'Electoral Competition and Coalition Bargaining in Multiparty Systems', *Journal of Theoretical Politics*, 8: 499–525.

Nash, J. 1953. 'Two Person Cooperative Games', *Econometrica*, 21: 128–140.

Neumann, S. 1956. *Modern Political Parties*. Chicago: The University of Chicago Press.

Neustadt, R. E. 1990. *Presidential Power and the Modern Presidents*. New York: The Free Press.

Noble, M. and Smith, G. 1996. 'Two Nations? Changing Patterns of Income and Wealth in Two Contrasting Areas', in Hills, J., ed., *New Inequalities*. Cambridge: Cambridge University Press.

Noel, S. J. R. 1993. 'Canadian Responses to Ethnic Conflict: Consociationalism, Federalism and Control', in McGarry, J. and O'Leary, B., eds., *The Politics of Ethnic Conflict Regulation: Case Studies of Protracted Ethnic Conflict*. London: Routledge.

Nordhaus, W. 1975. 'The Political Business Cycle', *Review of Economic Studies*, 42: 169–190.

Norris, P. 1995. 'May's Law of Curvilinear Disparity Revisited', *Party Politics*, 1: 29–47.

North, D. 1990. *Institutions, Institutional Change and Economic Performance*. Cambridge: Cambridge University Press.

Norton, P. 1978. *Conservative Dissidents*. London: Temple Smith.

1990. 'The Lady's Not for Turning but What About the Rest? Margaret Thatcher and the Conservative Party 1979–1989', *Parliamentary Affairs*, 43: 47–48.

O'Connell, D. 1991. 'Party Reform: Debates and Dilemmas, 1958–1991', in Whitlam, G., ed., *A Century of Social Change*. Sydney: Pluto Press.

O'Connor, J., Orloff, A. S. and Shaver, S. 1998. *States, Markets, Families: Gender, Liberalism and Social Policy in Australia, Canada, Great Britain and the United States*. Cambridge: Cambridge University Press.

OECD 1982. *The OECD List of Social Indicators*. Paris.

1991. *Trends in International Migration: Continuous Reporting System on Migration*. Paris.

1993. *Employment Outlook*. Paris.

1996. 'Social Transfers: Spending Patterns, Institutional Arrangements and Policy Responses', *OECD Economic Studies*, No 27.

Ogus, A. I., Barendt, E. M. and Buck, T. G., eds. 1988. *The Law of Social Security*. London: Butterworth.

O'Leary, B. 1991. 'An Taoiseach: The Irish Prime Minister', *West European Politics*, 133–162.

O'Leary, J. and Sharp, R., eds. 1991. *Inequality in Australia*. Melbourne: Heinemann.

O'Neill, D. and Sweetman, O. 1995. 'The Persistence of Poverty in Britain: Evidence from Patterns of Intergenerational Mobility', Mimeo, Department of Economics, Maynooth College, Ireland.

Orloff, A. S. 1988. 'Origins of America's Welfare State', in Weir, M., Orloff, A. S. and Skocpol, T. eds., *The Politics of Social Policy in the United States*. Princeton: Princeton University Press.

1993. *The Politics of Pensions: A Comparative Analysis of Britain, Canada and the United States, 1880–1940*. Madison: University of Wisconsin Press.

1996. 'Gender and the Welfare State', *Annual Review of Sociology*, 22: 51–70.

Osberg, L., Erksoy, S. and Phipps, S. 1997. 'Unemployment, Unemployment Insurance and the Distribution of Income in Canada in the 1980s', Gottschalk, P., Gustafsson, B. and Palmer, E., eds., *Changing Patterns in the Distribution of Economic Welfare. An International Perspective*. Cambridge: Cambridge University Press.

Osborne, M. and Rubinstein, A. 1994. *A Course in Game Theory*. Cambridge, MA: MIT Press.

Ostrogorski, M. I. 1902. *Democracy and the Organization of Political Parties*. London: Macmillan.

Overbye, E. 1994. 'Convergence in Policy Outcomes: Social Security Systems in Perspective', *Journal of Public Policy*, 14: 147–174.

Owens, J. E. 1997. 'The Return of Party Government in the House of Representatives: Central Leadership-Committee Relations in the 104th Congress', *British Journal of Political Science*, 27: 247–272.

Page, B. I. and Shapiro, R. Y. 1992. *The Rational Public: Fifty Years of Trends in Americans' Policy Preferences*. Chicago: University of Chicago Press.

Painter, M. 1996. 'Economic Policy, Market Liberalism and the "End of Australian Politics"', *Australian Journal of Political Science*, 31: 287–299.

1998. *Collaborative Federalism: Economic Reform in Australia in the 1990s*. Cambridge: Cambridge University Press.

Panebianco, A. 1988. *Political Parties: Organization and Power*. Cambridge: Cambridge University Press.

van Parijs, P. 1995. *Real Freedom for All*. Oxford: Oxford University Press.

Parkin, M. and Bade, R. 1990. *Macroeconomics and the Australian Economy*. Sydney: Allen & Unwin.

Patterson, K. D. 1996. *Political Parties and the Maintenance of Liberal Democracy*. New York: Columbia University Press.

Patterson, S. C. and Caldeira, G. A. 1988. 'Party Voting in the United States Congress', *British Journal of Political Science*, 17: 111–131.

Payne, J. W., Bettman, J. R. and Luce, M. F. 1996. 'When Time is Money: Decision Behavior under Opportunity-Cost Time Pressure', *Organizational Behavior and Human Decision Processes*, 66: 131–152.

Pech, J. 1986. 'The "Greatest Asset Since Child Endowment"? A Study of Low Income Working Families Receiving Family Income Supplement', Department of Social Security, November 1986, Research Paper, Canberra.

Peetz, D. 1997. 'Why Bother? Union Membership and Apathy', Centre for Economic Policy Research, Discussion Paper No 357, Australian National University.

Penniman, H. R., ed. 1975. 'Canada at the Polls: The General Election of 1974', Washington, DC: American Enterprise Institute for Public Policy Research.

Perlin, G. 1980. *The Tory Syndrome: Leadership Politics in the Progressive Conservative Party of Canada*. Montreal: McGill-Queen's University Press.

Persson, T. and Tabellini, G. 1994. 'Is Inequality Harmful for Growth?', *American Economic Review*, 84: 600–621.

Pestieu, P. 1989. 'The Demographics of Inequality', *Journal of Population Economics*, 2: 3–24.

Peters, B. G. 1989. *The Politics of Bureaucracy: A Comparative Perspective*, 3rd edn. New York: Longman.

1998. *Comparative Politics: Theory and Methods*. London: Macmillan.

Peterson, M. A. 1990. *Legislating Together*. Cambridge MA: Harvard University Press.

1998. 'The Politics of Health Care Policy: Overreaching in an Age of Polarization', in Weir, M., ed., *The Social Divide. Political Parties and the Future of Activist Government*. Washinton, DC: The Brookings Institution Press.

Petrocik, J. R. 1981. *Party Coalitions: Realignment and the Decline of the New Deal Party System*. Chicago: University of Chicago Press.

Pétry, F. 1995. 'The Party or Agenda Model: Election Programmes and Government Spending in Canada', *Canadian Journal of Political Science*, 28: 51–84.

Pierson, C. 1998. 'Contemporary Challenges to Welfare State Development', *Political Studies*, 46: 777–794.

Pierson, P. 1994. *Dismantling the Welfare State? Reagan, Thatcher and the Politics of Retrenchment*. Cambridge: Cambridge University Press.

1995. Fragmented Welfare States: Federal Institutions and the Development of Social Policy, *Governance*, 8: 449–478.

1998. 'The Deficit and the Politics of Domestic Reform', in Weir, M. ed., *The Social Divide. Political Parties and the Future of Activist Government*. Washington, DC: Brookings Institution Press.

Piven, F. 1998. 'Welfare and the Transformation of Electoral Politics', in Lo, C. Y. H. and Schwartz, M., eds., *Social Policy and the Conservative Agenda*, Malden, MA and Oxford: Blackwell.

Piven, F. and Cloward, A. R. 1989. *Why Americans Don't Vote*. New York: Pantheon Books.

Polsby, N. W. 1983. *Consequences of Party Reform*. Oxford and New York: Oxford University Press.

Pomper, G. M. 1992. 'Concepts of Political Parties', *Journal of Theoretical Politics*, 4: 143–159.

Porter, J. 1965. *The Vertical Mosaic: An Analysis of Social Class and Power in Canada*. Toronto: University of Toronto Press.

Portes, A. and Zhou, M. 1996. 'Self-employment and the Earnings of Immigrants', *American Sociological Review*, 61: 219–230.

Prior, J. 1986. *A Balance of Power*. London: Hamish Hamilton.

Przeworski, A. and Sprague, J. 1986. *Paper Stones: A History of Electoral Socialism*. Chicago: Chicago University Press.

Przeworski, A. and Teune, H. 1970. *The Logic of Comparative Social Enquiry*. New York: John Wiley.

Punnett, R. M. 1993. 'Selecting the Party Leader in Britain', *European Journal of Political Research*, 24: 257–276.

Pusey, M. 1991. *Economic Rationalism in Canberra: A Nation Building State Changes Its Mind*. Cambridge: Cambridge University Press.

Pym, F. 1984. *The Politics of Consent*. London: Hamish Hamilton.

Quadagno, J. 1994. *The Color of Welfare: How Racism Undermined the War on Poverty*. Oxford University Press: Oxford.

1998. 'Social Security Policy and the Entitlement Debate. The New American Exceptionalism', in Lo, C. Y. H. and Schwartz, M. eds., *Social Policy and the Conservative Agenda*. Malden, MA. and Oxford: Blackwell.

Quiggin, J. 1998. 'Social Democracy and Market Reform in Australia and New Zealand', *Oxford Review of Economic Policy*, 14: 76–95.

Ragin, C. 1987. *The Comparative Method. Moving Beyond Qualitative and Quantitative*

Strategies. Berkeley: University of California Press.

Rainwater, L. 1993. 'The Social Wage in the Income Package of Working Parents', Luxembourg Income Study Working Paper, No. 89.

Rainwater, L. and Smeeding, T. M. 1995. 'Doing Poorly: The Real Income of American Children in a Comparative Perspective', Mimeo, Syracuse University.

Rasmussen, J. 1983. 'The Alliance Campaign. Watersheds and Landslides: Was 1983 a Fault Line in British Politics?', in Ranney, A. ed., *Britain at the Polls, 1983*. Durham: Duke University Press.

Ray, R. 1991. 'The Right Stuff', in Burchell, D. and Mathews, R., eds., *Labor's Troubled Times*. Sydney: Pluto Press.

Rhodes, M. 1996. 'Globalization and West European Welfare States: A Critical Review of Recent Debates', *Journal of European Social Policy*, 6: 305–327.

Richardson, J. 1994. 'Doing Less by Doing More: British Government 1979–1993', *West European Politics*, 17: 178–197.

Richardson, S. 1997. 'Inequality', Centre for Economic Policy Research, Discussion Paper No. 375, Australian National University.

Riddell, P. 1983. *The Thatcher Government*. Oxford: Robertson.

Riker, W. 1962. *The Theory of Political Coalitions*. New Haven: Yale University Press.

1986. *The Art of Political Manipulation*. New Haven: Yale University Press.

Ringen, S. 1987. *The Possibility of Politics*. Oxford: Clarendon Press.

Robertson, D. 1976. *A Theory of Party Competition*. London: John Wiley.

Roemer, J. 1994. 'The Strategic Role of Party Ideology When Voters are Uncertain about How the Economy Works', *American Political Science Review*, 88: 327–335.

1999. 'The Democratic Political Economy of Progressive Income Taxation', *Econometrica*, 67:1–19.

Rohde, D. 1991. *Parties and Leaders in the Postreform House*. Chicago: Chicago University Press.

Rose, R. 1964. 'Parties, Factions and Tendencies in Britain', *Political Studies*, 12: 34–46.

1974. *The Problem of Party Government*. London: Macmillan.

1984a. *Do Parties Make a Difference?*, 2nd edn. London: Macmillan.

1984b. *Understanding Big Government*. London and Los Angeles: Sage.

1995. *Can Government Go Bankrupt?*, 2nd edn. New York: Basic Books.

Roth, G. 1979. *The Social Democrats in Imperial Germany: A Study in Working-class Isolation and National Integration*. New York: Arno Press.

Rubinstein, A. 1982. 'Perfect Equilibrium in a Bargaining Model', *Econometrica*, 50: 97–110.

1991. 'Comments on the interpretation of game theory', *Econometrica*, 59: 909–924.

1998. *Modelling Bounded Rationality*. Cambridge, MA: The MIT Press.

Saint-Paul, G. and Thierry, V. 1992. 'Education, Democracy and Growth', Centre for Economic Policy Research, Discussion Paper No. 613, Paris.

Sala-i-Martin, X. 1997. 'Transfers, Social Safety Net and Economic Growth', *IMF Staff Papers*, 44: 81–102.

Sartori, G. 1976. *Parties and Party Systems: A Framework for Analysis*. Cambridge: Cambridge University Press.

1994. 'Compare Why and How: Comparing, Miscomparing and the Comparative Method', in Mattei, D. and Ali, K., eds., *Comparing Nations: Concepts, Strategies and Substance*. Oxford: Basil Blackwell.

Sartori, G. ed. 1984. *Social Science Concepts*. Beverly Hills: Sage.

Saunders, P. 1991. 'Selectivity and Targeting in Income Support: The Australian Experience', *Journal of Social Policy*, 20: 299–326.

1992. 'Income Distribution in Australia and New Zealand: Comparisons based on the Luxembourg Income Study', in Slottje, D. J. and Smeeding, T. M. eds. *Research on Income Inequality*, vol. III. Greenwich: JAI Press.

1994a, 'Immigrants and the Distribution of Income: National and International Comparisons', Social Policy Research Centre, University of New South Wales, Discussion Papers, No. 52.

1994b. *Welfare and Inequality*. Cambridge: Cambridge University Press.

1997. 'Economic Adjustment and Distributional Change: Income Inequality and Poverty in Australia in the 1980s', in Gottschalk, P., Gustafsson, B. and Palmer, E., eds., *Changing Patterns in the Distribution of Economic Welfare. An International Perspective*. Cambridge: Cambridge University Press.

Saunders, P. and Hobbs, G. 1988. 'Income Inequality in Australia in an International Comparative Perspective', *Australian Economic Review*, 3: 25–34.

Saunders, P., Stott, H. and Hobbes, G. 1991. 'Income Inequality in Australia and New Zealand: International Comparisons and Recent Trends', *Review of Income and Wealth*, 37: 63–79.

Sawer, M. 1998. 'A Question of Heartland? Women and the ALP', in Parkin, A. and Warhurst, J., eds., *The ALP towards 2000*. Sydney: Allen & Unwin.

Scarrow, S. 1996. *Parties and Their Members*. Oxford: Oxford University Press.

Scharpf, F. W. 1991. *Crisis and Choice in European Social Democracy*. Ithaca, New York: Cornell University Press.

1997. *Games Real Actors Play*. Boulder, CO: Westview Press.

Schelling, T. 1980. *The strategy of conflict*, 2nd edn. Cambridge, MA: Harvard University Press.

Schlesinger, J. 1974. *The Imperial Presidency*. London: Andre Deutch.

1991. *Political Parties and the Winning of Office*. Ann Arbor: The University of Michigan Press.

Schmidt, M. 1996. 'When Parties Matter: A Review of the Possibilities and Limits of Partisan Influence on Public Policy', *European Journal of Political Research*, 30: 155–183.

Schmitter, P. 1974. 'Still the Century of Corporatism', *Review of Politics*, 36: 85–131.

Schumpeter, J. 1954. 'The Crisis of the Tax State', *International Economic Papers*, 4: 5–30.

Schwartz, M. 1990. *The Party Network: The Robust Organization of Illinois Republicans*. Madison, Wis.: The University of Wisconsin Press.

1994. 'Electoral Success Versus Party Maintenance: National, State, and Local Party Contributions to Illinois Legislative Races', *Publius: The Journal of Federalism*, 24: 79–92.

1998. 'What Went Right?, Why the Clinton Administration Did Not Alter the Conservative Trajectory in Federal Policy', in Lo, C. Y. H. and Schwartz, M., eds., *Social Policy and the Conservative Agenda*. Oxford: Blackwell.

Scully, G. W. and Slottje, D. J. 1989. 'The Paradox of Politics and Policy in Redistributing Income', *Public Choice*, 60: 55–70.

Searing, D. D. 1994. *Westminster's World*. Cambridge, MA: Harvard University Press.

Shafer, B. E. 1997. '"We are all Southern Democrats Now": the Shape of American Politics in the Very Late Twentieth Century', in Shafer, B. E., ed., *Present Discontents*. Chatham, NJ: Chatham House.

Sharpe, L. J. and Newton, K. 1984. *Does Politics Matter?: The Determinants of Public Policy*. Oxford: Clarendon.

Shepherd, R. 1991. *The Power Brokers*. London: Hutchinson.

Shepsle, K. A. and Bonchek, M. S. 1997. *Analysing Politics*. New York: Norton.

Shribman, D. M. 1998. 'Era of Pretty Good Feelings: The Middle Way of Bill Clinton and America's Voters', in Maisel, S., ed., *The Parties Respond*. Boulder, CO: Westview Press.

Shubik, M. 1984. *Game Theory in the Social Sciences*. Cambridge, MA: MIT Press.

Simms, M. 1988. 'Political Review', *Australian Quarterly*, 60: 231–239.

1993. 'Two Steps Forward, One Step Back', in Lovenduski, J. and Norris, P., eds., *Gender and Party Politics*, London: Sage.

Simon, H. 1957. *Models of Man*. New York: J. Wiley.

Sinclair, B. 1990. 'The Congressional Party: Evolving Organizational, Agenda-Setting, and Policy Roles', in Maisel, S., ed., *The Parties Respond*, Boulder, CO: Westview Press.

1995. *Legislators, Leaders and Lawmaking*. Baltimore: Johns Hopkins University Press.

1998. 'Evolution or Revolution? Policy-oriented Congressional Parties in the 1990s', in Maisel, S., ed., *The Parties Respond*. Boulder, CO: Westview Press.

Singleton, G. 1990. *The Accord and the Australian Labour Movement*. Victoria: Melbourne University Press.

Sinnott, R. 1986. 'Party Differences and Spatial Representation: The Irish Case', *British Journal of Political Science*, 16: 217–241.

Skocpol, T. 1988. 'The Limits of the New Deal System and the Roots of Contemporary Welfare Dilemmas', in Weir, M., Orloff, A. S. and Skocpol, T., eds., *The Politics of Social Policy in the United States*. Princeton: Princeton University Press.

1995. *Social Policy in the United States: Future Possibilities in Historical Perspective*. Princeton: Princeton University Press.

    1996. *Boomerang: Clinton's Health Security Effort and the Turn Against Government in US Politics*. New York: W. W. Norton.

Smeeding, T. 1997. 'American Income Inequality in a Cross-National Perspective', Luxembourg Income Study Working Paper No. 157.

Smeeding, T. M., Rainwater, L. and Torrey, B. B. 1993. 'Going to Extremes: The US Elderly in an International Context', Luxembourg Income Study Working Paper No. 89.

Smiley, D. V. 1980. *Canada in Question: Federalism in the Eighties*, 3rd edn. Toronto: McGraw-Hill Ryerson.

Smith, D. 1973. *A Gentle Portrait. A Political Biography of Walter Gordon*. Edmonton: Hurting Publishers.

Stark, T. 1989. 'The Changing Distribution of Income Under Mrs. Thatcher', in Green, F., ed., *The Restructuring of the UK Economy*. London: Harvester Wheatsheaf.

Stewart, G. T. 1986. *The Origins of Canadian Politics. A Comparative Approach*. Vancouver: University of British Columbia Press.

Stewart III, C. H. 1991. 'The Politics of Tax Reform in the 1980s', in Alesina, A. and Carliner, G., eds., *Politics and Economics in the Eighties*. Chicago: University of Chicago Press.

Stigler, G. 1970. 'Director's Law of Public Income Redistribution', *Journal of Law and Economics*, 13: 1–10.

Stilwell, F. 1993. *Economic Inequality*. Sydney: Pluto Press.

Stokes, G. and Cox, R. 1981. 'The Governing Party: The ALP and the Politics of Consensus', in Parkin, A. and Allan, P., eds, *The Dunstan Decade*. Melbourne: Longman.

Stone, S. A. 1998. 'Comment of Vanberg. Rules, Dispute Resolution, and Strategic Behavior', *Journal of Theoretical Politics*, 10: 327–338.

Strange, S. 1996. *The Retreat of the State: the Diffusion of Power in the World Economy*. Cambridge: Cambridge University Press.

Strøm, K. 1989. 'A Behavioral Theory of Competitive Political Parties', *American Journal of Political Science*, 34: 565–598.

    1998. 'Institutions and Strategy in Parliamentary Democracy: Review Article', *Legislative Studies Quarterly*, 23: 128–143.

Struthers, J. 1989. 'Federalism and the Evolution of Social Policy and the Welfare State', in Hodgins, B. W., ed., *Federalism in Canada and Australia: Historical Perspectives*. Peterborough: Broadview Press.

Studlar, D. T. and Matland, R. E. 1996. 'The Dynamics of Women's Representation in the Canadian Provinces: 1975–1994', *Canadian Journal of Political Science*, 29: 269–294.

Stutchbury, M. 1990. 'Macroeconomic Policy', in Jennet, C. and Stewart, R. G., eds, *Hawke and Australian Public Policy*. Melbourne: Macmillan.

Sundquist, J. L. 1981. *The Decline and Resurgence of Congress*. Washinton, DC: Brookings Institution.

Sundquist, J. L. 1993. *Beyond Gridlock?* Washington, DC: Brookings Institution.

Swank, D. H. 1992. 'Electoral and Partisan Influences on Australian Fiscal

Policy from Menzies to Hawke', *Australian Journal of Political Science*, 27: 414–433.

1998. 'Funding the Welfare State: Globalization and the Taxation of Business in Advanced Market Economies', *Political Studies*, 46: 671–692.

Tanner, L. 1991. 'Labourism in Retreat', in Burchell, D. and Mathews, R., eds., *Labor's Troubled Times*. Sydney: Pluto Press.

Taylor, M. 1970. 'The Problem of Salience in the Theory of Collective Decision-Making', *Behavioral Science*, 15: 415–430.

Thatcher, M. 1993. *The Downing Street Years*. London: HarperCollins.

Thorburn, H. 1979. *Party Politics in Canada*. Scarborough: Prentice-Hall of Canada.

Toso, S. 1997. *Selettività e universalismo nel ridisegno delle politiche della spesa di welfare*. *Ministero del Tesoro*, Commissione Tecnica Per la Spesa Pubblica, November.

Travers, P. and Richardson, S. 1993. *Living Decently*. Melbourne: Oxford University Press.

Trudeau, P. 1993. *Memoirs*. Toronto: McClelland & Stewart.

Tsebelis, G. 1990. *Nested Games: Rational Choice in Comparative Politics*. Berkeley: California University Press.

Tufte, E. 1978. *Political Control of the Economy*. Princeton: Princeton University Press.

Tullock, G. 1983. *Economics of Income Redistribution*. Boston: Kluwer.

Uhr, J. 1998. *Deliberative Democracy in Australia: The Changing Place of Parliament*. Cambridge: Cambridge University Press.

van der Veen, R. 1998. 'Real Freedom Versus Reciprocity: Competing Views on the Justice of Unconditional Basic Income', *Political Studies*, 46: 140–163.

Vowles, J. and McAllister, I. 1996. 'Electoral Foundations and Electoral Consequences: from Convergence to Divergence', in Castles, F. G., Gerristen, R. and Vowles, J., eds., *The Great Experiment*. Sydney: Allen & Unwin.

Walker, A. 1987. 'Conclusion I: A Divided Britain', in Walker, A. and Walker, C., eds., *The Growing Divide. A Social Audit 1979–1987*. London: Child Poverty Action Group.

Walker, A. and Walker C., eds., 1987. *The Growing Divide. A Social Audit 1979–1987*. London: Child Poverty Action Group.

Walters, R. 1998. 'The Democratic Party and the Politics of Welfare Reform', in Lo, C. Y. H. and Schwartz, M., eds., *Social Policy and the Conservative Agenda*. Malden, MA and Oxford: Blackwell.

Ward, D. 1993. 'The Continuing Search for Party Influence in Government', *Legislative Studies Quarterly*, 18: 211–230.

Ward, H. 1995. 'Game theory and the Politics of Global Warming: The State of Play and Beyond', Paper delivered at the Rational Choice Panel at the Political Studies Association Conference, York, 18–20 April.

Ware, A. 1985. *The Breakdown of Democratic Party Organization, 1940–1980*. Oxford: Clarendon Press.

1992. 'Activist-Leader Relations and the Structure of Political Parties: "Exchange" Models and Vote-Seeking Behaviour in Parties', *British Journal of Political Science*, 22: 47–68.

1996. *Political Parties and Party Systems*. Oxford: Oxford University Press.

Ware, A. ed. 1987. *Political Parties: Electoral Change and Structural Responses*. Oxford: Blackwell.

Warhurst, J. 1996. 'Transitional Hero: Gough Whitlam and the Australian Labor Party', *Australian Journal of Political Science*, 31: 243–252.

Wattenberg, M. 1997. *The Decline of American Political Parties*, 5th edn. Cambridge, MA: Harvard University Press.

Weale, A. 1990. 'Social Policy', in Dunleavy, P., Gamble, A. and Peele, G., eds., *Developments in British Politics*, London: Macmillan.

Wearing, J. 1981. *The L-Shaped Party: the Liberal Party of Canada 1958–1980*. Toronto: McGraw-Hill.

Weaver, K. 1995. 'The Politics of Welfare Reform', in Weaver, K. and Dickens, W. T. eds. *Looking Before We Leap: Social Science and Welfare Reform*. Washington, D. C: Brookings Institution.

1998. 'Ending Welfare as We Know It', in Weir, M., ed., *The Social Divide. Political Parties and the Future of Activist Government*. Washington DC: Brookings Institution.

Webb, P. D. 1994. 'Party Organizational Change in Britain: The Iron Law of Centralization?', in Katz, R. and Mair, P., eds., *How Parties Organize: Change and Adaptation in Party Organizations in Western Democracies*. London: Sage.

Weber, M. 1968. *Economy and Society*. New York: Bedminster Press.

Weingast, B. and Marshall, W. 1988. 'The Industrial Organization of Congress', *Journal of Political Economy*, 96: 132–163.

Weir, M. 1998. 'Political Parties and Social Policymaking', in Weir, M., ed., *The Social Divide. Political Parties and the Future of Activist Government*. Washington, DC: The Brookings Institution.

Weir, M., Orloff, A. S. and Skocpol, T. 1988. *The Politics of Social Policy in the United States*. Princeton: Princeton University Press.

von Weizächer, R. K. 1995. 'Public Pension Reform, Demographics and Inequality. Distributional Analysis Research Programme', DARP-11, STICERD, London School of Economics and Political Science.

Weller, P. 1985. *First Among Equals: Prime Ministers in Westminster Systems*. Sydney: Allen & Unwin.

Wes, M. 1996. *Globalization. Winners and Losers*. London, IPPR, Commission on Public Policy and British Business.

Wharhurst, J. 1988. 'The ALP Campaign', in McAllister, I. and Warhurst, J., eds., *Australia Votes*. Sydney: Longman.

Wheelwright, T. 1983. 'New South Wales: the Dominant Right', in Parkin, A. and Warhurst, J. eds., *Machine Politics*. Sydney: Allen & Unwin.

Whitaker, R. 1977. *The Government Party: Organizing and Financing the Liberal Party of Canada, 1930–1958*. Toronto: University of Toronto Press.

Whiteley, P. 1983. *The Labour Party in Crisis*. London: Methuen.

Whiteley, P., Seyd, P. and Parry, J. 1996. *Labour and Conservative Party Members 1990–1992: Social Characteristics, Political Attitudes and Activities*. Aldershot: Dartmouth.

Whiteley, P., Seyd, P. and Richardson, J. 1994. *True Blues: The Politics of Conservative Party Membership*. Oxford: Clarendon Press.

Whiteley, P., Seyd, P., Richardson, J. and Bissell, P. 1993. 'Explaining Party Activism: The Case of the British Conservative Party', *British Journal of Political Science*, 24: 79–94.

Wilenski, P. 1986. *Public Power and Public Administration*. Sydney: Hale & Iremonger.

Williams, L. F. 1998. 'Race and the Politics of Social Policy', in Weir, M., ed., *The Social Divide. Political Parties and the Future of Activist Government*. Washington, DC: The Brookings Institution.

Wilson, J. 1995. *Political Organizations*, 2nd edn. New Haven: Princeton University Press.

Wolfson, M. C. 1993. 'When Inequalities Diverge', Statistics Canada and Canadian Institute for Advanced Research, mimeo, November.

Wood, A. 1994. *North–South Trade, Employment and Inequality: Changing Fortunes in a Skill-Driven World*. Oxford: Clarendon Press.

Wright, J. F. H. 1986. Australian Experience with Majority-Preferential and Quota-Preferential Systems', in Grofman, B. and Lijphart, A., eds., *Electoral Laws and their Political Consequences*. New York: Agathon Press.

Young, H. 1991. *One of Us: A Bibliography of Margaret Thatcher*. London: Macmillan.

Young, L. 1998. 'Party, State and Political Competition in Canada', *Canadian Journal of Political Science*, 31: 339–358.

Zaller, J. R. 1992. *The Nature and Origins of Mass Opinion*. Cambridge: Cambridge University Press.

Index